Martin Sökefeld (ed.)
Spaces of Conflict in Everyday Life

Culture and Social Practice

Martin Sökefeld (ed.)
Spaces of Conflict in Everyday Life
Perspectives across Asia

[transcript]

SPONSORED BY THE

Federal Ministry
of Education
and Research

CROSSROADS
ASIA
Conflict · Migration · Development

Bibliographic information published by the Deutsche Nationalbibliothek
The Deutsche Nationalbibliothek lists this publication in the Deutsche Nationalbibliografie; detailed bibliographic data are available in the Internet at http://dnb.d-nb.de

© 2015 transcript Verlag, Bielefeld

All rights reserved. No part of this book may be reprinted or reproduced or utilized in any form or by any electronic, mechanical, or other means, now known or hereafter invented, including photocopying and recording, or in any information storage or retrieval system, without permission in writing from the publisher.

Cover layout: Kordula Röckenhaus, Bielefeld
Printed in Germany
Print-ISBN 978-3-8376-3024-4
PDF-ISBN 978-3-8394-3024-8

Contents

Acknowledgements | 7

Spaces of Conflict in Everyday Life:
An Introduction
Martin Sökefeld | 9

Shifting Borders:
Coping Strategies of Inhabitants in the Aftermath
of the Osh Conflict, Kyrgyzstan
Aksana Ismailbekova | 33

Understanding Mobilisation Processes in Conflict through
Framing: The Case of Inter-Communal Conflict in the Batken
Province, Kyrgyzstan
Khushbakht Hojiev | 57

Institution-Centred Conflict Research:
A Methodological Approach and its Application in East
Afghanistan
Jan Koehler | 83

Land-based Conflict in Afghanistan:
On the Right of Pre-emption (shuf'a) as
'Back-Channel' Diplomacy and a Show of Indignation
Nick Miszak | 115

Not in the Master Plan:
Dimensions of Exclusion in Kabul
Katja Mielke | 135

Negotiating Space in the Conflict Zone of Kashmir:
The Borderlanders' Perspective
Debidatta Aurobinda Mahapatra | 163

Exclusionary Infrastructures:
Crisis and the Rise of Sectarian Hospitals in Northern Pakistan
Emma Varley | 187

Notes on the Contributors | 221

Acknowledgements

This book is an outcome of the research network Crossroads Asia, which has just entered its second phase and includes the Bonn International Center for Conversion, the Center for Development Research and the Institute of Oriental and Asian Studies, both based at the University of Bonn, the Center for Development Studies of Freie Universität Berlin, the Zentralasien-Seminar of Humboldt University Berlin, the Zentrum Moderner Orient and the Department of Social and Cultural Anthropology of Ludwig-Maximilians-University Munich. In the first phase the Institute of Geography at the University of Cologne and the Department of Social and Cultural Anthropology at Tübingen University were also part of the network. Since 2011, Crossroads Asia has been funded very generously by the German Federal Ministry of Education and Research. This also includes funding of the conference Spaces of Conflict in Everyday Life, which took place on October 11, 2014, at the Department of Social and Cultural Anthropology of Ludwig-Maximilians-University Munich, and from which this book developed.

First of all I would like to thank the Federal Ministry of Education and Research for its extremely generous support. Many thanks go also to the Crossroads Asia coordination office in Bonn, for its administrative assistance, and to all members of the network for continuous cooperation. I am further very grateful to all those who presented their papers at the conference and who took part in the lively debate. Last but not least, I would like to thank Mark Jones for proofreading and Beatrice Odierna for further copyediting and checking the layout of the book.

Munich, June 2015
Martin Sökefeld

Spaces of Conflict in Everyday Life: An Introduction

Martin Sökefeld

This volume presents contributions made to a conference hosted and run by the research network "Crossroads Asia," which took place in Munich in October 2014. The goal of the Crossroads Asia network is to enhance the understanding of the geographic area that stretches from eastern Iran to western China and from the Aral Sea to northern India. This part of Asia falls through the cracks of conventionally defined research areas, in that it is not entirely situated in South Asia, West Asia or Central Asia but intersects and partly overlaps these 'disciplinary' regions of area studies. Nevertheless, it makes a good deal of sense to take a cross-cutting perspective, simply because many social and political relations and processes intersect and connect significant parts of these conventionally delimited areas. The world is not a mosaic of containers, and while the critique of methodological nationalism (Wimmer/Glick Schiller 2002) has become widely accepted in academia, a critique of methodological (and disciplinary) 'regionalism' is equally necessary. Accordingly, Crossroads Asia challenges the validity of the traditional approach of area studies, namely of dividing the world into clearly delimited segments which are then examined by specialised and institutionalised disciplines, for example 'South Asian Studies' or 'Central Asian Studies', without looking much beyond these limits. In contrast, Crossroads Asia's counter-approach proposes to carry out research against the grain of conventionally defined areas, following dynamics that do not necessarily stop at the borders of nation states or areas.

Mobility is a key dynamic in this regard: people, as well as goods and ideas, are extremely mobile in the areas under study, in spite of an environment characterised by high mountain systems and deserts, which for outsiders rather seem to inhibit or even foreclose movement. Nevertheless, it is not only physical movements, such as migration, trade, nomadism and other forms of "wayfaring" (Ingold 2009), which are central in this regard. The network also departs from an understanding of the social that is centred on processes and emphasises social mobility and movement. Processual dynamics and social movements are, in most cases, intimately connected with conflicts; indeed, the area studied by the Crossroads network is one of the most conflict-ridden parts of the world. For instance, one just has to think of the civil war in Tajikistan, the Kashmir conflict between India and Pakistan and the insurgency and ongoing protest in the Kashmir Valley against Indian control, the conflict in Afghanistan and the war between the Taliban and the Pakistani army that is so intimately tied to the situation in Afghanistan. Thus, conflict has almost 'naturally' become a central concern of the Crossroads Network, albeit without limiting the focus to macro-level conflicts. However, macro-level conflicts form a significant context for contestations at the meso and micro levels; in fact, all levels intersect. Furthermore, instead of focusing on states and actors, we were interested in the everyday life of conflicts – or rather everyday life in the context of conflicts. While Georg Elwert (2004) maintains that conflicts are socially embedded, we emphasise that in the contexts we studied, social life is always embedded in conflicts.

As Crossroad Asia's basic approach to conflict has been laid out previously in a concept paper (Crossroads Asia Working Group Conflict 2012), I shall only summarise some of the major points here. First of all, conflict is seen as a 'normal' and universal aspect of social life and not as an exceptional occurrence and deviation away from a 'normal' state of social order. Conflicts and the necessity to deal with them are part of everyday social life, and they may have integrative or destructive functions for society; furthermore, they are not restricted to a narrowly defined realm of politics (centring on issues related to the state and security). Departing from an extended concept of politics that draws on a broad concept of power as a significant dimension of all social relations, 'social' conflicts are also 'political'. Given the situation in the areas studied, it is quite obvious that social relations, including relations of conflict, do not stop at the borders of the nation state, and so in order to conceive of the social we took inspiration from Norbert Elias's concept of figurations, to which I shall return below.

Emphasising conflicts as processes, we are of the opinion that the search for the causes (and consequences, for that matter) of conflicts is often not analytically useful. In many cases it is even impossible to identify causes, because conflicts frequently have neither a clear beginning nor an end. Rather, "conflicts follow conflicts," in that they feed into and intersect one another. Distinguishing between the causes of conflict, as well as for the purpose of analytical categorisation ('ethnic conflicts', 'resource conflicts', 'religious conflicts', etc.), often runs the danger of simplifying highly complex situations regarding intersecting antagonisms. This implies that in the endeavour to understand conflicts, emic perspectives have to be taken seriously and must not be obscured by the imposition of macro-perspective categories like, for instance, the distinction between 'Taliban' and 'civilians' in Afghanistan. Furthermore, conflicts are not simply about 'objects of conflict' but have a significant communicative dimension. Often, the discursive construction of a conflict is itself disputed, so we need to take not only symbolic action, including rituals surrounding conflicts, into account, but also non-communication, silence and discursive taboos.

CONFLICTS AS FIGURATIONS

The approach to conflicts suggested herein takes the conflicting actors seriously. Norbert Elias was one of the first social scientists to focus on individuals as social actors. He refused to privilege or reify 'society' or 'the social' – or 'structure', we could say – or to separate it from the individual human being; rather, he emphasised the necessity to think about both together: the individual human being/actor embedded in social relationships and the social composed of individual human beings and resulting from their interaction. Elias can be seen as a precursor to later practice theory. For him, neither methodological individualism nor methodological holism was a viable option for sociology. He suggested the concept of *figuration* in order to refer to the 'middle ground' of social formations that come into being through the interaction of individuals and which in turn strongly influence individual action. Elias takes the example of a game of cards – or rather of individuals *playing* cards – in order to explain what he means by figuration (Elias 2009: 141f). The people playing form a figuration. Their interaction is interdependent, i.e. the acts of each of these individuals depend on the acts of others, to which they respond and which set certain conditions to which they re-act in turn. The game is not an abstraction or an ideal type but a concrete event and process. The game is also not reducible to a set of rules; it is rather the enactment and interpretation of these rules in the particular event of playing. The game does not exist independently of the playing individuals and vice versa, i.e. the individuals are not independent of this situation, as they become and are players only through their interaction. Such a figuration has no fixed boundaries. While we can limit our view to the players, we could also take into consideration the larger space in which they are playing, perhaps a pub or a living room. Again, we will discover concrete interdependencies with other actors in this room and beyond, discovering larger networks of interaction. However, even if we follow these interdependencies of interaction further, we trace a specific and concrete figuration and do not arrive at the abstraction of 'the social' or 'society'. Through tracing the figuration we learn about interdependencies and are able to discover connections which in the beginning might have been out of sight. Elias emphasises that figurations are changeable patterns that implicate individuals, not only intellectually, but also as 'whole persons' (ibid. 142) – with their bodies and senses, we should add. He further points out that two or more groups composed of interdependent individuals may be intertwined in a figuration. He takes the example of two football teams that play against one another. The interdependencies and interactions of the players within each of the teams can only be understood with reference to their interactions with the opposing team. To this figuration we can add the spectators and fans, who in turn respond to the unfolding of the game on the field. We could also extend this notion by taking into account other football teams and their followers and arrive at the larger figuration of a football league – a figuration of the figurations of individual teams and games. Figurations are not clearly bounded but extend in space and time, and they cannot be defined by drawing limits but rather by pointing out core events and issues. The connectedness of figurations – which also implies specific closures and disjunctions – corroborates Crossroads Asia's emphasis of mobility and trans-border relations.

Taking inspiration from Elias's conceptualisation, we consider conflicts as figurations or as significant nodes of larger figurations where multiple networks of interaction and interdependency collide. Just like Elias's example of the football game, conflicts come into being through interacting individuals that form oppositions and/or alliances. Also, conflict figurations branch out and extend over time and space; they have particular histories and connect with other issues and figurations.

Following Latour, we cannot limit the analysis of figurations to the acting individuals involved – we also have to take *things*, objects, into account. Elias overlooked that the players in his game of cards actually needed a material deck of cards, without which they would be engaged in a very different activity. Similarly, objects such as a ball, goals, a field and, perhaps even a stadium are necessary elements for the figuration of a football game. Just as Elias refused to strictly separate 'the social' from 'the individual', Latour refuses to separate 'human beings' from 'non-human beings'. This is highly relevant for the analysis of conflicts, as they have their own material conditions and paraphernalia. Take Latour's famous example of the gun: a human being with a gun is not the same as a human being without a gun. Although the gun does nothing by itself (shoot people), the possession of a gun transforms the human being; it changes the range of action (Latour 2002: 214ff). People carrying guns and who interact with one another form a quite different configuration than people without guns. Yet the significance of material things for conflicts is not limited to the obvious case of weapons. Other things such as roads, mobile phones and cars equally play significant roles in figurations, figurations of conflict included, and they enable different ways to perform the action, extend the range of action and transform actors in various ways. Many such things in particular transform the relation of actors and agents with space, in that they enable the bridging of distance and facilitate the connection between distant places, or they reduce the time needed to do so. Thus, they enable the extension of figurations.

Given the particular emphasis of the Crossroads Asia network on questions of mobility and space, I will focus on these issues in the rest of this introduction, departing from the discussion of a conflict which I have followed, more or less continuously, over the last two and a half decades, namely the conflict between Sunnis and Shias in Gilgit, the capital city of the high mountain area of Gilgit-Baltistan, to which Emma Varley's chapter in this collection also refers. This conflict can be viewed as a local figuration that overlaps with other figurations in time and space and which also has strong effects on local space, transforming, in fact, spatial organisation.

Conflict, Space and Mobility: Shias and Sunnis in Gilgit

Everyday life in Gilgit is strongly affected by Sunni-Shia violence. Since the late 1980s, periods of violence, which are known locally as *tensions*, have occurred every few years, or sometimes even more frequently. In 2012, for instance, there were three periods of tensions. In contrast to earlier cases, the events of violence that produced tensions did not happen in Gilgit town itself, but Shia passengers were attacked on buses coming from or going to Gilgit on the Karakorum Highway (in February and May 2012) or near the Babusar Pass (in September 2012). Nevertheless, these attacks had strong repercussions in the town. Because counter-violence is expected after such attacks, curfews are imposed on the town which often last for several weeks. Life in Gilgit comes to a halt. Traffic on the Karakorum Highway, the lifeline on which Gilgit-Baltistan depends for the supply of food and other essentials, is closed or strongly restricted. The bazaar is closed and people have to live for days on whatever they happen to store in their houses. Even when, after some time, the curfew is relaxed or lifted, movement remains restrained, as people fear further violence. The atmosphere in the town remains very tense, and often it takes weeks or even months until life becomes 'normal' again.

The conflict between Shias and Sunnis in Gilgit does not have a definite beginning, although in local discourse 1988 is often given as the year in which the troubles started. Nonetheless, this year marks the escalation of Sunni-Shia violence rather than the actual beginning of the conflict. Of course, the Shia-Sunni issue originates in the dispute about the succession of the Prophet Mohammad and is therefore almost as old as Islam itself. Shia-Sunni antagonism is a global concomitant of Islam that has diverse local manifestations. In Gilgit-Baltistan, for instance, the two sects are unevenly distributed area-wise. This spatial distribution of Shias and Sunnis (and Ismailis, the third Muslim sect in Gilgit-Baltistan, which is not directly involved in the antagonism) originates from the differential Islamisation of the region. Roughly, Sunni missionaries came from the south, Shias from the East and Ismailis from the North. Thus, very roughly, the south of Gilgit-Baltistan, Diamer District, is purely Sunni, while to the east, Baltistan, is mostly – though not exclusively – Shia, while the northern part of the area, Hunza, is mostly Ismaili. Gilgit town is mixed and surrounded by villages populated by members of all sects. 'Mixed' does not mean that the sects are evenly distributed throughout the town; rather, Shias and Sunnis are concentrated in particular areas, and mixed neighbourhoods are actually the great exception. This spatial configuration of Shias and Sunnis living in close proximity, and yet in separate – and often spatially opposed – neighbourhoods of the town, is probably one significant precondition that has been highly conducive to the escalation of the conflict. Increasing spatial separation, however, is also a significant outcome of conflict.

In local discourse, people mostly emphasise that there was no conflict "in the past," that Shias and Sunnis were closely related, marriages included, that they lived amicably side by side and that in many cases one even did not know whether a person was Shia or Sunni. Two dichotomies (beside the Shia-Sunni dichotomy itself) dominate the discourse about sectarian conflict in Gilgit, both of which support one another: past vs. present and inside vs. outside. While the past was peaceful, the present is violent. Similarly, it is said that people from Gilgit are peaceful, and it was in fact outsiders who brought conflict and violence to the area. Taken together, both dichotomies rather exonerate the local people of Gilgit, in that they are not responsible for Sunni-Shia violence that has befallen the town over the last decades. When I first started fieldwork in Gilgit, in 1991, I was told that Shias and Sunnis had even prayed together in the same mosque. The beginning of the separation of Shias and Sunnis in ritual gatherings was attributed to Sardar Mohammad Akbar Khan, who was the *Wazir-e-Wazarat* (Governor) of the Maharaja in Gilgit in the first decade of the 20th century. I was told that the same mosque in Gilgit's bazaar was used by Shias and Sunnis for prayer, but that the governor initiated the construction of a Shia Imambarga, a hall which Shias use especially for the commemoration of the martyrdom of the Imam Hussain during Muharram, the month of mourning. Thus, separate places were allocated to Sunnis and Shias, though they still often shared mosques until the 1970s.

The first incidents of violence occurred in the 1970s. On Ashura, the 10th of the month of Muharram, Shias mourn the martyrdom of the Imam Hussain in Kerbela in 680 in a public *julus* (procession). Ashura mourning practices include self-flagellation (*zanjiri matam*). The *julus* used to end in a reunion at the central bazaar of Gilgit, in front of the Sunni *jama masjid* (main mosque). In 1972, the Qazi of the Sunni protested against the assembly in this place, arguing that the *julus* disturbed prayer in the mosque and that the blood of the Shias defiled the space around the building. The Shias, however, refused to change the course of the Ashura *julus*. The dispute continued over the following years. In 1975, the Shia *julus* was shot at from the Sunni mosque. The Sunni Qazi was arrested, following which armed Sunnis from Kohistan and Diamer marched towards Gilgit, in order to free the Qazi. Similarly, armed Shias started out from Nager, in order to defend Shias in Gilgit. Both groups were stopped by local paramilitary troops, the Gilgit Scouts, before they reached the town. In the following years, the administration did not allow the Shias to assemble in front of the Sunni mosque. As the Shias refused to gather at another place, the *julus* was prohibited for the next two years, until the Shias gave in. Muharram remains a very tense time in Gilgit up to today. The bloodshed that was prevented in 1975 occurred in 1988. In this year, Shias ended Ramadan, the month of fasting, a day earlier than the Sunnis. While Sunnis were still fasting, young Shia men rejoiced in the main bazaar, by smoking and eating. The Sunnis felt deeply offended, there was a local fight and when the news of this reached the Sunni areas of Diamer and Kohistan, armed *lashkar* ('warriors') again made their way toward Gilgit. This time they were not stopped, as the Gilgit Scouts in the interim period had been disbanded and the regular army would take no action. The Sunni *lashkar* did not enter Gilgit town but devastated Shia villages, such as Jalalabad and Sakwar, close to the town.

Why did the dispute over the *julus* develop in the 1970s? Many people in Gilgit – Shias, Sunnis and Ismailis alike – draw a line from politics to religion. In early 1971, the town saw a brief but massive uprising against the Pakistani domination of the area. A minor dispute between a local teacher and a Punjabi army officer grew into the open expression of discontent with the area's political status: having been part of the State of Jammu and Kashmir before the partition of the subcontinent in 1947, Gilgit-Baltistan was (and still is) under Pakistani control and administration, yet it was not a constitutional part of the country and lacked any representation in the Pakistani political setup (Sökefeld 2005). There was a huge demonstration. In order to free a political leader who had been arrested, the police station in Gilgit was stormed and then set on fire. The Gilgit Scouts refused to use force to control the situation, and finally troops from outside were called in to put down the insurgency. Thereafter, Sunni *ulema* from outside came to Gilgit and started to preach against Shias, calling them 'apostates' and 'non-Muslims'. For many people in Gilgit it made perfect sense that these *ulema* were brought in by the government in order to execute a divide-and-rule strategy, that is, to pit Sunnis against Shias, in order to prevent further united mobilisation against Pakistan's control. Although this allegation cannot be proven, it is a clear indication of mistrust vis-à-vis the government of Pakistan. In any case, since the mid-1970s, alienation between Shias and Sunnis has grown into inter-sectarian violence.

The events of 1988 ruptured Shia-Sunni relations and had long-lasting effects. While before, Shia-Sunni relations had been one issue among others in the town, the sectarian antagonism now became a premise for social life in Gilgit. Segregation, spatial as well as social, between both groups increased, and Shias living in villages close to the town or in parts of the city where they were in a minority position – and therefore allegedly vulnerable to further attack by Sunnis – moved to other places that were inhabited by a Shia or Ismaili majority and which felt safe. Similarly, Sunnis also concentrated in Sunni areas. In effect, villages and neighbourhoods became unmixed, and nowadays, in periods of tension, people will often, for weeks, refuse to go to their workplaces if these happen to be in a majority area of the other sect. In her contribution to this volume, Emma Varley vividly describes the grave effects of these dynamics of vulnerability and separation on the health sector in Gilgit. A similar dynamic applies to schools, whereby parents send their children to institutes that they consider safe because they are situated in a neighbourhood dominated by their own sect. Thus, many schools become increasingly homogeneous in terms of the sectarian affiliation of their students. In acute periods of tension, people even avoid moving through areas dominated by the other sect. Moreover, in 2012, after the bus attacks mentioned earlier, public transport in Gilgit was separated according to sect, although this was stopped by the government after just a few days (Grieser/Sökefeld 2015). Together with this increasing spatial separation of Shias and Sunnis comes a growing social distance between the two sects, due in part to the fact that for almost three decades no cross-sectarian marriages have been concluded. Many people have relatives in the other sect, yet social contact has decreased greatly. Everyday life is increasingly sectarianised, meaning that sectarian affiliation becomes significant in more and more areas of life (Grieser/Sökefeld 2015: 83).

The social dynamics of sectarianisation can be described succinctly through Leo Kuper's concept of polarisation. Kuper uses the concept for

"an intensification of conflict by aggressive action and reaction. Polarization, then, is a process of increasing aggregation of the members of the society into exclusive and mutually hostile groups, entailing the elimination of the middle-ground and of mediating relationships. Episodes of conflict accumulate. There are corresponding ideologies […] presenting simplified conceptions of the society as already polarized into two antagonistic groups with incompatible and irreconcilable interests, rendering inevitable the resort to violence." (Kuper 1977: 128)

Although sectarian violence is not a daily affair in Gilgit, in the sense that somebody is attacked or killed every day, events of violence and conflict have mounted up due to growing antagonism and separation. Both groups rely on (religious) ideologies that legitimise this antagonism and interpret the violent action of the other group as a validation of their own position. Most importantly, the 'middle-ground' has been largely erased in Gilgit – both spatially and in terms of intermediate social relations. In fact, few places are left where Shias and Sunnis interact on a daily basis. To some extent the central bazaar is one such place, although customers tend to frequent 'same-sect' shops if they are not looking for specialised goods. Nonetheless, the bazaar is also seen as a very dangerous area, and it is the first place that people vacate unanimously when violence occurs. Another place of cross-sectarian interaction is Gilgit's university, the Karakorum International University (KIU), which struggles to keep sectarianism out of its precincts, and not always successfully. In 2012 and 2013, for instance, Shia students celebrated *yom-e-Hussain* (the day of the Imam Hussain) in commemoration of the martyrdom of the third Shia Imam at the university, in reaction to which Sunni students protested. In 2012, clashes followed, and in both years the KIU was closed for a number weeks, in order to prevent further escalation. A 'sectarian logic' is forced on the university and on other institutions. In an article, Nosheen Ali describes how the university is pressurised into maintaining a 'sectarian balance' in terms of employment or prizes awarded, whereby all three sects, Ismailis included, have to be considered on equal terms, in order to avoid protests (Ali 2010: 744f). This sectarian logic has become a premise for social life, an a priori notion that shapes the perception of events, so that every incident of violence that occurs is first interpreted within the Shia-Sunni framework: if the victim is a Shia, it is assumed that the perpetrator is a Sunni, or the other way round, until it often turns out that the incident was perhaps a family issue completely unrelated to sectarianism.

The sectarian logic is pervasive. Although most inhabitants of the town regret this state of affairs, and only a few people in Gilgit are die-hard partisans in relation to their own sect, they cannot escape the separating dynamics of polarisation. Sectarian 'un-mixing' is not produced by bureaucratic efforts or by the coordinated use of violence for this purpose, as in cases of "ethnic cleansing" (e.g. Hayden 1996) – it occurs rather as a kind of self-organisation that is driven by sentiments of fear and insecurity. In spite of the strong dynamics of polarisation, there are always actors who try to overcome the sectarian divide and who exert great effort in working towards reconciliation; yet, they often also succumb to sectarian logic. Thus, Nosheen Ali points out that it was a peace *jirga* (peace council) that forced the 'sectarian balance' on KIU and demanded that members of all sects have to be equally represented in the awards process. Interestingly, it is especially the 'nationalists' of Gilgit-Baltistan, i.e. those political groups that strongly criticise Pakistan's control over the area and that demand real autonomy or even independence, that most openly reject sectarian logic. For them, the imposition of sectarian logic is a nefarious strategy of control that goes way beyond 'divide and rule' tactics, as violence and insecurity provide a convincing legitimisation to tighten the surveillance, control and militarisation of the area further (Ali 2013).

SECTARIANISM IN GILGIT AS FIGURATION

Sectarianism in Gilgit can be read as a figuration in which many issues overlap and interconnect. It is of course a much more complex figuration than Norbert Elias's simple example of the games of cards or football, as sectarianism draws on a long history of Shia-Sunni antagonism in Islam, though it is not reducible purely to this particular issue. Shia-Sunni antagonism is not a pre-existing coercive structure that leaves individual actors no choice but to fight each other; rather, sectarian logic, which today indeed has acquired a certain coercive power – especially as a cognitive framework of interpretation –, developed over time as a consequence of the accumulation of conflict interaction and experience. Individual actors act in response to the actions of members of their own and of the other sect, including their expectations of the actions of others. Thus, the un-mixing of Shias and Sunnis is a consequence of the experience of insecurity and the expectation of further violence. It had the consequence of erasing a middle-ground where members of both sects could meet and interact beyond the premise of antagonism. The dynamic of polarisation, once triggered, is difficult to stop.

Also, in the figuration of Sunni-Shia violence, material things are a significant part of the game. This is most obvious in the case of automatic weapons, which are used in events of violence and without which the escalation of the antagonism would have been impossible. Since the 1990s, Sunni-Shia resentment has been linked discursively to the so-called 'Kalashnikov culture' that prevailed in many parts of Pakistan. Nowadays, one could speak instead of a 'bomb culture' that haunts the country, and recently grenades have also been used in Shia-Sunni violence in Gilgit. Besides weapons, infrastructure and means of transportation also play a significant role, both as transport for attackers – the violence of 1988 would not have been possible without cars – and as targets for attack. Thus, in 2012, Shias were assaulted on buses while passing through Sunni areas. Perhaps the most important implements for the conflict today are mobile phones, as attacks are coordinated through mobile communication. Young men especially, who have to pass through areas dominated by the other sect, are highly suspicious of mobiles: when they see somebody starting to talk on the phone while they are passing by, they often change their route or even abort their trip altogether, because they fear that someone might have been alerted of their approach, in order to shoot them. Furthermore, mobile communication enables the easy circulation of news and rumours that may trigger further violence. The attack on Shia passengers travelling on buses on the Karakorum Highway by people of Chilas, the Sunni town in the south of Gilgit, in April 2012, was triggered by the rather exaggerated 'news' spread by text messages that many Sunnis had been killed at a demonstration in Gilgit. When violence occurs, the authorities therefore usually shut down mobile services, just as they close down or at least strictly control traffic on the Karakorum highway. Such measures, however, add to the atmosphere of insecurity, as it becomes more difficult to get reliable information and also because the supply of provisions is stopped and becomes precarious.

Importantly, the figuration of Sunni-Shia conflict in Gilgit intersects and overlaps with other issues, most significantly with the dispute about the political status of the area. While any involvement of state and government in the triggering of violence cannot be verified, the discursive intersection of politics and the Shia-Sunni issue has very practical results. Local elections, for instance, generally follow the sectarian logic, and often candidates quite explicitly use sectarian affiliation as a means of mobilising support. Furthermore, as I pointed out previously, governmental efforts to curb Sunni-Shia violence add to the militarisation and control of the area by all kinds of 'security' agencies, which strongly add to a widespread feeling of insecurity, marginalisation and disenfranchising domination by Pakistan.

It noteworthy that the Shia-Sunni figuration emerges not only from the action of those who somehow actively take part in the antagonism, as perpetrators of violence or as producers of sectarian discourse as preachers in mosques, for instance, but also the figuration creates a 'space of conflict' in Gilgit in which everyday life takes place – a space of conflict in the dual sense of *physical space*, as a series of places in which people live and through which they pass, and of *social space*, made up of social positions and relationships that people occupy and spin through their interaction. In their daily action, in most realms of life, people in the town have to take into account the conflict and the pervasive logic of sectarianism and reproduce it accordingly. People's actions are not determined, but their choices are limited by the conflict in regards to where they move in the town, to which school they send their children, which doctor they see in case of illness, where they look for possible marriage partners – all of which is affected by sectarian considerations. To allude to Georg Elwert again, social life in Gilgit is embedded in this space of sectarian conflict.

Nevertheless, the Shia-Sunni figuration in Gilgit goes beyond the local space of conflict and connects with sectarianism in other places in Pakistan. Politics in Pakistan, most importantly the politics of Islamisation that was executed by General Zia ul Haq after 1979 and which solely promoted a specific Sunni interpretation of Islam, have strongly fostered Gilgit Shias' self-perception of being marginalised and being constantly under threat. In Pakistan, anti-Shia violence is not limited to Gilgit-Baltistan. In recent years, for instance, especially Shias in Baluchistan, most of them Hazaras originating from Afghanistan, have become victims of merciless massacres. In November 2013, clashes emerged around the Ashura procession in Rawalpindi, which resulted in severe violence in which at least eight persons were killed and many more injured. Often, people in Gilgit-Baltistan react to such incidents. After the Rawalpindi attacks, there was a huge demonstration in the Sunni town Chilas protesting against Shia attacks on a Sunni mosque and madrasa in Rawalpindi. At the same time, Shias in Gilgit condemned attacks on a Shia *imambarga* in Rawalpindi. Both a Sunni and a Shia party called for a "shutter-down strike," and bazaars in Gilgit and Chilas were closed. The authorities also blocked traffic on the Karakorum Highway, in order to prevent retaliatory violence.

Furthermore, Shias and Sunnis in Gilgit are embedded in far-reaching religious networks. This is not a new development; in fact, the ideological separation of Sunnis and Shias is largely the consequence of the increasing translocal connection of their *ulema* (religious scholars) to their respective centres of learning. Sunnis in Gilgit are today almost exclusively followers of the School of Deoband – a relationship which dates back to the 1920s when, for the first time, two Sunnis from the Gilgit area went to study at the famous madrasa in the north Indian town of Deoband and subsequently taught their version of Islam in Gilgit. For Shias, the decisive relation is with Iran. In 1937, an Iranian *alim* (scholar) who settled in the town initiated the construction of the present-day Shia *jama masjid* and became its first imam (Sökefeld 1997: 187f). Subsequently, almost all Shia *ulema* from Gilgit have been to Iran for religious studies, and as a consequence of the greater centralisation of Shia Islam, almost all Shias in Gilgit have personal connections to Iran because they are *muqallidun* (followers, implying a relation of personal faithfulness) of a Shia ayatollah in the country. The Shia networks connect what in area studies are usually separated as South and West Asia.

Another overarching context in which the Shia-Sunni issue is embedded is the Kashmir conflict. I have already pointed out that the Shia-Sunni conflict is locally interpreted with reference to the specific political predicament of Gilgit-Baltistan as being controlled by Pakistan, which is based on the Kashmir dispute. Yet, the conflict in Gilgit also feeds back into the Kashmir dispute. Thus, local nationalism that postulates the nation of Gilgit-Baltistan as distinct from Pakistan, as well as from Kashmir, and which is entitled to self-determination, or at least real autonomy, and that thereby challenges the conventional framing of the Kashmir conflict, also derives from the experience of Pakistan's divisive politics of religion. This nationalism proposes to overcome such divisions through the identification with a nation that – unlike Pakistan – is not based on religious affiliation in the first place.

SPACE AND PLACE, MOBILITY AND MOBILISATION

The sectarian figuration in Gilgit is linked intimately and in multiple ways with issues of space and mobility. Sectarianisation is first of all the sectarianisation of *places*. This started with Wazir-e-Wazarat Sardar Mohammad

Akbar Khan in the early 20th century, who assigned separate places for Shia and Sunni ritual gatherings. Conflict over the Ashura *julus* in the 1970s was essentially over movement and space, whereby Sunnis considered the movement of the Shia *julus* near to their mosque an infringement on their space, while Shias insisted on their right to move across the city space. Nonetheless, through the ongoing dynamics of polarisation the urban space of Gilgit has become increasingly subject to sectarian division. Polarisation implies sectarian place-making and the increasing congruence of group boundaries and spatial boundaries. Many parts of the city have become marked as either Sunni or Shia space, in which the movement of members of the respective other group is considered unsafe. This is not only crucial for quotidian movement, since many people have moved house in order to leave places that they consider unsafe. Movement is restricted especially in times of tension, but a considerable degree of (self-)restriction remains effective also when an acute period of conflict is over. Furthermore, violent events are linked directly with movement, as people need to move in order to attack. Accordingly, the authorities try to control space and movement through a dense network of checkpoints and the imposition of curfews, i.e. prohibiting people from moving outside of their house, in periods of violence. The loss of the middle-ground in the process of polarisation means that neutral sites have become reduced and contested; antagonists try to mark neutral places as their own space. Beyond literal movement in physical space, the Shia-Sunni issue is also linked with issues of mobilisation in social and political space. On the one hand, actors have to be mobilised in order to side with the antagonists in one way or the other, but on the other hand this inter-sect bitterness is also employed as a means of mobilisation in other affairs such as elections.

The close linkage between space/place and conflict is not accidental; rather, it is the consequence of the fact that all human action 'takes place' in places – even if in virtual ones. Place is a crucial resource for action and is therefore almost necessarily disputed in cases of unrest. Disputes about places can take many forms, such as conflicts about territory and borders, or about the right to move or the right to stay. Thus, the relation between conflict and space/place is of course a dual one: conflicts take place *in* space and at particular places, but they are also *about* space and places that are claimed by the antagonists. Often, conflict is also inscribed in places through symbolic markings or the drawing of physical boundaries. Similarly, movement and mobility are not only significant aspects of conflict action, but they are also affected by conflict.

I think a brief note on the relation of 'space' and 'place' is required here. Tim Ingold (2009) is right, in that there is no 'space' in practice: as soon as action 'takes place', 'space' is converted into concrete places – it is appropriated as particular places. Movement does not take place in space but from place to place. Conceiving of place as 'space' is therefore the philosophers' fallacy – the fallacy of those philosophers who 'take the people out,' to refer to Ingold's beautiful definition of anthropology as "philosophy with the people in" (Ingold 1992: 695-6). Still, I think, we need a word on the abstract condition of space – a kind of pre-social notion. Turning Ingold against Lefebvre (1991), we could suggest that space is never constructed, because as soon as it is constructed, i.e. subject to social action, it becomes a place(s). Consequentially, space is not contested – except in abstract discourse. What are always subject to disputes, though, are particular places.

THE CONTRIBUTIONS IN THIS VOLUME

Issues of space and place, of movement and mobility, are the common denominators for the contributors to this volume, who deal with contested places and movements, including land as the most concrete place as an object of dispute, with the difficulty of mobilising resources in marginalised spaces, and with the effects of displacement from a contested border zone.

Aksana Ismailbekova's contribution, *Shifting Borders: Coping Strategies of Inhabitants in the Aftermath of the Osh Conflict, Kyrgyzstan*, is about the 'ethnic' division of Kyrgyzstan's second-largest city as a consequence of violent conflict. She analyses how Kyrgyz and Uzbek inhabitants coped with the 'ethnic' violence that occurred in 1990 and 2010. Historically, Uzbeks had largely been city-dwellers, while the Kyrgyz lived as nomads; yet, the two groups were not always completely separate, as there were intermarriages, and to some extent 'ethnic' identity was a matter of economic specialisation. Soviet processes of modernisation, which focused especially on the development of cities, brought both groups closer together and separated them at the same time. Driven by Soviet urban planning, Kyrgyz moved into the city, often occupying 'modern' apartment buildings that replaced 'traditional' Uzbek neighbourhoods, while Uzbeks were pushed towards the margins. Thus, land became contentious and was overtly ethnicised, especially in the post-Soviet period. Complex social relations were increasingly reduced to a Kyrgyz-Uzbek dichotomy, and especially the violence of 2010 triggered the further displacement of Uzbeks – often to neighbouring Uzbekistan – and consolidated the Kyrgyz domination of Osh. For Uzbeks, moving out of mixed neighbourhoods was a kind of survival strategy. Following a Kyrgyz real-estate agent, who took advantage of the Uzbeks' urge to sell their properties in order to move to safer areas, the chapter provides insights into the dynamics behind the spatial separation of Uzbek and Kyrgyz. Besides housing, segregation also affects businesses and even mosques. The city major's attempts to promote ethnically mixed 'friendship houses' could not stop the dynamics of segregation, and both Uzbeks and Kyrgyz felt compelled instead to take the side of their respective groups, in order to avoid further violence. Interestingly, however, these segregation dynamics did not affect all parts of Osh equally, and some neighbourhoods were able to prevent violence – and therefore segregation – by stressing a shared identity of "being from Osh" at the expense of ethnic particularism.

In his article, *Understanding Mobilisation Processes in Conflict through Framing: The Case of inter-communal Conflict in the Batken Province, Kyrgyzstan*, Khushbakht Hojiev analyses the dynamics of a local conflict between Tajiks and Kyrgyz in a village of southern Kyrgyzstan. What started as a brawl between a few young men threatened to escalate into a larger, violent fight in which the antagonists literally opposed one another in space. Nevertheless, efforts made by local elders at mediation, and later the arrival of security forces, prevented this escalation. Hojiev asks why this conflict was considered locally as an ethnic conflict, and he applies framing analysis, derived from social movement theory, to this case. Following Hartmut Esser, he defines framing as an inter-subjective process of definition, perception and identification of a conflict situation and argues that a focus on framing helps to bridge the 'instrumentalist-interpretivist' divide in conflict analysis and to emphasise an action and process-oriented perspective. Framing is an active and constitutive process that draws on broader cognitive models and public sentiments. Both Kyrgyz and Tajiks applied an ethnic frame to the incident in question, relating to the broader model of the titular nation, from the Kyrgyz perspective, and to the model of minority, from the Tajik point of view. Hojiev points out that especially three referencing mechanisms were significant in the process of framing:

the use of the symbolic dimension of violence, othering and alignment with the larger political discourse, especially the ethno-nationalist discourse at the national level of Kyrgyzstan. Here also reference to the violent conflict in Osh plays an important role, though framing is not necessarily uncontested. In this particular case, elders and representatives of the local authorities were able to reframe the incident successfully as an ordinary tussle between young men. Framing is a complex process, the analysis of which helps to improve understanding of conflict situations.

Taking a different methodological and theoretical approach, Jan Koehler asks about the role of social order and social institutions in relation to conflicts. In *Institution-Centred Conflict Research: A Methodological Approach and its Application in East Afghanistan*, drawing on classical contributions to conflict theory from Coser and Dahrendorf about the question whether conflict is disruptive or integrative in the first place, Koehler argues that the institutionalisation of unavoidable conflicts as a constitutive element of society fosters social cohesion. However, while other authors have drawn this conclusion for 'modern', industrialised and state-centred societies, he sets out to test this proposition for the rather volatile social setting in Afghanistan. Asking how conflicts are processed, what role institutions play in conflict and how conflict-processing impacts on social order, Koehler draws on material from a larger, comparative research process but focuses in this contribution on a case of land-grabbing in a district of the Nangarhar province of north-eastern Afghanistan. The dispute is about a piece of land that was owned by a clan but then claimed by a military commander. In the vicissitudes of Afghanistan's political situation, land ownership changed sides several time. The case involves different institutions, such as *jirgas* and formal land titles, and strategies, such as patronage and self-help. The development of the conflict shows that power and force are not enough to secure land: claims have to respect certain rules. Thus, the powerful commander also took steps to secure formal title to the land in question. Koehler reaches the conclusion that local conflict-processing institutions survive war and social fragmentation. The case indicates that violence is constrained even in situations of gross power difference, if in the long run the interests of the more powerful party require acceptance within the institutional context. However, procedures such as *jirgas* legitimate claims rather than contain violence, and so they are more an instrument of those in power than a means to limit and control such power.

Nick Miszak's chapter on *Land-based Conflict in Afghanistan: On the Right of Pre-emption (shuf'a) as 'back-channel' Diplomacy and a Show of Indignation* analyses another case of land conflict. Land is the most important object of dispute in the area, as it is a significant resource for people's social position and power. Furthermore, it is linked closely with the concept of *namus*, signifying properties that men have to defend in order to protect their honour. Land has become particularly conflictual in Afghanistan, as after the beginning of the US-led military intervention the country was literally flooded with international funds and many Afghan refugees returned home. In a case study, again from the province of Nagrahar in Eastern Afghanistan, Miszak focuses in particular on the role of the right of pre-emption (*shuf'a*) in land conflicts. The conflict in question relates to a piece of land close to the Torkham border crossing with Pakistan, the most important entry point for NATO supplies to Afghanistan, which is therefore of particular value for business. Rumours that a township would be constructed in this place further enhanced the value of the plot in question. In 2002, a group of people called *Pekhawal* started to construct shops on this plot overnight, knowing that eviction is difficult once labour and materials have been invested in a piece of land. The next day, a group of Mohmandara went to the location and tried to stop construction work, claiming that the Pekhawals' occupation was illegal. As neighbours of the plot, the Mohmandara claimed to be *shuf'adar*, which meant that they would reserve the right to benefit from the land to them. However, through the intervention of the police, only a kind of standstill between both parties could be achieved. In the changing constellations of power the Mohmandara did not pursue their case through the courts (neither of the groups had a formal title for the land) or a *jirga* but sought rather to influence the executive through roadblocks and other action, thereby arousing public interest by what Miszak calls 'back-channel diplomacy' – a series of meetings with different politicians who the Mohmandaras tried to convince of their own perspective. The Mohmandaras' campaign rested especially on their interpretation of the right of pre-emption, *shuf'a*, an important concept of Islamic property law. Nevertheless, the occupying Pekhawals also produced historical narratives, in order to establish their own right of pre-emption and to reject that of the Mohmandaras. Miszak details how narratives and counter-narratives are constructed. Thus, both parties accept the general validity of *shuf'a* and the relation to the land becomes the source of the legitimacy of claims. Although after more than ten years the conflict is still not solved,

Miszak argues that, in spite of all narratives to the contrary, Afghanistan is by no means simply a country where violence and lawlessness reign supreme. Corroborating Jan Koehler's findings, Miszak concludes that while a threat to use force is often present in conflicts, force does not overrule legitimacy, and it is legitimacy in the first place that people attempt to construct for their claims.

Katja Mielke's chapter, *Not in in the Master Plan: Dimensions of Exclusion in Kabul*, takes a different approach. Instead of focusing on a particular conflict, she analyses a conflictual field, namely urban infrastructural development in District 13 on the outskirts of Afghanistan's capital city. "D13" is a rapidly urbanising district, mostly populated by Hazaras, which has been largely ignored by Kabul's infrastructural development. The Hazara inhabitants transfer their identity as a discriminated-against minority in Afghanistan onto the urban district. For them, their state of being disadvantaged and marginalised is epitomised in the fact that D13 has not been included in Kabul's master plan, which in turn is regarded as the reason why the municipality shows little interest in the district's development. The Hazaras' perception of exclusion has been exacerbated by rapid construction of a township of Kuchis in D13 which is well-serviced and supported by international donor agencies. Mielke considers D13 as a 'core figuration' which is part of larger figurations at the scale of the city and beyond. Asking how residents and representatives struggle regarding access to services and resources, she analyses the positionalities and relationships of actors that hinder or enable such access vis-à-vis the at-best disinterested municipality. In particular, she discusses the successful work of a rather young neighbourhood head (*wakil-e guzar*), who has been able to secure a number of projects for his area. Mielke shows that this *wakil-e guzar* is well-connected beyond D13 and can draw on national and even international support. Following Elias she argues that power imbalances cannot be reduced to ethnic differences, and she concludes that dynamics within D13 cannot be understood in an isolated manner: processes in the core figuration do not make sense if the wider figurational context – the social, spatial and temporal interdependencies in which the core figuration is imbedded – is ignored.

With Debidatta Aurobinda Mahapatra's chapter, *Negotiating Space in the Conflict Zone of Kashmir: The Borderlanders' Perspective*, we enter into a pervasive long-term conflict, namely the Kashmir dispute. Deploring the fact that the discourse on Kashmir centres on security issues and the state-perspectives of India and Pakistan, Mahapatra turns to the people who live(d) in the immediate vicinity on the Line of Control (LoC) between Indian- and Pakistan-controlled parts of the erstwhile princely state and who are immediately affected by violence, division and insecurity. These 'borderlanders' are not part of the mainstream discourse on Kashmir. Mahapatra argues that the border in Kashmir needs to be problematised and that the perspective of the borderlanders is crucial to this end. The article focuses on borderlanders on the Indian side of the LoC and is based on fieldwork that took place both at the border and in a number of refugee camps. Drawing on Martinez, Mahapatra analyses the border zone of Kashmir as an 'alienated borderland' characterised by most unfavourable conditions for those who live on the border. Based mostly on interviews, he describes the conditions of the borderlanders, focusing especially on the experiences of war, including the fortification of the LoC, as well as (multiple) displacement and life in the camps. In conclusion he points out that Kashmir's borders contradict much of the current border discourse, which focuses much more on the permeability and flexibility of borders than on their divisiveness and rigidity.

Through Emma Varley's chapter *Exclusionary Infrastructures: Crisis and the Rise of Sectarian Hospitals in Northern Pakistan*, we re-enter Gilgit. Varley analyses the effects of Shia-Sunni sectarianism on Gilgit's healthcare system, pointing out how healthcare itself has been sectarianised. She discusses especially events that were the consequence of the assassination of the Shia Imam Syed Zia-ud-din Rizvi in January 2005 and the subsequent retaliatory violence of Shias against Sunnis in the town. This violence also targeted Sunni doctors and patients at Gilgit's District Headquarters Hospital (DHQ), situated in a Shia majority neighbourhood. Although the DHQ theoretically offered its services to all people in Gilgit, Sunnis considered it an insecure place and were practically excluded. Thus, while public healthcare in Gilgit was originally insufficient anyway, access became even worse for Sunnis. Nevertheless, Shia patients also suffered because Sunni medical personnel often refused to work at the DHQ for lack of security. In order to overcome the lack of healthcare for Sunnis, a separate hospital was established in 2005 – on a private initiative – in the Sunni neighbourhood of Kashrote. This Kashrote hospital was subsequently extended and received government funding, yet essential facilities for diagnostics and treatment were lacking. Thus, the medical infrastructure of Gilgit became highly sectarianised, whereby the hospital sites became strictly associated with one or the other sect. Varley argues that the development of sect-specific medical infrastructure strongly affects everyday life in the town, thus exacerbating insecurity and contributing further to the lack of efficient medical services. This is particularly so after (or rather between) acute periods of tension, and therefore she calls the usual distinction between conflict and post-conflict states into question. The sectarianisation of healthcare demonstrates the state's inability to provide public security, and instead of being neutral sites of service, the hospitals serve as 'sites for identity formation and the emergence of novel forms of sectarian sociality', as Varley concludes.

REFERENCES

Ali, Nosheen (2010): "Sectarian Imaginaries: The Micropolitics of Sectarianism and State-making in Northern Pakistan." In: Current Sociology 58, pp. 738–754.
Ali, Nosheen (2013): "Grounding Militarism: Structures of Feeling and Force in Gilgit-Baltistan." In: Kamala Visweswaran (ed.), Everyday Occupations: Experiencing Militarism in South Asia and the Middle East, Philadelphia: University of Pennsylvania Press, pp. 85-110.
Crossroads Asia Working Group Conflict (2012): Conflict Research on Crossroads Asia – A Conceptual Approach. In: Crossroads Asia Concept Paper Series, No. 1. (http://crossroads-asia.de/veroeffentlichungen/concept-papers/concept-paper-conflict.html; accessed May 1, 2015.
Elias, Norbert (2009): Was ist Soziologie? Weinheim and Munich: Juventa.
Elwert, Georg (2004): „Anthropologische Perspektiven auf Konfikt." In: Julia Eckert (ed.), Anthropologie der Konflikte. Georg Elwerts konflikttheoretische Thesen in der Diskussion, Bielefeld: transcript, pp. 26-38.
Grieser, Anna/Sökefeld, Martin (2015): "Intersections of sectarian dynamics and spatial mobility in Gilgit-Baltistan." In: Stefan Conermann and Elena Smolarz (eds.), Mobilizing Religion: Networks and Mobility, Berlin: EB-Verlag, pp. 83-110.
Hayden, Robert M. (1996): "Imagined communities and real victims: Self-determination and ethnic cleansing in Yugoslavia." In: American Ethnologist 23, pp. 783-801.
Ingold, Tim (1992): "Editorial." In: Man 27, pp. 693-696.

Ingold, Tim (2009): "Against space: Place, movement, knowledge." In: Peter Wynn Kirby (ed.), Boundless Worlds: An Anthropological Approach to Movement, New York: Berghahn, pp. 29-43.

Kuper, Leo (1977): The Pity of it All: Polarisation of Racial and Ethnic Relations, London: Duckworth.

Latour, Bruno (2002): Die Hoffnung der Pandora, Frankfurt: Suhrkamp.

Lefebvre, Henri (1991): The Production of Space, Oxford: Blackwell.

Mielke, Katja/Hornidge, Anna-Katharina (2014): "Crossroads Studies: From Spatial Containers to Interactions in Differentiated Spatialities." In: Crossroads Asia Working Paper Series, No. 15. (http://crossroads-asia.de/fileadmin/user_upload/publications/Xroads_Working_Paper_15_Mielke_Hornidge_Crossroads_Studi.pdf; accessed May 1, 2015).

Sökefeld, Martin (1997): Ein Labyrinth von Identitäten in Nordpakistan: Zwischen Landbesitz, Religion und Kaschmir-Konflikt, Köln: Köppe.

Sökefeld, Martin (2005): "From Colonialism to Postcolonial Colonialism: Changing Modes of Domination in the Northern Areas of Pakistan." In: Journal of Asian Studies 64, pp. 939-974.

Wimmer, Andreas/Glick Schiller, Nina (2002): "Methodological Nationalism and Beyond: Nation-State Building, Migration and the Social Sciences." In: Global Networks 2, pp. 301-334.

Shifting Borders: Coping Strategies of Inhabitants in the Aftermath of the Osh Conflict, Kyrgyzstan

AKSANA ISMAILBEKOVA

INTRODUCTION

Osh is the second largest city in Kyrgyzstan. It is located in the Fergana Valley and is often referred to as the 'capital' of the south, because it is a focal point for broad-ranging familial, religious and exchange networks. Osh is home to nearly equal proportions of the country's two main ethnic groups – Kyrgyz and Uzbeks[1] – both of which have enjoyed a long history of peaceful coexistence in the city and across the Fergana Valley, marked by interethnic marriages, friendships and a broad range of social and economic interactions. Nevertheless, ethnic tensions have occurred since the late Soviet period, related partly to Soviet nation-building projects and partly to the new state's efforts to establish its independence. In 1990, and again in 2010, Osh gained international attention because of the eruption of extensive armed violence and large-scale destruction.

In these two episodes of conflict, groups of ethnic Kyrgyz and Uzbeks fought each other in Osh and neighbouring towns like Jalal-Abad and Su-

---

1 Ethnic Kyrgyz make up 72 per cent of the population in Kyrgyzstan. The largest minority are the Uzbeks, comprising 14 per cent of the population. The pre-conflict population of Osh numbered 258.000 individuals, with almost equal ethnic proportions of Uzbeks (48 per cent) and Kyrgyz (43 per cent) (National Census 2009).

zak. In both 1990 and 2010, hundreds of people were killed or injured, thousands of homes were razed and property worth millions of US Dollars was looted. The first conflict erupted in June 1990 in the context of land disputes emerging as a result of the collapse of the Soviet Union, but on this occasion Soviet troops intervened and stopped the violence. The second period of riots occurred exactly twenty years later, in June 2010, as a result of a recent political crisis, during which Kyrgyzstan's president was ousted, and the subsequent involvement of criminal groupings. Urban violence led to a widening emotional gap between Uzbeks and Kyrgyz and disseminated tension amongst the city's population (Megoran 2012, 2013). During the conflict in 2010, non-inhabitants flocked into the city and took part in the fighting.

The conflict of 2010 was dramatic but not homogenous, since not all of the city's neighbourhoods and surrounding areas were affected equally by the traumatising violence and destruction; in fact, the southern parts of Osh remained quite peaceful. Most notably, a number of ethnically mixed settlements did not experience any sort of violence, while others saw some damage to property but no fatalities, especially in the northern part of the city (Kutmanaliev, forthcoming). Towns like Uzgen were proud of having prevented conflict and remaining peaceful despite massive attempts by outsiders to incite violence. I agree with Kutmanaliev that some parts of the city have become spaces of 'ethnic division' between Uzbek *mahalla* and Kyrgyz *raion* (the Uzbek and Kyrgyz words for neighbourhood, respectively), while other parts have not been affected by this segregation. While some neighbourhoods have stayed together, other areas have become forcibly segregated by many factors such as state policy, local leadership, housing, the economy and a desire for safety. I argue that in segregated areas, people were forced to 'take sides' in order to survive, and in some parts of the city itself, Uzbeks and Kyrgyz reproduced their own spaces after the conflict, dividing these areas along 'ethnic' lines. Social interaction across the ethnic divide became extremely limited, as even former contexts of interethnic interaction, such as mosques and the transportation system, became segregated.

The events of 1990 and 2010 highlight that ethnic relations in Osh and the Fergana Valley are highly significant, not only for Kyrgyzstan's national stability but also for regional and human security. Conflict in the Kyrgyz part of the ethnically heterogeneous Fergana Valley also impacts interethnic relations and political processes in the Uzbek and Tajik parts of the region where the Kyrgyz are a minority. Violence and the aggravating processes of fighting easily spill over and lead to further interethnic conflicts, and so effective conflict management in Osh and its surrounding areas is vital for regional stability, even though numerous factors work against it. For instance, the number of unemployed young men is growing, thereby producing a large number of dissatisfied and easily mobilised aggressors, and the state promotes aggressive ethno-national ideologies that incite the antagonism of Kyrgyz towards minorities. The wider problems of discrimination and the exclusion of minority groups also threaten to raise broader human security issues.

In this chapter, I examine how the Uzbek minority and the Kyrgyz majority have coped in the aftermath of the recent Osh troubles in multiethnic Kyrgyzstan and their distinct ways of adapting and rearranging their lives in the aftermath thereof. The conflict provided powerful narratives (Megoran 2013), forcing local inhabitants to change their ideas regarding community, ethnicity and authority, and to re-build conflict-affected and severely damaged districts such as Shark, Cheremushka, Kyzyl-Kyshtak, Sheit-Tebe, Amir-Temur, Furkat, Sulaiman-Too and Ak-Buura along 'ethnic' lines. As a result, inhabitants of the conflict-affected areas have accommodated new conditions and incorporated them into their everyday lives.

Most of the literature on conflicts points to segregation being detrimental to inter-communal peace (Björkdahl 2013; Aggestam/Björkdahl 2013), yet it is important to draw a distinction between a short-term and a longer-term outcome. Ethnically-fuelled divisions can be observed also in other parts of the world, such as the Western Balkans, i.e. Bosnia and Herzegovina, Macedonia and Kosovo (Bieber/Daskalovski 2003; Aggestam/Björkdahl 2013); however, categories of identity alone cannot serve as causal explanations for conflict, since such categories are not invested with agency themselves, despite the fact that they are often attributed with the power and capacity to influence behaviour and action (Schlee 2008).

My main argument is that most ethnic Uzbeks and Kyrgyz follow a strategy of taking sides in violent conflicts. Schlee (2008) combines 'cost-benefit calculations' and social structures and their cognitive representations, in order to explain why and how people take sides during clashes. Following this explanatory framework, I argue that whether or not people take sides along ethnic lines – especially in times of conflict – is linked to advancing group interests and protecting one's own security. As a result, this kind of decision-making (taking sides) can be illustrated through the process of identification (Schlee 2008: 15). As Schlee argues, it is important to distinguish two aspects in this respect:

> "One has to do with concept and categories. The way in which people classify themselves and others tend to be of a systematic nature, and employs a certain logic and plausibility structure. […]. The other type of reason concerns the advantages and disadvantages that may arise from such identifications and such decisions to take sides: in other words with the cost and benefits of taking sides. It is to be expected that the two types of reason interpenetrate each other. Where there is room for identity work, i.e. for people reasoning about their identities and changing them, categories can be expected to be replaced or stretched to fit the needs of actors. These needs often have to do with the size of a group or alliance: one either seeks a wider alliance or tries to keep others out, to exclude them for sharing in certain benefits." (2008: 15)

This chapter is based on ethnographic research carried out in Osh, which I started in 2011 when I visited the city for three summer months, and continued in 2012 for three more summer months.[2] The methods I used during my ethnographic research were mostly in depth-interviewing and participant observation. During my research, I focused my attention mostly on the districts that were severely damaged. Due to time constraints I could not carry out research in all the parts of Osh, as it is particularly large city. I relate my contemporary ethnographic findings as well to the shared Soviet past of the region. In the next section I will draw attention to the Soviet construction of an urban planning policy that contributed to the emergence of social tension between the two ethnic groups in question.

---

2   The research was conducted in the framework of the Crossroads Asia competence network. The author is grateful to the German Federal Ministry of Education and Research (BMBF) for funding the ethnographic research in Kyrgyzstan from 2011-2014.

The Osh Conflict in 1990

The ethnic history of urban Osh is crucial for understanding the most recent violent conflicts. Kyrgyz and Uzbeks have enjoyed a long history of peaceful coexistence in the Fergana Valley, and more particularly in Osh (Reeves 2005; Megoran 2002; Liu 2012). This long history of synchronicity is rooted in the two groups' different ecological adaptations whereby nomads (Kyrgyz) used to reside primarily in the mountains, and the settled population (Uzbeks) used to live in the towns, farm irrigated land and practice trades and crafts. Moreover, there were intermarriages, fluent knowledge of both languages by the representatives of each ethnic group and the practicing of the same religion. To some degree, ethnic identity was a matter of belonging to a certain economic segment (Liu 2012: 26; Starr et.al 2011). Such divisions were not an obstacle for inter-ethnic marriages and cohabitation, though, and individuals could move between ethnic, religious and regional identities over their life course (Reeves 2005; Roberts 2010; Liu 2012; Ismailbekova 2012, 2013).

In the late 19th century, Central Asia experienced the expansion of the Russian Empire, during which time Russian administrative centres were established in old cities, such as Osh. As with French colonialism in North Africa, where *villes nouvelles* were built near to the Arab medina (Wright 1991; Rabinow 1989; Abu-Lughod 1980), Russian colonial cities in Central Asia were divided and consisted of indigenous settlements and European sectors (King 1976; Galitskyi/Ploskikh 1987). This kind of separation and segregation evoked an alienated urban geography through the presence of colonisers living beside natives. Moreover, this presence produced social tensions between Russians and the natives of the city as a result of the city's expansion, the unequal distribution of land and the destruction of the old municipality due to industrialisation and modernisation (Sahadeo 2007). It is important to consider comparative postcolonial orders and urban violence in other contexts such as Arabian and Iranian cities (Freitag/Lafi/Riedler 2014).

In the case of a mainly agrarian and nomadic-pastoralist region like Central Asia, the Soviet state invested great resources into the development of cities, in order to integrate them into the Soviet Union's urban hierarchies of administration, socio-cultural production and centralised economic networks. Cities were the main motor of Soviet modernisation, especially in Central Asia (Alexander/Buchli/Humphrey 2007), and Osh became the key urban anchor and administrative capital in southern Kyrgyzstan. Through the city's rapid development, especially its infrastructure and institutions, one can see the Soviet vision of progress. State urban planning replaced the *mahalla* (local neighbourhood) with apartment buildings in an effort to develop industry, cultivate a labour force and make people more visible to the administrative apparatus of the state (Liu 2012).

The question of land use was a big issue in the city's Soviet-era development. Osh's industrial and population boom began in the late 1950s, and by the late 20th century the city's form and demography had changed as a result of urban expansion, which included distributing land for housing, farming and industry (Liu 2012). The idea was that a Soviet city would not only provide the infrastructure for modern life, but it would also help to raise the cultural and educational level of the population. Every institution was a part of urban design and was elaborately developed with the aim of regulating and channelling the everyday lives of the Soviet citizenry. Usually, the Communist Party would decide where people worked and lived, and whether they received an education, in order to shape progressive, hard-working, selfless, efficient and healthy Soviet citizens (Fitzpatrick 1999; Kotkin 1995). Humphrey argues that the city environment indeed influenced the conceptual worlds of Soviet people (Humphrey 2005).

Soviet urban planning also had the effect of changing the ethnic profile of cities. In Osh, for instance, some of the old Uzbek *mahalla* and mosques in the city centre were destroyed in the 1960s to make way for multi-storey apartment buildings that would house the new industrial workers pouring in from rural areas. These new workers were mostly ethnic Kyrgyz. Displaced Uzbeks were given new flats on the outskirts of the city, but many refused to take them because they were outside Osh's administrative jurisdiction, thus making Uzbeks 'rural'. At the same time, non-contiguous Kyrgyz villages near Osh were incorporated into the urban framework, thus intensifying the "Kyrgyz-isation" of the city (Liu 2012).

In the intervening decades, competition for scarce land between Uzbeks and Kyrgyz contributed to the emergence of social tension between the two ethnic groups. In 1990, growing tensions over the evident anti-Uzbek sentiments of urban planning erupted in riots over a land dispute between new Kyrgyz workers and Uzbek urban dwellers (Tishkov 1997). Demand for residential land (even in overcrowded Uzbek and Kyrgyz neighbourhoods) continues to be problematic for the post-Soviet administration in Osh, and any claim for land now has ethnicised political overtones whereby the city's very borders are an ongoing source of political debate. These factors must be taken into consideration when analysing the current dynamics of the city.

THE OSH CONFLICT IN 2010

The conflict of summer 2010 in southern Kyrgyzstan was the worst unrest in years and saw the first eruption of inter-communal violence since 1990. Fighting erupted two months after President Kurmanbek Bakiyev was ousted in a popular revolt. The president's departure created a power vacuum, and – according to an international inquiry into the events –competition between some Uzbek leaders (i.e. separatists who formed the provisional government), President Bakiyev's family and assorted criminals was responsible for instigating the violence (IICI 2011).[3] The conflict between Uzbeks and Kyrgyz started in Osh and spread to the neighbouring regions of Jalal-Abad and Bazar-Korgon. Although these clashes between Uzbek and Kyrgyz cohorts around Osh may appear to have been a micro-political drama, with only two ethnic groups and competing political factions of one nation state on the stage, closer examination of the events highlights the subtle, yet effectual, influences of other forces. The conflict was a multilayered (local, regional and national) result of competing interests, but it effectively further reduced social and political complexity within and around Osh in relation to the 'Kyrgyz' and 'Uzbek' ethnic categories. As elsewhere, complex, messy and deeply political dynamics led to the progressive ethnicisation of conflict (Reeves 2010). Similar dynamics in which conflict among political elites rapidly 'spirals' into ethnic conflict, have been observed across former Soviet states, including Moldova and Ukraine (e.g. Kaufman 1996; Osipian/Osipian 2012).

In one week, more than 470 people were killed and thousands were injured. Hundreds of private homes were burned and properties looted. The Independent International Commission of Inquiry (IICI) determined that Uzbeks made up nearly 75 per cent of the 470 people killed, and a 'dispro-

---

3   The Independent International Commission of Inquiry into the events in southern Kyrgyzstan was established at the request of the subsequent president. President Rosa Otunbaeva asked Dr. Kimmo Kiljunen, Special Representative for Central Asia in the OSCE Parliamentary Assembly, to coordinate it (IICI 2011).

portionately high number' of Uzbek-owned properties were among those destroyed. The more dramatic effects of the conflict appeared in the displacement of local populations. During and after the conflict, thousands of ethnic Uzbeks and Kyrgyz tried to escape from southern Kyrgyzstan. About 111.000 people fled temporarily to Uzbekistan, and a further 300.000 were internally displaced (IICI 2011).

Although the high rates of displacement suggest that both ethnic groups fled the violence in equal numbers, the reconstruction of Osh has furthered the agenda of Kyrgyz ethno-nationalism. Wachtel (2013: 9) argued that the outbreak of violence – and post-violence reconstruction – diminished Uzbek influence in the city and allowed power-holders to reclaim Osh symbolically as ethnic Kyrgyz territory, which has been done by building various kinds of monuments in public spaces, initiated by the mayor, in order to display the importance of the Kyrgyz nation. Megoran (2013) and Wachtel (2013) share the opinion that Uzbeks are viewed by state officials in Kyrgyzstan as the main danger to the Kyrgyz state, while Uzbeks (especially their elites) are envisioned as representatives of intimidation aimed at the Kyrgyz state, because they are allied with international organisations and foreign countries,[4] and they do not devote enough effort to the project of national unity. This perceived danger is considered as a security issue, and Uzbek minorities are treated as an internal threat to the state's integrity.

Osh may therefore represent the tale of two different ethnic groups, as Liu (2012) and Megoran (2013) have highlighted in their recent works, whereby the city serves as a site for building relationships along and across ethnic lines as well as dividing relationships in the same way. Both scholars suggest, as does public opinion, that each ethnic group is attached to its own location, i.e. Uzbeks to their own *mahalla*s and Kyrgyz to their own Soviet-style neighbourhoods. And it would seem that further division, competition over the city's territory and escalation of ethnic conflicts are inevitable.

As mentioned above, the northern and southern parts of the city, each with its own ethnically heterogeneous population, have experienced different outcomes during periods of ethnic escalation and non-escalation. In the sections below I will describe in detail how land and houses were sold, how the internal mobility of urban dwellers was stifled, how public space was

---

4 The basis of this accusation comes from the relative openness of Uzbeks to international journalists and support from international organisations.

dominated by the representatives of one ethnic group (Kyrgyz) at the exclusion of another ethnic group (Uzbeks) and what the role of the state administration was in this matter. Finally, I will discuss how some parts of Osh were divided along ethnic lines and how other parts remained undivided.

BUYING A PLOT OF LAND: THE IMPACT OF MIGRATION ON THE CITY IN KYZYL KYSHTAK

In this section I will provide ethnographic examples, in order to illustrate how people dealt with the conflict on the ground and to understand the reasoning behind their actions.

My Kyrgyz informant, Murat (a pseudonym), had worked as a real estate agent for a long time, but his business increased significantly after the conflict. Many Uzbeks sold him their land or other assets in the districts Kyzyl-Kyshtak, Sheit-Tebe, Amir-Temur and Furkat, for relatively low prices, in order to move to an Uzbek-populated neighbourhood, On-Adyr, and to be as far away as possible from the Kyrgyz residential area, thus avoiding any potential fighting (Kyrg. and Uzb. *urush*) between neighbours. Other Uzbeks sold their assets and properties and moved to Russia, in order to secure a life free from persecution in Kyrgyzstan (Ismailbekova 2013). Conversely, many Kyrgyz moved out of Uzbek neighbourhoods. In the conflict, many Uzbeks lost their businesses and properties, due to arson or robbery, and subsequently they sold their land and houses in Kyzyl Kyshtak due to the fear of living alongside Kyrgyz neighbours, even though they had not been attacked; rather, land in this neighbourhood belonged to the Uzbeks according to the law, since they had been born in that district.[5] This was not the case everywhere, though, and so it is important to mention here that there are also counter-examples of areas where people protected each other and stayed together.

Murat started buying land off Uzbek clients and re-selling it to young Kyrgyz migrants working in Russia. In Osh, these Kyrgyz migrants had enough money to buy land and houses at short notice, because they earned better money in Russia than in Kyrgyzstan. However, it is important to mention here that Murat's position was ambiguous. On the one hand, he

---

5   According to the law, land in this area belonged to those who were born on that land. In this particular case, it was Uzbeks who were born in this area.

had intentionally sold land only to Kyrgyz migrants and not to Uzbeks, in order to side with the Kyrgyz and support his Kyrgyz co-residence. Murat's main argument was that Uzbeks should leave Osh completely, or that those who could not leave the city should live in separate neighbourhoods. During the conflict he supported young Kyrgyz men in attacking Uzbek neighbourhoods and protecting his own neighbourhood. However, after the conflict, he became a mediator between the two ethnic groups, due to his profitable business, language skills and extended networks in the city, especially with the state administration. Murat's network of Uzbek friends helped him to find land and houses.

The Kyzyl Kyshtak neighbourhood was situated at the far edge of Osh with far-reaching views of the surrounding countryside. All houses in this new locality were empty due to the absence of infrastructure and services such as electricity, water and roads, and also because the new owners were actually in Russia. This area was located not far from a small supermarket, a petrol station, a bar and a bakery, all of which were approximately ten minutes away by car. The majority of house owners were relatively young men between twenty and thirty years old, most of whom had not yet married. However, family members looked after the houses from time to time.

Murat told me that "conflict [is] not only good for my business, but for all Kyrgyz in Osh generally." Many Uzbeks, according to him, finally started to sell their properties to Kyrgyz people so that Kyrgyz could leave their Soviet high-rise apartments and move to bigger houses in the city; the Kyrgyz resented having to live in Soviet buildings for a long time, particularly on the outskirts of the city. Many Uzbeks also sold profitable businesses, such as shops, restaurants and market pitches to Kyrgyz for relatively low prices. Again, Kyrgyz working in Russia sent money to their relatives in Osh and tried to buy cheap properties from the Uzbeks, which would not have been possible had it not been for the conflict.

Seeing my interest in these changes of ownership in the aftermath of the troubles, Murat's wife, Nurilya (a pseudonym), asked me whether I would be interested in visiting her older sister's new house. I agreed immediately and went to meet two of Murat's wife's older sisters, Maripa and Nurgul (pseudonyms). Nurilya told me that her first older sister, Maripa, had bought a house in 2011 in the Tash Komur area, which was occupied exclusively by newly rich Kyrgyz. In this district a few Uzbeks had also built new houses in 2012. After the conflict, however, they sold their houses and moved either to Russia or to On-Adyr.

According to Maripa, they had been living in a Soviet apartment building for many years because that was all they could afford at the time. Among the Kyrgyz, it is important to live in one house with one's extended kinship networks. The conflict had provided a welcome opportunity which allowed them to buy a huge house from an Uzbek at a low rate. The desires and family patterns of Kyrgyz and Uzbeks are very similar – it is just their spatial and political positions in city that are different. Maripa and her husband did not have enough money to buy this house immediately, even though the price was lower than the market rate, but thankfully their son, who was working in Russia at that time, sent them money so that they would not miss out on buying such a cheap property.

Maripa told me that the previous owner of her neighbour's property was an Uzbek who sold his half-finished house for only $20.000. While discussing the beautiful architecture and ornaments adorning the Uzbek houses, the second older sister of Murat's wife, Nurgul, told me that she had also asked Murat to help her family to find a cheap house, as she was tired of living in her Soviet apartment block since the early 1980s.

The flow of Kyrgyz money from Russia was not surprising, especially when it came to buying up the assets of Uzbeks, Murat told me. Buying assets had always been an important motivation of Kyrgyz migrants working abroad (Reeves 2012), but this time Osh-Kyrgyz migrants started to help other Kyrgyz friends and kinsmen to buy Uzbek properties. In the Kyrgyz narrative of Osh as a contested space – as Megoran puts it – the Kyrgyz regarded this as the right time to claim what they felt rightly belonged to their ethnic group; therefore, helping each other to obtain land was an expression of ethnic solidarity. As Murat explained, he wanted to buy Uzbek property and to sell it only to Kyrgyz, and, if necessary, even to wait for payment. In the next section, I will discuss how Uzbeks are currently moving into the On-Adyr neighbourhood.

Isolated On-Adyr Mahalla

During my research I heard from many Kyrgyz that a significant number of Uzbeks were leaving their houses in the centre of Osh city and moving to live in On-Adyr. One of my Uzbek informants, Nodira (a pseudonym), asked me whether I would be interested in talking to her uncle, who was the deputy of the city as well as of the On-Adyr district. On-Adyr is the main secure place for Uzbeks in Osh. It is located ten kilometres away from the centre and isolated from the rest of the city, and it is exactly the kind of place Osh Uzbeks had refused to move to before. On-Adyr is an extremely sad sight – it does not have water, electricity, roads or even trees. The nearest bazaar and elementary school are located three kilometres away, and the only bus stop is situated at a distance of one kilometre.

I visited Nodira's uncle, Farhod (pseudonym), who was the main leader of the *mahalla* and a deputy of the city. He told me that he had had to sell his large house in the centre of the city urgently, out of fear of the illegal seizure of his home, and move to his second house in On-Adyr. Farhod told me that police officers threatened him that he should sell the house for a low price or face the consequences. He had joined the new *mahalla* alongside other relatives who had also moved from their old houses to the new houses. According to Farhod, Kyrgyz who had been living in On-Adyr for a long time had to move to Kyrgyz neighbourhoods and sell their houses to Uzbeks moving into the area. There was no physical pressure on them to do so; rather, the atmosphere of distrust and fear had forced them to move. Apart from trying to live separately, some Uzbeks were afraid of going into the city centre in the evenings.

The reason behind this fear was that many nightspots were in the centre of the city, and it was considered important that the young people of two ethnic groups should not meet, especially at nighttime. Furthermore, many local people feared that violence might erupt and they would be unable to help their children if they were in the city centre, and women or older people were freer to move around, because usually only men were involved in violence. Because the city centre was out of reach for Uzbeks, small entertainment venues emerged in On-Adyr – new cafes, a small market, a DVD rental shop, play stations, karaoke and billiard bars – following the ideas put forward Farhod. Seeing the atmosphere of mistrust in the city and a lack of nightspots for young Uzbek youth, Farhod felt that this was the only realistic solution from a short-term perspective, if the two ethnic groups wanted to live side by side in the long run. Nowadays, the youth of On-Adyr do not venture outside of their *mahalla*, because this neighbourhood has everything necessary for their entertainment. In addition, a bank, a hospital and an exchange office were opened after the conflict.

Nodira (pseudonym), a student, and some of her fellow students went to eat *samsy* (baked pastry with savory filling) at the main cafe in On-Adyr. The students confirmed that they were afraid of going to the centre of the city; a few of them used to travel to the centre by car, but they were reluctant to do so now. Furthermore, it was not considered acceptable for young women to be in the centre, even during daytime, and they generally had to be home by 16.00, otherwise their parents would start to worry. However, this fear and distrust was not limited to young Uzbek people – it was also evident among young Kyrgyz, who were equally afraid of going to an Uzbek *mahalla*.

So far I have looked at how Uzbeks have found ways to survive hard socio-economic pressure in the main city centre, due to the destruction of business and the fear of living side by side with Kyrgyz. Osh Uzbeks take the side of the Uzbek community and express their preference to move from mixed areas to purely Uzbek-dominated districts, in order to feel more secure and be protected within their community, rather than being open to the insecure and unprotected environment in the city. Now I will move on to examine the state's attempt to build peace and prevent future violence in the city, as well as local responses to such attempts.

WHY THE EMERGENCE OF 'FRIENDSHIP HOUSES'?

After the recent conflicts, both conflict management and urban development were on the agenda of Melis Myrzakmatov, Osh city mayor, who is ethnically Kyrgyz. Violence transformed the physical landscape of the city, due to the destruction of many houses and other big buildings in the city. His role as a politician in the southern Kyrgyzstan was to control the people of Osh, and so he used the 'Soviet Master Plan', which was originally designed in 1978, for mixing two ethnic groups, destroying some *mahallas*' houses and rebuilding the city according to a Kyrgyz ethnic 'nationalistic' style scenario after the conflict. This was done by relocating residents to new neighbourhoods that would consist of mixed houses which were home to both the Uzbek and Kyrgyz ethnic groups. This was announced under the 'House of Friendship' umbrella, which was meant to celebrate inter-ethnic tolerance. Nevertheless, Myrzakmatov could not stop the Uzbeks from segregating themselves in Osh. According to my informants, contemporary and future urban planning and reconstruction has the potential to escalate the conflict in Osh.

The future urban plan envisaged multi-story buildings. According to the plan, apartment buildings would be constructed in what were once principally Uzbek neighbourhoods made up of single-family homes. As the apartment buildings were meant to accommodate both Uzbeks and Kyrgyz, Uzbek *mahallas* would be replaced by ethnically mixed neighbourhoods. Many Uzbeks complained that they were being forcibly evicted from their homes, and they also suggested that the violence in June had been planned in order to facilitate this relocation, based on the fact that before the conflict, Myrzakmatov had already announced his desire to build apartment buildings in Uzbek neighbourhoods.

New apartment buildings were constructed especially for victims of the violence. Many Uzbek as well as Kyrgyz victims were given apartments in the same blocks, mostly in the Anar and Hoz byt kombinat (HBK) neighbourhoods; yet, both Uzbeks and Kyrgyz were reluctant to live in these new residences, as high-rise blocks rather contradicted Uzbek ideas about how they should live their lives, and the Kyrgyz were extremely reluctant to live alongside Uzbeks. Behind the idea of cohabitation in shared apartment blocks was the initiative of the state administration, which aimed at building peace by *forcing* members of the two ethnic groups to live side by side. However, the victims' wounds were very fresh, and people constantly questioned how the two factions could live together when they had all lost wives, husbands and children at the hands of the respective other.

This resistance to living together was accompanied by the 'emptiness' of these newly built apartments, even though they were apparently fully furnished and were connected to water, electricity and gas supplies. State officials would visit these houses, in order to present the residences to an international audience of journalists and capital administrators from Bishkek. Once state officials had inspected the apartment block and its residents, the dwellers would immediately disappear into their own *mahallas* in other parts of the city.

However, the state administration tried to encourage Uzbeks and Kyrgyz to live together by building friendship houses for the victims of both groups who, however, ended up resisting this initiative and ignoring it completely. This resistance was not open or public; in fact, it was almost imperceptible, because the residents would appear in the apartments when state officials informed them about upcoming inspections, and then they would completely disappear afterwards. These apartments were given for free, but the conditions under which they were provided stipulated that the new homeowners must have lost family members during the violence, which had to be proven by a death certificate issued by the government.

Here I have illustrated the responses of Uzbeks and Kyrgyz to the state's attempts to build peace by forcing people to live in shared houses. Yet, for the people, it was too early to overcome the pain of loss and to start living together as before on the basis of a shared Osh or Muslim identity. Instead, people heavily stressed ethnic identities and refused to live together under the same roof.

In the next section I will illustrate that the people of Osh have also segregated themselves by means other than selling and buying property. They listen to different kinds of music, buy goods at the ethnically homogeneous market and attend different mosques. The following journey through the public space of Osh reveals another interesting aspect of segregation and its social relevance for urban dwellers.

SEGREGATION ALONG ETHNIC LINES

During my visit to Osh, before the conflict, the city's cultural diversity amazed me. There were shops and cafes in and around the main central market which were loudly playing Uzbek, Russian and Kyrgyz pop music. My post-conflict experience at the marketplace was in sharp contrast, in that the Kyrgyz soundscape dominated most public places such as the market, public transportation, shops and cafes. My Kyrgyz informant, Burul (fifty years old, a pseudonym), told me:

"Many Uzbeks started speaking the Kyrgyz language and listening to Kyrgyz radio in the marshrutka (minibus). Before, it was not possible to listen to Kyrgyz music in the main market, because Uzbeks would not allow us to listen to it; only Uzbek music would play everywhere. Before, no wedding toi (feast) would start without the Uzbek toi music, but now any Kyrgyz wedding exclusively features only Kyrgyz music, speech and other relevant lifecycle rituals. Before, we would try to be flexible and incorporate Uzbek rituals into our weddings, but now Uzbeks have started to respect Kyrgyz people and their traditions as well."

However, Uzbek music has not completely disappeared; rather, it has become less public and moved more into the private domain. Uzbeks might comment on the statement above, saying that they do not *respect* but rather *fear* the Kyrgyz now. When I interviewed Uzbeks in the Uzbek Cheremushka *mahalla*, I heard Uzbek music in the small gardens, especially that of a famous Uzbekistani singer, Yulduz Osmonova. The music was not particularly loud, but it was still being played. The Uzbeks' concern is to keep peace and not to trigger further violence. This was obvious from an interview with the head (*ming boshu*) of the Cheremushka *mahalla* community, who told me that many of his relatives, friends and neighbours had complained to him about the constant harassment meted out by Kyrgyz young men, to which he suggested they should react with patience (*soburdu*) and tolerance.

While walking around the city in 2011-12, after the violent conflicts, not only could I not hear the diverse music of Osh as before, but also I could not take a public minibus and enjoy the previous ethnic diversity of its passengers. Many Uzbek drivers had changed their routes around the city, so that now they only connected one Uzbek neighbourhood to another Uzbek neighbourhood. The same changes had also been made by their Kyrgyz counterparts. The Uzbek driver of the *marshrutka*, Azim, told me that before the violence his bus route had run from On-Adyr (a predominantly Uzbek neighbourhood) to the city centre and then out from the centre to Tash Komur (a predominantly Kyrgyz neighbourhood). But he could not continue working in this manner, because many Kyrgyz passengers would not take his *marshrutka*, and on some occasions they would even refuse to pay. His family also suggested changing his route exclusively to the Uzbek neighbourhoods, and he felt particularly insecure while driving in and around Kyrgyz areas. The atmosphere of distrust and hatred predominates in the city and is obvious in every aspect of city life. Many Uzbeks describe their relationships with Kyrgyz as "cold" (*muzdak*) and not "hot" (*yssyk*) as before.

Public minibuses are not the only example of this form of segregation. There is very strong ethnic concentration in the marketplace, too. My informant, Nurgul (Kyrgyz by ethnicity, thirty years old), told me the following:

"Many Uzbeks support each other and protect their own communities by not allowing outsiders to enter. Uzbeks do not betray one another. If you ask any Uzbeks to help them to find any person within their mahalla, they will not tell you the house of that person. We Kyrgyz are open and tell everything to outsiders, even showing them the exact door. Kyrgyz would never protect their own communities as the Uzbeks do. However, after the violence, many Kyrgyz started showing their solidarity to each other and they would mobilise at very short notice. During the conflict, the

Kyrgyz residents of Tash Komur, especially women, united and prepared borsok (fired bread) and cooked food for complete Kyrgyz strangers from Alai, knowing that they would be hungry and had come from far away to protect Kyrgyz Osh residents from the Uzbeks."

This solidarity was also evident when I wanted to buy Uzbek clothes from a local businesswoman. My Kyrgyz informant suggested that I should not buy clothes in the Uzbek style. Many Kyrgyz preferred to support each other by buying only from Kyrgyz traders, and in turn many Uzbeks preferred not to buy from Kyrgyz. *Samsy* sellers and influential Uzbek entrepreneurs told me their clients used to be only Kyrgyz before the conflict, but thereafter Kyrgyz customers virtually disappeared altogether. The same applied to the other side.

The majority of the Uzbeks that I interviewed had lost their places in the main market of the city as well as small businesses in the centre, such as *samsykana* (a cafe where one can eat Uzbek pie with meat and potatoes), *tandyrkana* (a cafe where one can buy bread) and the sewing centre. As a result, many Uzbeks remained unemployed, although in some instances Uzbek businesses could be saved by bribing state officials or criminal groups. In other instances, however, Uzbek entrepreneurs had to change the names of their restaurants or shops to Kyrgyz names and hire Kyrgyz workers instead of Uzbeks. I visited a famous Uzbek café, 'Kyrgyzstan', but it was protected by a Kyrgyz criminal group, which the owner of the cafe had hired to protect his business – not the police or other Uzbek groups, because only they had enough power to resist both Kyrgyz young men, state officials and other contenders who could seriously affect the business or even completely close it down.

The mosque is another place which clearly highlights ethnic segregation, but this was not the case before the conflict occurred, as people themselves told me by comparing and contrasting the situation of the mosque and its ethnically divided attendees before and after the violence. Both Uzbeks and Kyrgyz were shocked to hear on the nights of June 10-11, 2010 the early *azan* prayer being heralded at 2am (although the prayer is usually announced at 5.15am), openly informing people in neighbourhoods near to the mosque of the upcoming violence. As a result, many Kyrgyz and Uzbeks did not trust the mosques, whose imam could represent either ethnic group. The deputy of the city, Farhod, told me that "Uzbeks started attending their own mosques, located in their own respective neighbourhoods. Kyrgyz attended their own mosques."

Even though the mosques could play a crucial role in building peace between two ethnic groups by stressing their Muslim Kyrgyz and Uzbek identities, this attempt made by the local *mullahs* nevertheless was not successful. From my observation, among those who attended the mosque in the Uzbek neighbourhood of Cheremushka, the majority were Uzbeks and there were very few Kyrgyz. The present picture indicates that the mosque in Cheremushka is dominated by Uzbeks, whereas the central mosque of Osh is attended mainly by Kyrgyz. Many mullahs from Uzbek mosques which are situated in Uzbek *mahalla*s have been replaced by Kyrgyz – a move initiated by the state – and this has further exacerbated the situation for Uzbeks, many of whom now only attend Uzbek mosques with an Uzbek imam, because they do not trust the Kyrgyz.

Finally, the main state administration also added to segregation along ethnic lines. Many police officers, hospitals and university staff are now Kyrgyz, whereas Uzbeks used to dominate these professions (Reeves 2010; Liu 2012). In an interview with the mullah and local doctor, Muhtar, I was told that many Uzbeks preferred to see private Uzbek doctors if they had health problems, rather than Kyrgyz doctors at the public hospitals. Many had psychological problems, for which he prescribed Uzbek medicinal plants. An Uzbek school graduate complained to me that he had not been accepted to the city's university because of his ethnic affiliations. My Kyrgyz informant, Nurgul, emphatically corroborated this statement.

I have provided herein a few situations that describe the segregation implemented by Kyrgyz state officials, all of which are to the detriment of Uzbek people, who lost trade and their businesses after the conflict.

Conclusion

This chapter has concentrated on various experiences affecting the lives of those living in Osh after 2010. The inhabitants of Osh have tried to separate themselves ethnically, in order to prevent conflict and save lives within the limits of their ability and from a short-term perspective. However, the outcome of this division in the long term might prevent people from future integration. Some areas of Osh opted for segregation as a coping strategy by siding with their own community, while other areas decided not to segregate as a strategy of prevention. Consequently, depending on the locations of the residents and the degree to which they were affected by the conflict, strategies are diverse. I have shown not only that this is a matter of mutual segregation, but also that Uzbeks are being marginalised and forcibly pushed out. This division goes against the state's attempt to build 'peace' by encouraging two ethnic groups to live together through the construction of friendship houses and supporting inter-ethnic marriages. This can be related back to the Soviet era city planning ideas.

Dividing some people along 'ethnic' lines and nationalistic forces goes against such attempts; however, it is not as simple as it seems to be; rather, it is quite involuntary on the part of Uzbeks. Ordinary local people have weakened their positions and lost access to resources previously available to them. Both local ordinary Kyrgyz and Uzbeks would prefer to live in harmony and inter-ethnic solidarity and support the centuries-long inter-ethnic symbiosis. As a result of the conflict, though, two ethnic groups have been cut off from their neighbours and close friends of the opposite ethnic group and have had to sell land at low prices, lose businesses and move to non-prestigious neighbourhoods.

Forced segregation has created the emergence of a new division along ethnic lines in the most conflict-affected areas of the city, which makes people concerned about the whole situation and life in general in Osh. Inter-ethnic harmony that has been preserved by two ethnic groups for a long time seems to have dissolved. This division was not voluntary; rather, it was done or practiced as a result of a lack of available alternatives. However, there are Kyrgyz and Uzbeks leaders interested in and gaining from the conflict.

By applying Schlee's theoretical model, I would argue first that any claims to identity made by Uzbeks and Kyrgyz have to meet certain conventions, and above all they have to be plausible to be of any use, for example in mobilising people or creating solidarity along or beyond ethnic lines. In this chapter, Uzbeks and Kyrgyz identify themselves using criteria of ethnicity (Kyrgyz, Uzbek) and beyond ethnicity (Muslim, Osh) as sources of identification. There is clear evidence that amongst the Kyrgyz and Uzbeks, ethnicity and other markers were manipulated – depending on the context and situation. That is, people were capable of broadening their ethnicity or going beyond it, albeit based on a shared scheme or model. The ways in which people identify themselves depend on the available resources and their specific interests. In such situations, social actors rely on their ethnic groups or ethnically mixed groups.

The most conflict-affected Osh Kyrgyz and Uzbeks have followed the logic of cost and benefit calculations by taking the sides with their own respective ethnic communities. This decision was the best option in times of chaos and insecurity, because belonging to one's own community would increase security as well as protection, without necessarily expending much time and energy. During the conflict, people did not trust and in fact feared one another, due to the inability to recognise who was an enemy and who was a friend. Therefore, taking the side of one's own community would provide them with safety and trust at a low cost. The ways in which people identify themselves and their ethnicity depends on their available resources and their specific interests, such as creating solidarity or mobilising people. Consequently, 'taking sides' has been the best and most effective way of protecting themselves from the disaster of conflict and ongoing tension.

It should be noted that taking sides with one's own ethnic community was not an issue in other parts of the city, where being together against others was the best decision and the best way to protect local people from the ravages of conflict. A number of ethnically mixed settlements in Osh did not experience any sort of violence, and so they have refused to divide and have opted for alternative strategies such as being united and protecting themselves from outsiders under the umbrella of 'being from Osh' and enjoying a 'shared Muslim identity'. Here, identification along ethnic lines was not beneficial for people; instead, they opted for an alternative identification which would go beyond ethnic identity. By only being part of mixed communities can both Kyrgyz and Uzbeks better secure themselves from outside threats and prevent ethnic segregation. Depending on the locations of the residents and the degree to which they were affected by the conflict, strategies are diverse. Therefore, one can observe how people shifted their identities depending on their situation and needs.

References

Abu-Lughod, Janet L. (1980): Rabat, Urban Apartheid in Morocco. Princeton, NJ: Princeton University Press.

Aggestam, Karin/Björkdahl, Annika (2013): Rethinking Peacebuilding: The Quest for Just Peace in the Middle East and the Western Balkans, London: Routledge

Alexander, Catherine/Buchli, Victor/Humphrey, Caroline (2007): Urban Life in Post-Soviet Asia, London: I.B. Tauris.

Bieber, F./Daskalovski, Z. (2003): Understanding the War in Kosovo, London: Frank Cass Publishers.

Björkdahl, Annika (2013): "Urban Peacebuilding." In: Peacebuilding 1/2, pp. 207-221.

Fitzpatrick, Sheila (1999): Everyday Stalinism: Ordinary Life in Extraordinary Times: Soviet Russia in the 1930s, New York: Oxford University Press.

Freitag, Ulrike/Fuhrmann, Malte/Lafi, Nora/Riedler, Florian (2011): The City in the Ottoman Empire: Migration and the Making of Urban Modernity, London: Routledge Taylor and Francis Group.

Galitskyi, Vladimir/Ploskih, V.M. (1987): Starinnyi Osh: ocherk istorii, Frunze: Izd-vo "Ilim".

Humphrey, Caroline (2005): "Ideology in Infrastructure: Architecture and Soviet Imagination." In: Journal of the Royal Anthropological Institute 11, pp. 39-58.

Ismailbekova, Aksana (2012):"Dynamika mejetnichekih brakov posle konflikta v Oshe [Dynamics of interethnic marriages in the aftermath of conflict in Osh]." In: Etnograficheskoe Obozrenie 6, pp. 84-98.

Ismailbekova, Aksana (2013): "Coping Strategies: Migration, Public Avoidance, and Marriage in the Aftermath of the Osh Conflict, Fergana Valley." In: Nationalities Papers 41/1, pp. 109-127.

Kaufman, Stuart (1996): "Spiraling to ethnic war: Elites, masses, and Moscow in Moldova's civil war." In: International Security 21/2, pp. 108-138.

King, Anthony (1976): Colonial Urban Development: Culture, Social Power, and Environment, London: Routledge and Kegan Paul.

Kotkin, Stephan (1995): Magnetic Mountain: Stalinism as a Civilization, Berkeley: University of California Press.

Kutmanaliev, Joldon (2015 forthcoming): Ethnic Violence and Peace in Southern Kyrgyzstan. PhD dissertation, The European University Institute, Italy.

Liu, Morgan (2012): Under Solomon's Throne. Uzbek Vision of Renewal in Osh, Pittsburgh, Pa.: University of Pittsburgh Press.

Megoran, Nick (2002): The Borders of Eternal Friendship? The Politics and Pain of Nationalism and Identity along the Uzbekistan–Kyrgyzstan Fergana Valley Boundary, 1999–2000. PhD dissertation, University of Cambridge.

Megoran, Nick (2012): "Averting Violence in Kyrgyzstan: Understanding and Responding to Nationalism." In: Russia and Eurasia Programme Paper, 2012/03, Chatham House.

Megoran, Nick (2013): "Shared space, divided space: narrating ethnic histories of Osh." In: Environmental and Planning A 45, pp. 892-907.

National Statistical Committee of Kyrgyz Republic (2009): National Census 2009. Vol. III (tables), Regions of Kyrgyzstan, Osh city.

Osipian, Ararat/Osipian, Alexandr (2012): "Regional Diversity and Divided Memories in Ukraine: Contested Past as Electoral Resource, 2004-2010." In: East European Politics and Societies 26/3, pp. 616-642.

Rabinow, Paul (1989): French Modern: Norms and Forms of the Social Environment, Cambridge/MA: MIT Press.

Reeves, Madeleine (2005): "Locating danger: Konfliktologiia and the search for fixity in the Ferghana Valley borderlands." In: Central Asian Survey 24/1, pp. 67–81.

Reeves, Madeleine (2010): "The ethnicisation of violence in Southern Kyrgyzstan.", June 21, 2010 (https://www.opendemocracy.net/od-russia/madeleine-reeves/ethnicisation-of-violence-in-southern-kyrgyzstan-0; accessed February 2, 2012).

Reeves, Madeleine (2012): "Black Work, Green Money: Remittances, Ritual, and Domestic Economies in Southern Kyrgyzstan." In: Slavic Review 71, pp. 108-134.

Roberts, Sean R. (2010): "Why is Ethnic Violence Erupting Between Kyrgyz and Uzbeks in Southern Kyrgyzstan?" (http://roberts-report.blogspot.com; accessed December 27, 2010).

Sahadeo, Jeff (2007): Russian Colonial Society in Tashkent: 1865-1923. Bloomington: Indiana University Press.

Schlee, Guenther (2008): How Enemies Are Made: Towards a Theory of Ethnic and Religious Conflict, Oxford and New York: Berghahn Books.

Starr, Frederick/Beshimov, Baktybek/Bobokulov, Inomjon/Shozimov, Pulat (2011): Ferghana Valley: The Heart of Central Asia. Armonk, New York: M.E. Sharpe.

The Independent International Commission of Inquiry (IICI) (2011): "Report of the Independent International Commission of Inquiry into the Events in Southern Kyrgyzstan in June 2010." (http://reliefweb.int/sites/reliefweb.int/files/resources/Full_Report_490.pdf; accessed June 17, 2015).

Tishkov, Valery (1997): Ethnicity, Nationalism and Conflict After The Soviet Union, London: Sage Publications.

Wachtel, Andrew Baruch (2013): "Kyrgyzstan between democratization and ethnic intolerance, Nationalities Papers." In: The Journal of Nationalism and Ethnicity 1/16, pp. 971-986.

Wright, Gwendolyn (1991): The Politics of Design in French Colonial Urbanism, Chicago: University of Chicago Press.

Understanding Mobilisation Processes in Conflict through Framing: The Case of Inter-Communal Conflict in the Batken Province, Kyrgyzstan[1]

KHUSHBAKHT HOJIEV

On the afternoon of December 29, 2011, in a small village marketplace in Andarak, four young men of Tajik ethnicity set upon two schoolboys of Kyrgyz ethnicity, inflicting bodily harm on them.[2] Andarak – a solely Tajik-populated village in the Leilek district of the Batken province in southern Kyrgyzstan – shares one common road with the following three downstream Kyrgyz-populated villages: Iskra, Kommuna and Kektash.

---

1 This article is based on field research conducted in the Leilak district of the Batken province in Kyrgyzstan from May to Oktober 2012. I am particularly grateful to Katja Mielke, Martin Sökefeld and Aksana Ismailbekova for insights into and reviews of early drafts of this paper. Due to sensitivity of the topic, all names of informants have been anonymised.
2 The terms "Tajik" and "Kyrgyz" (standing for people of Tajik and Kyrgyz ethnicity) are deliberately used throughout the paper to differentiate the residents of two neighbouring villages according to their ethnic origins. This is a primary form of differentiation applied by local communities, not only in their reflection on past incidents of conflict, but also in general communication and day-to-day interaction. The usage of these terms also aims at incorporating the terminology used actively by members of local communities/my respondents in the narration of the conflict events analysed in this paper.

It is difficult to draw any border between Andarak and its immediate neighbouring village Iskra, as the people of both villages, divided only by their ethnic origin (Tajik and Kyrgyz), have been living side by side for many years and thus make up a single multiethnic community. The brawl at the marketplace is said to have occurred after repeated incidents of quarrels and misunderstandings between Tajik and Kyrgyz youths that had happened in the recent past. As a result of this unrest, one of the Kyrgyz teenagers was hospitalized, while the other managed to escape from the scene. In response to this incident parents and relatives of the teenagers immediately referred to the neighbourhood inspector, a police officer who is responsible for both villages. Anticipating trouble, he quickly arrested two of the young Tajik men that were involved in the brawl. Soon, however, a group of Tajik men arrived at the police station and negotiated the release of the arrested young people.

This immediately mobilised a crowd of local Kyrgyz villagers that soon gathered at the police station, demanding the police to re-arrest the perpetrators of the violent act. Though small in number, these Kyrgyz villagers were angry and determined to riot if the police did not fulfill their demand. The agitated crowd, in response to a lack of action by the neighbourhood police officer, moved to the central part of Iskra, situated approximately one-and-a-half kilometres from the marketplace in Andarak, and blocking the only road leading to Andarak, they started to mobilise more people. Meanwhile, word spread inside and outside the village that "they" had attacked "two of us".[3] Over the following hours, Kyrgyz men from neighbouring areas gathered in Iskra. In response, a Tajik crowd also formed and mobilised men in Andarak at the other end of the road.[4] The atmosphere grew tense, and the mobs from both sides were armed with staves and metal bars, prepared for a clash.

Although the conflict initially fitted the 'everyday conflict' model[5] (*"konflikt na bitovoy pochve"* in Russian, as termed by locals), as gatherings like this were a fairly common occurrence in southern Kyrgyzstan in

---

3   Interviews with members of the local Kyrgyz community (Iskra, Kommuna, Isfana, September 2012).

4   Interviews with members of the local Tajik community (Andarak, July 2012).

5   Such conflicts, occurring from time to time, have been perceived largely as limited and comprising containable violence, thus initially not causing serious concern for authorities or communities.

the post-Osh 2010 period[6], unrest and the probability of a violent clash between the two cohorts increased as mobilisation continued and conflict dynamics intensified. Given that Kyrgyz villagers constituted a minority in the area compared to the Tajik community living in their immediate neighbourhood, the Kyrgyz horde mobilised armed supporters from outside the village, including neighbouring communities, the district centre and the western villages of Leilek district, located at a distance of about 15-20 kilometres from Andarak.

The Tajik community, as an ethnic minority in the country, could not gain external support, as the road was blocked. Even local Tajiks that were in the district centre at that point in time could not re-enter the village. Hence, the Tajik crowd relied on internal resources and mobilised all men in the village to ready themselves for a possible clash. At 9pm, both groups, each comprising between 300 and 600 people according to different estimations, started to advance on the other, moving from two sides of the main road towards its centre.

This triggered further agitation, intensifying the mobilisation of both factions through self-arming with sticks and metal bars. Before long, both sets of armed men faced each other, leaving only twenty metres between them and waiting for the right moment to launch an attack. Accusations were shouted across the road in increasingly agitated tones, signalling the readiness of both crowds to fight. Mediation efforts, which were started by local leaders and community elders, involving front-row activists[7] from

---

6   Violent clashes between the Kyrgyz and Uzbek populations in the southern city of Osh in June 2010 contributed to the largest inter-ethnic conflict in Kyrgyzstan in last two decades. Similar large-scale violence happened in June 1990 in Osh and Uzgen cities of southern Kyrgyzstan (cf. Tishkov 1995). The violence and pogroms that exploded on June 10, 2010 resulted in several hundred human casualties, estimated by different sources at between 460 to 2000 people, and destroyed hundreds of homes and whole neighbourhoods. About 120.000 Uzbek refugees, composed mostly of children and women, fled during the violence across the border to Uzbekistan, and 400.000 people were internally displaced as a result of the conflict (ICG 2010: 19).

7   The term "activist(s)" is used in the context of this case study for active members of both crowds that mobilised other conflict participants or members of conflict groups. This usage of the term helps to distinguish the so-called mobilisers and leaders of both groups, who were more actively involved in the fram-

both sides and which were complemented later by the arrival of law enforcement units from Batken, eventually prevented a violent encounter, although three shops belonging to Tajik residents and two houses in the village were set on fire.

Though no human casualties were recorded, about sixty soldiers belonging to Ministry of the Interior and the State Committee on National Security forces were deployed in Andarak the next day, to monitor the situation and to maintain order in the following weeks. Private duty posts, established by community members on both sides, were also on alert twenty-four hours a day for about another twenty days.

Though this conflict can be approached from different angles, the choice of social categorisation, which the mobilisers and the mobilised associated with the initial violence between the young people from the two neighbouring communities, was crucial in this process of conflict escalation. The original brawl was understood as 'ethnic' violence, and this interpretation was also applied to the subsequent mobilisation. Why was the 'ethnic' frame applied to these events, and how can the analysis of this framing help to understand the dynamics involved?

Framing, which emerges from actors' and observers' interpretations of conflict events, not only refers to the mode of interpretation through which actors involved in a conflict make sense of a situation, but also includes a discursive dimension through which they define conflicts, causes and actions within narratives selected or generated by them (Esser 1999; Benford/Snow 2000; Snow/Byrd 2007).

Framing has significant implications for conflict processes. In this chapter, I will argue that the framing of the 'Andarak events'[8], as a discursive work, determined the scope of mobilisation throughout the conflict process. Hence, I aim to illustrate how framing theory, derived primarily from the social movement literature, produces fruitful insights for conflict studies by addressing the generation of mobilising and counter-mobilising ideas, their public reception and 'maintenance' as well as the resulting processes of mobilisation in conflict events. The role of actors' framing, seen as the pro-

---

ing process, from ordinary conflict participants and group members that were simply involved in the crowd. The latter are often termed "followers" in the literature.

8 The unrest which involved the Kyrgyz and Tajik communities in Andarak became known locally as "Andarak events".

duction of meaning by these actors (Benford/Snow 2000), can be taken as a point of departure to explain mobilisation processes and the dimensions of conflict escalation, as well as to develop framing as a theoretical approach for studying conflicts from a process perspective.

The argument will be made in four stages. First, I will elaborate on the concept of framing as an approach that can be applied to analyse conflict processes; second I will analyse the framing of the conflict in Andarak and its implications for subsequent mobilisation based on the narratives of conflict activists; third, I will describe a viable framing process structure that one can draw from this example and fourth, I will conclude that framing as a theoretical approach allows better understanding of mobilisation and other dynamics involved in conflict.[9]

FRAMING IN CONFLICT PROCESSES

Conflict studies have been dominated by causal inquiry, on the one hand, and a persistent divide between instrumentalist (rational choice) and interpretivist (social-psychological) camps, on the other. This divide has been particularly obvious in studies of (inter-)communal conflicts emerging in multiethnic societies, where scholars of the two camps claim the priority of either rationality or contested social settings in explaining conflict.

Yet, this divide, similarly to approaches seeking 'root causes' of conflict, restricts our understanding of conflict dynamics, because ignoring either of the two notions – the rational choices of goal-oriented actors and the effects of the contested social setting – may result in consciously overlooking essential aspects of a conflict.

---

9 My findings from the Andarak case study are based on field research conducted in the conflict area during 2012. The first source of data comprises narratives on conflict made by actors and observers from both Kyrgyz and Tajik communities and obtained through unstructured narrative interviews several months after the conflict took place. These narratives are supplemented by secondary sources – primarily media reports on the case, online forum discussions (at www.diesel.elcat.kg), analysis of the conflict developed by local analysts and reports written by non-governmental organisations and an official state Commission established to investigate the incident in Andarak.

A number of authors have attempted to bridge this divide by thinking across the 'instrumentalist-interpretative divide' in the analysis of inter-communal conflicts (Bates et al. 1998; Horowitz 1998; Esser 1999; Fearon/Laitin 2000; Desrosiers 2011).

Framing can contribute to comprehending conflict from a process perspective and offers an approach that bridges this conventional dichotomy in conflict theorising (Desrosiers 2011). According to this approach, conflict dynamics and processes involved in inter-communal conflict are the result of the purposeful behaviour of actors that takes place against the background of a constraining and constitutive social setting. At the same time, processes involved in inter-communal conflict and communal violence, including transition from one stage of escalation to another, are not free from irregularities and digressions. The scrutiny of mobilisation in conflicts requires taking into account, among other things, discursive dynamics, such as contested meanings and worldviews, discourses, norms and structures of power relations and their implications for the actions of the actors involved.

Furthermore, framing is an inter-subjective process of definition, perception and identification of a conflict situation or event in which a certain cognitive model of the situation (*Modell der Situation*) is produced with informative and guiding functions (Esser 1999).[10] In this sense it designates the active role of conflict actors in reality construction and defining the conflict situation, and it presupposes framing to be a verb – as something that actors *do*. Frames, as mobilising (or demobilising) ideas, are produced as action-oriented "schemata" (Goffman 1974) within the existing social environment that organise experience and guide the actions of actors in conflict processes, as well as mobilise the community and resources. In conflicts, actors act as signifying agents engaged actively in this process of signification (Benford/Snow 2000: 613), and the frames of a conflict produced by actors are consequential. The causative nature of frames is determined by their embeddedness in conflict dynamics and the wider political and social processes surrounding the conflict. The resonance of these frames, generated in how a conflict event is defined, predefines conflict dy-

---

10 I take Esser's proposition of "*Situationslogik*," in which he elaborated his understanding of framing in ethnic conflicts as a point of departure.

namics and the processes involved therein, including the escalation or de-escalation of violence.[11]

Taking this notion another step forward, framing involves frame generation, on the one hand, and frame reception and enacting, i.e. mobilisation based on the frame, on the other.[12] A conflict event is defined by an actor or an observer on the basis of the social environment and institutional setting that shape social relations. Hence, a frame of a conflict event has to be aligned to the social environment in order to be successful. From this viewpoint, frames of conflict are generated on the basis of already existing larger "cognitive models," as well as those that are ingrained in the minds, perceptions and understandings of people and embedded as meaningful structures in the social environment (Esser 1999: 247-249).[13] These larger cognitive models can be myths relating to ethnic identity, traditions and norms governing inter-communal relations, the history of past violence or the like. Actors within a conflict frame the situation based on already existing, greater cognitive models, in order to make them acceptable by the community involved through alignment with common concerns and beliefs (Snow et al. 1986). Frames can also rely on more than one such larger cognitive model already internalised by the given community.

In order to activate and strengthen the framing of the given conflict situation, actors also rely on symbolically dramatised depictions of common concerns and interests (including material interests), often depicted as collective group interests and apprehensions, through reflection on the wrongdoings of the other side.

---

11 The aspect of de-escalation in conflict dynamics is beyond the scope of this chapter.
12 Snow et al. (1986) define these processes within their concept of "frame alignment."
13 Such larger cognitive models are defined variously by others, for instance lifeworld by Schütz and worldviews by Mielke et al. (2011). Larger cognitive models also include notions of self-identification, as well as the cognitive orientation of oneself to the social world. This feature makes them broader than the concept of master frames, which refers to a "generic type of collective action frame that is wider in scope and influence than run-of-the-mill social movement frames" (Snow/Benford 1992).

This way, the cognitive aspect of framing involves cognition in broader terms, which also includes argumentative and symbolic aspects, and enables their communicative reception by the public (Esser 1999: 248).

Following the resonance of a given frame, the actions that certain framing suggests in a conflict situation, i.e. mobilisation for violence, counterattacks and the like, have to be perceived as suitable by the public that is later involved in the mobilisation; at the very least there should not be massive opposition against it. The suitability of presupposed action might be measured through a fully conscious reflexive mode or supported in a semi-automated way, depending on how the given frame is aligned with public sentiments, collective identity and transcendent interests (Esser 1999: 249). This aspect of the framing process builds up the latent readiness of the conflict groups and defines the scope of the following mobilisation that occurs as a result. The task of conflict actors involved in framing is to increase the numbers of group members, in order to demonstrate some form of readiness to act. Frames become important for conflict mobilisation insofar as they are shared by enough people to channel individual behaviour into collective action in conflict processes.

As a result of such differentiation between two central aspects – frame generation and enacting – framing theory modifies strict rationalist assumptions about conflict actors from the point of view of agent-oriented constructivism and the cognitive paradigm (Esser 1999). Within the framing process, actors involved in mobilisation instead follow a form of what can be described as 'soft rationalism', which derives from the influence of ingrained, larger cognitive models in their behaviour and thus assumes intentionality. This assumption about intentionality does not make an arbitrary distinction between the rational and irrational, the strategic and non-strategic, actions of conflict actors (Desrosiers 2011: 7); rather, it assumes the "purposeful choices" of actors in conflict that can be both strategic and non-strategic, while the term 'strategic' means not only a reflection of actors' goals (both material and symbolic), but also their anticipation about others' choices (Lepgold/Lamborn 2001:8).

Hence, by framing the conflict situation or conflict event, these actors act within soft rationalism amidst both a constraining social structure and around (their anticipation about) interaction with others' actions.

Due to such concerns, not all frames will be successful or resonate among the community concerned and lead to mobilisation in conflict situations. Variations in frame resonance allow for accounting for disparities in the mobilisation process in conflict, based on frame variations generated and adopted by actors.

Thus, framing in mobilisation processes and conflict in general defines not only conflict situations, but is also an active and constitutive process that includes alignment with broader cognitive models, public sentiments, perceived transcendent collective interests, suitable modes of action vis-à-vis the action of the other side as well as its successful resonance in the community concerned. At the same time, the effects and ramifications of framing for conflict dynamics are not always predictable, as it is often contested and intersected with counter-framing. Furthermore, new and transformed frames may emerge throughout the course of conflict development.

FRAMING OF CONFLICT IN ANDARAK

As mentioned above, despite the nature of the event that triggered the clashes, i.e. a skirmish among young people from two neighbouring communities, the conflict and the initial violence in Andarak was defined in ethnic terms. Kyrgyz activists, including many of those that were at the police station, framed the attack on the schoolboys as an act of disrespect by ethnic outsiders, namely Tajiks, in respect to Kyrgyz people that had provoked inescapable and legitimate retaliation. They argued that this act was the latest in a series of acts of disrespect committed by Tajiks against members of the local Kyrgyz community. The result of such ethnic categorisation was to link explicitly the unrest to an incursion into Kyrgyz indigenous status, honour and dignity in the land of Kyrgyz people.

According to one of the Kyrgyz activists, "the cause of the conflict is that the Tajiks got rich, and they started behaving disrespectfully towards Kyrgyz people. It was not the first time that they had attacked Kyrgyz boys in Andarak. Living in the land of Kyrgyz, people they need to behave and, first of all, respect Kyrgyz people."[14]

The rhetoric of the Tajik group, in turn, focused on themes related to their minority position as well as the aggressive attempts of the Kyrgyz to dominate, pressure exerted by the Kyrgyz population and local government over the local Tajik community and confiscating the economic resources of

---

14 Interviews with activists from the local Kyrgyz community (Iskra, Kommuna, September 2012).

Tajiks. Hence, the mobilisation of the Kyrgyz mob in response to the initial violence between the young people was framed by Tajik activists within the oppressive approach and the relation of the Kyrgyz community with the Tajik minority group and its attempt to punish Tajiks. According to one Tajik participant in the skirmish, "local Kyrgyz did not like the fact that Tajiks were better off. They tried to use any possible situation as an excuse to put pressure on Tajiks. In every suitable situation the Tajiks are reminded that this is Kyrgyz land and they have to respect them, speak Kyrgyz [...]."[15]

Thus, the ethnic framing of conflict was part of the broader cognitive *titulnaya nasiya* (meaning 'titular nation') and ethnic minority models. The narrative of *titulnaya nasiya* vs. ethnic minority takes its roots from the Soviet period and is prominent in Russian-language academia. Local politicians and members of local communities still refer to it most of the time in the Russian language, even when the conversation is led in one of the local languages. The concept of *titulnaya nasiya* developed during the Soviet period and denoted nations of autonomous entities, such as republics and autonomous republics, within the Soviet Union. An *ethnos* (Bromlei 1983) had to satisfy certain criteria related to the size of the population and the compactness of its settlement, in order to become *titulnaya nasiya*.

Given inherent dominance in regard to access to power and resources presumed for a titular nation, the concept of titulnaya nasiya constituted underlying inequality in multiethnic societies. In the case of the scuffle under investigation in this chapter, the rhetoric followed the pattern of titulnaya nasiya vs. ethnic minority when the issue of resources, as is traditionally done in explanations of conflicts in the Ferghana valley, was added to such frames by observers; for instance, the local NGO Foundation for Tolerance International, reporting on the unrest, framed it as a conflict between local Kyrgyz people and the Tajik minority over water and land resources (Foundation for Tolerance International 2012).

Such an ethnic categorisation had far-reaching consequences for the following mobilisation processes, particularly due to the recent history of large-scale, inter-ethnic violence in Osh city that resulted in about 400 casualties (Human Rights Watch 2010; cf. Reeves 2010). Further interpretations of the initial violence that developed during mobilisation came in the

---

15 Interview with a conflict activist from the Tajik community (Andarak, September 2012).

form of rumours that have been formed through narratives and enabled the mobilisation.

Referencing Mechanisms in the Framing Process

An examination of this case suggests that three referencing mechanisms were particularly relevant in explaining the generation and enactment of further interpretations (frames) of the event in Andarak: (1) the use of the symbolic dimension of violence (memories of past unrest), (2) *othering*, through blame displacement and victimisation, and (3) alignment with larger political discourses (pertinent in the country at that particular period of time). These three referencing mechanisms explain, specifically, how the framing of the skirmish was used successfully for mobilisation, or in other words for conflict escalation or de-escalation.

The Use of the Symbolic Dimension of Violence

The symbolic dimension of violence became an important asset that enabled the quick mobilisation of support for the Kyrgyz group. Although Tajiks are one of smallest national minorities in Kyrgyzstan, the Tajik community of Andarak is almost double the population of its immediate Kyrgyz neighbours in Iskra. Consequently, the Kyrgyz activists had to rely on the external support of Kyrgyz men from outside of the village. The two nearby Kyrgyz-populated villages of Kommuna and Kektash were an immediate source of support, though the mobilisation of Kyrgyz men from more distant locations had been an established practice in earlier ethnically-framed conflicts (i.e. June 2010 Osh violence, Aidarkan riot of January 26, 2012, other small-scale incidents in Leilek).

Two of the rumours spread throughout the Kyrgyz crowd were particularly influential for mobilising support from both inside and outside of Iskra: namely that "Tajiks raped a Kyrgyz woman in Andarak" and "Tajiks killed a Kyrgyz schoolboy". These rumours represented the interpretation of the conflict event by some Kyrgyz activists. Being culturally and contextually specific to the situation in Kyrgyzstan, these rumours mobilised outrageous support for the Kyrgyz group, with men arriving in groups from neighbouring villages and distanced locations. For Talantbek, a young Kyrgyz man from the neighbouring village of Kommuna, who arrived in Iskra with a group of men after hearing about "the incident of rape by Tajiks," this act was "the worst offence and humiliation to Kyrgyz people and could not leave anyone unconcerned," although there had been quarrels and skirmishes with Tajiks before.[16] Similarly, the rumour about the purported killing of a schoolboy mobilised a group of men from neighbouring villages via networks of kinship and peers of young men to "punish Tajiks for this cruel act." According to various estimations, at least 200 men armed with metal bars and sticks arrived from other villages and the district centre in Andarak to join the Kyrgyz mob.

Such ethnic framing not only strengthened the group's shared identity, but it also created legitimacy for a violent response. Beyond the general symbolic function that rape has in situations of conflict as a degrading act (Wimmer/Schetter 2003), for the Kyrgyz community the perception of rape and killing in the conflict in Andarak was shaped by cognitive models formed by the memory of recent violence between Kyrgyz and Uzbek residents in Osh in June 2010, which left several hundred people dead (KIC 2011). The essence of the narrative of the Osh violence was, for most of the Kyrgyz in the Leilek district and especially in Isfana, a town where Uzbeks form the majority, that "Kyrgyz people won the war in Osh and punished the Uzbeks for their cruel acts."[17] Uzbeks in this narrative were perceived as the perpetrators of cruel crimes, including rape and mass murder in Osh, whereas Kyrgyz men, who fought against them, were regarded as defenders of their community in their own country. Moreover, the first mass mobilisation of Kyrgyz groups in Osh (in June 2010) was in response to the alleged mass raping of young Kyrgyz women by Uzbek men in a student dormitory (International Crisis Group 2010: 12). Hence, for Kyrgyz, the meaning of rape more than ever comprised great humiliation and dishonouring of their community by *others*, not to speak of the sacred role of women in the traditional Central Asian societies to which rural Kyrgyz also belong. Thus, the particular meaning of the term 'rape' was its close attachment to recent brutal inter-ethnic violence. The memory of the rape of Kyrgyz women and mass killings by the *others* was spread not only by narratives, but also through reports in the written and visual media. For instance, one widespread visual source involved documentaries about the Osh violence that were distributed throughout the country in the form of CDs (known locally as CDs of Osh events/*diski Oshskikh sobytiy* in Russian). Some of these

---

16 Interview with conflict participants and a member of the local community from Kommuna (September 2012).
17 Interview with 'R.K.' (Isfana, September 2012).

documentaries reported the unrest in a biased manner, reflected a one-sided perspective and contained outrageous images of killed and burned people. Copies of these CDs were available to the public in local internet cafes and small CD shops soon after the clashes. One of these documentaries, which was widely disseminated in Leilek district and could still be purchased in some internet cafes (though it was not sold openly), blamed Uzbeks for all the damage and casualties, while showing images of the dead, allegedly raped and burned Kyrgyz women.[18] The Kyrgyz people of Leilek district, who did not actually witness the conflict in Osh, had open access to this documentary and its video images that could potentially inflame hatred and foster a negative attitude towards Uzbeks and any other nationalities fighting against the Kyrgyz people. Perhaps it was due to this CD that some of the young men from the district centre turned up in Andarak purely on the basis that they had heard rumours of a clash between Tajiks and Kyrgyz, while the cause of the clash was of no importance to them at all.[19] The Kyrgyz men acting violently against the Tajiks in Andarak felt their actions were justified and legitimate – very much in the same way as the violence against Uzbeks in Osh in 2010.

With such framing and the spreading of rumours, the mobilisation of a Kyrgyz crowd in Andarak relied on ethnic solidarity based on kinship ties and networks of friends.

'Othering' through Blame Displacement and Victimisation

The mobilisation of the Tajik group was based on framing the situation as a threat deriving from the 'other side', in connection with increasing fear and mistrust of the other group. The Tajik community of Andarak can be characterised by multiple identities that resonate differently depending on the circumstances. Living in the territory of Kyrgyzstan, and claiming that the first people to settle in Andarak were of Tajik ethnicity, members of the Tajik community of Andarak have Kyrgyz citizenship, speak the Kyrgyz language fluently and participate in the political life of the country by claiming

---

18 Several of my informants in Leilek claimed that they had a copy of this CD at home. One of them insistently gave me one of the two copies she possessed, asking me to see for myself "what had really happened".

19 Interview with T.R., a Kyrgyz conflict participant arriving from the district centre (Isfana, September 2012).

their rights as citizens of Kyrgyzstan. Hence, most of the time, they regard themselves as being part of the "people of Kyrgyzstan".[20]

Yet, the framing of the other group as a threat to the Tajik community, to which I refer in this context as a process of 'othering', enabled significant mobilisation of support for the Tajik group: "The Kyrgyz are getting ready for *jang*" (a Tajik term meaning both a war and a fight) was a frame that the activists returning from the police station employed to mobilise Tajik men in the marketplace.[21] This interpretation was not mere rumour but rather an exaggerated depiction of the state of conflict escalation, which called upon all Tajik men in Andarak to protect their homes and families.

Through this framing, Tajik activists relied on the mobilisation of group solidarity and cohesion, on the one hand, and blame displacement, on the other, while protecting their homes from Kyrgyz attack meant an acknowledgement of a real threat. This perception of a threat was once again based on already existing cognitive frames and memories of past violence. The Tajik community of Andarak also perceived the Osh battles as a "victory for the Kyrgyz people over the Uzbeks," yet, in their perception, the Uzbeks were the victims of violent attacks made by Kyrgyz groups, and not the perpetrators of cruel acts, as perceived by Kyrgyz people. For the Tajiks, their interpretation of this past violent conflict was tied to a minority perspective. Hence, being a much smaller national minority than the Uzbeks in Kyrgyzstan, Tajik activists framed a possible attack by the Kyrgyz crowd as a repetition of majority-minority clashes in the context of increasing nationalist discourse in the country. Some of the Tajiks that took part in the conflict underlined that they had seen what "Kyrgyz people did to Uzbeks in Osh" and that they would never allow them to do the same to Tajiks in Andarak. For the majority of the Tajiks the quick mobilisation of armed Kyrgyz men meant also an attempt "to punish Tajiks," where punishment, in essence, was understood as a repetition on a smaller scale of what happened with the Uzbeks in Osh.

The resultant interpretation of the conflict, based on 'othering', blame displacement and victimisation, enabled the quick gathering of an armed Tajik crowd, and it was this mobilisation which allegedly played an important role in preventing the Kyrgyz crowd from actually attacking. One of Tajik participants, for instance, believed that "if the Tajiks had not been

---

20 Interview with local elders in Andarak (Andarak, July 2012).
21 Interview with E.M., a Tajik activist in the conflict (Andarak, August 2012).

ready to resist with a relatively equal force, the Kyrgyz crowd would have definitely attacked the Tajik community in Andarak."[22]

Thus, group cohesion among the Tajik community was built by framing a threat deriving from the other side and building an image of *others* based on self-victimisation. Blame displacement was an essential component of this point, as the mobilisation of the Kyrgyz crowd was framed rather as an "attempt to punish Tajiks" and not as a consequence of the incident between the young boys at the marketplace.

Alignment with Larger Political Discourses

In addition to aligning the frames of the skirmish and its context with larger cognitive models such as ethnic identity and an imaginary of past violence, Kyrgyz activists also successfully aligned it with more significant political discourses at the national level and continued, from the reception of these discourses, at the local level. While framing the unrest, the rhetoric on the Kyrgyz side invoked claims such as "this is the land of Kyrgyz people" and that minorities, like the Tajiks, first of all had to respect them.

The initial violence was principally interpreted as an act of disrespect by a national minority against *titul'naya natsiya*. The legitimation of some form of 'punishment' for this disrespect resonated with the positive reception and internalisation of the political discourse of ethno-nationalism, which gained particular popularity at the national level, especially in the south, after the 2010 violence in Osh.

Ethnicity-driven politics at the national level, gathering pace after the violence of June 2010, and its subsequent incorporation in local politics, enabled the successful internalisation of nationalist rhetoric (as a cognitive model) by the majority of the population, including communities at the local level (cf. Laruelle 2012; Megoran 2012; Wachtel 2013). The parliamentary (October 10, 2010) and presidential (October 30, 2011) elections that took place after the violence in Osh polarised key political parties in line with ethnic groups in Kyrgyzstan. The south-north division that dominated political dynamics throughout the country's independent history, including both the 2005 and 2010 revolutions[23,] was supplemented by the instrumen-

---

22 Interview with 'R.S.' (Andarak, June 2012).
23 Since the year 2005 Kyrgyzstan overcame two revolutions, both resulting in change of political leadership of the country and making Kyrgyzstan the only Central Asian state that followed the chain of color revolutions in Georgia in

talisation of ethnic hatred and the juxtaposition of ethnic Uzbeks and Kyrgyz that resulted from the violence of June 2010.

Political parties invoked the interests of sub-groups within the national electorate on the basis of ethnicity (Dzhuraev 2012). Hence, unsurprisingly, a new political party, *Ata Jurt* (homeland), won most of the seats with a nationalist rhetoric targeting the Kyrgyz population of the south as victims of the Uzbeks, a notion that Kyrgyz activists and informants repeated many times during my interviews. During the election campaign, the leadership of *Ata Jurt*, especially its co-leader Kamchibek Tashiyev, openly promoted the notion that in Kyrgyzstan the *"titulnaya nasiya*, i.e. ethnic Kyrgyz, should be indeed titular, and other ethnicities [should not be considered as] equal with or higher than the Kyrgyz" (Ivashenko 2010). Such rhetoric gained prominence and promoted nationalistic narratives among the population of the south, and it also created a significant group of new political elite in the country, on the one hand, and resulted in the division of the electorate on the basis of ethnicity, on the other.

2003 and Ukraine in 2004. In March 2005 former President of Kyrgyzstan Askar Akayev was ousted in the result of so called "Tulip Revolution" by a broad coalition of then oppositional forces. Back then some of the observers assessed this event as a return to democratization (Juraev 2010, cf. Cummings (ed.) 2009) in the land that had been occasionally called an island of democracy in Central Asia. Yet, the second revolution on April 6-7, 2010 and appeals of protesters against the post-Akayev leadership of the country headed by President Kurmanbek Bakiev proved, the least to say, the opposite. In comparison to the Tulip Revolution the second revolution in April 2010 occurred to be rather violent with clashes erupting across Kyrgyzstan and protesters violently demanding resignation of President Bakiyev. Clashes and protests during this revolution left about 80 dead and around 1000 wounded (ICG 2010). In addition to the substantial role of clan politics and political patronage in both revolutions in Kyrgyzstan, the events during the revolution in 2010 had direct impact on the interethnic violence that erupted in June of the same year between Kyrgyz and Uzbek residents of Osh city as well as the discourse of nationalism that has been influential in the society since (cf. Matveeva 2010, Matveeva et al. 2012, McGlinchey 2011).

The presidential elections of October 2011 continued the dynamics of political development in this spirit of "parochialisation of political legitimacy" (Dzhuraev 2012: 3). Mainly, polarisation along the lines of regional division prevailed, as in the past, during these elections, thereby dividing the votes of the ethnic Kyrgyz electorate between candidates from the south and a candidate from the north. The Kyrgyz population of Jalalabad, Osh and Batken provinces preferred candidates from the right-wing parties *Ata Jurt* and *Butun Kyrgyzstan* (*United Kyrgyzstan*), Kamchibek Tashiev and Adakhan Madumarov, respectively, whereas Kyrgyz from northern regions voted ostensibly for the candidate of the centrist Social Democratic Party of Kyrgyzstan, Almazbek Atambayev. Given the prominence of ethno-nationalist discourse among the southern candidates and its popularity in the south, local support groups, made up exclusively of ethnic Kyrgyz, mobilised easily in the southern districts. For the same reason, and because of the fear of possible violence, the ethnic Uzbek population of the southern regions either abstained from the elections or voted for the northerner Almazbek Atambayev, who did not campaign with the same narrative (Rahmetov 2011; Ismailbekova 2012). The Tajik minority in the Leilek district of Batken province, where Adakhan Madumarov was leading, also voted for Atambayev (the current President)[24] for the same reason.[25]

Hence, during the conflict in Andarak, the ethno-nationalist discourse was not only significant at the national level, but also its public reception at the local level in the southern regions was well-facilitated. Kyrgyz activists framed the unrest within this discourse and thereby achieved its successful

---

24 Interview with the head of the Tajik diaspora (Isfana, June 2012).

25 The specifically localised nature of the mobilisation of support in the election period makes this choice an important factor for inter-communal relations. At the district, vicinity and village levels, local elders usually advise insufficiently informed residents on the "right candidate" and guide them toward collective voting for this preferred person. On the other hand, according to my informants, buying votes through immaterial (e.g. promises made by candidates to local leaders) and material (e.g. payment of a certain amount of money to each family for their vote) support was practiced during the aforementioned presidential elections as well. Hence, local leaders recognise easily when a portion of the minority community votes for a candidate other than the preferred one. See Radnitz (2010) for a discussion on the localised nature of political mobilisation in Kyrgyzstan.

alignment with current public sentiments as well as with memories of past violence. This in turn made framing of the conflict within the ethno-nationalist rhetoric of "Kyrgyzstan as the land of Kyrgyz people" successful and added more legitimacy to the action presupposed by suggested frames.

Contestations and Re-Framing in Conflict Processes

Although ethnic framing of the skirmish and its subsequent implications held strategic advantages for both groups in the mobilisation process, framing processes in Andarak were also characterised by contestation and re-framing. Such small-scale conflicts between members of the 'titular nation' and 'ethnic minorities' (both Tajik and Uzbek) were not uncommon in Leilek, and so non-ethnic framing of the standoff, attempted by local communities, aimed at enabling some form of de-escalation. Community leaders, elders and local authority representatives that initiated mediation efforts to prevent an outbreak of mass violence framed it as an ordinary tussle between young people aligned with provocation by criminal groups' intent on inflaming another instance of inter-ethnic violence in southern Kyrgyzstan. According to the report of a local NGO, members of an informal criminal group, consisting of young sportsmen, jobless youth and drug dealers, were seemingly engaged on the side of the Tajiks. Furthermore, a number of ex-convicts were allegedly seen in the two crowds, "mobilising people and setting Kyrgyz against Tajiks – and vice versa" (Leilek Danishmani 2012: 3). The shared Muslim identity of both communities and their history of previous peaceful co-habitation in the area were particularly highlighted as legitimate references for the non-ethnic framing of the conflict by local elders of both communities, who had observed the mobilisation processes.

This re-framing was effective in enabling mediation efforts through the traditional institution of elders[26] and state intervention in the conflict, as it

---

26 In both Kyrgyz and Tajik society, traditional institutions have long worked as arbitrators and mediators during conflicts and disputes within and between the communities. For rural communities, village leaders (both informal and formally elected ones) and elders are trusted people to whom villagers turn, in order to resolve conflicts and to guide community interactions. For example, the Court of Elders – Aksakal sotu – has been long considered a legitimate local institution by villagers, although elders that represent it lack basic legal training and

threatened to escalate to a violent clash between the Kyrgyz and Tajik crowds. It also shaped the state discourse about the conflict in Andarak, which was based on the 'third force' hypothesis, i.e. the idea that interethnic violence had been provoked by a group of criminals or outsiders in order to inflame inter-ethnic conflict, which in turn led to the direct intervention of law-enforcement agencies in order to prevent a violent clash, yet did not change communal sentiments about ethnic contestations.[27]

---

education. An important position of aksakals (elders) is based on the respect shown to them by the people and the common belief, both in Tajik and Kyrgyz societies, that older people are wiser and known much more than younger ones. Community leaders that are elected in Kyrgyzstan as mingbashi (head of thousand), ke'chebashi (head of street), elikbashi (head of fifty) are also chosen from among the respected members of the community. Community leaders often involve elders and religious celebrities, such as the imam of the village mosque, in mediation due to the persisting respect of the communities for these traditional institutions.

27 In this regard, one can draw an analogy with the framing of the violence in Osh by the authorities and its influence on public discourses after the conflict. The framing of the June 2010 violence in Osh by members of the-then provisional government that shaped media discourse after the event was also centred on the "third force hypothesis". This was confirmed by the results of a media review focusing on the depiction of the Osh conflict in the national media from May to August 2010, conducted by the author. While suggesting various causes of the conflict and also preceding events of April and May in Jalalabad and Osh, the provisional government insisted that the escalation of inter-ethnic clashes resulted from a "provocation by third forces" and "special unknown groups" which led to the deterioration of the situation in the epicentres of the conflict in the wake of political turbulence and regime change in Kyrgyzstan. This framing persisted particularly after the conflict in light of claims made by both residents of Osh and national and international observers about the inaction of the provisional authorities and their failure to prevent inter-ethnic violence, about the involvement of the state in pogroms in Uzbek-populated districts in Osh as well as acts of crime committed by state agencies during and in the aftermath of the conflict (HRW 2010; KIC 2011: 5; Matveeva et.al. 2012).

How Do References Structure Framing?

Larger cognitive models, broader political discourses and memories of past violence can be defined for the purpose of understanding the working structure of the framing process as references of the frame. In conflict processes, frame generation and resonance are supported mainly by or based on the references of the frame.

Going back to the discussion of framing in conflict studies based on this brief elaboration on framing in mobilisation processes in Andarak, one can draw some conclusions about the mechanisms of frame generation and frame enactment in conflict dynamics. As mentioned above, framing is a rather complex process that can combine several points of reference. Accordingly, one could break down larger cognitive patterns or models into more specific references.

As the framing approach is aimed at bridging macro, meso and micro processes in conflict analysis, thus arguing for the interrelatedness of all three dimensions in inter-communal conflicts, for instance in contrast to the level analysis approach for conflict studies proposed by Cordell/Wolf (2010), references should be formulated in such a way that they are able to intersect all three levels.

The first reference of a frame is the more significant cognitive patterns that shape the self-identification of conflict actors. The main concern selecting this reference is conflict group formation. Collective identities are typically selected as a greater cognitive pattern in the framing process that shapes the mode of group formation in a situation of conflict. Group formation in conflict is based on the chosen collective identity and its positioning in relation to the opposite conflict group. The framing process in clashes often starts with self-identification and confrontation building in relations with the other group. The second reference is the broader political discourse and political processes that flow beyond (or parallel to) inter-communal unrest. It is obvious that inter-communal conflict does not evolve in isolation from other political processes or from the effects of both communities involved. This presupposes that, although the study of conflicts within the scope of these elaborations does not adhere to normative constellations of the nation-state framework, the state as the actor enjoying a monopoly of violence in Weberian terms cannot be excluded from the analysis of inter-communal conflicts. This does not suggest that the state should be necessarily considered as a separate third actor; rather, it is meant to propose that frames are often influenced by those larger national-level political discourses that are internalised at the local communal level through communicative reception. The effect of such discourses on framing needs to be analysed by treating them as one of the references.

The third reference is memory of past violence, which can be activated through imaginaries and their symbolic dimension. Although memory can also be seen as a superior cognitive pattern, memory of past violence is typically used as a reference with a distinctive function. As Halbwachs argues, collective memory of past events is reproduced within shared social frames, thus depicting active individual engagement in social frames and processes (1992). Hence, if on the one hand memory of past violence effectively enables the formation of *we-ness* and essentially contributes to the *othering* process in building an image of the opposing protagonist, on the other hand it serves to select the form of response action and justifies its suitability. To exercise violence, it first has to be perceived as being justified by the majority of actors involved in the conflict and/or the community concerned. Treating memory as a separate reference allows scrutinising the ramifications of past violence in order to shape current conflict dynamics.

Accounting for these three references as integral elements of mechanisms of frame generation and its implementation enables a better comprehension of two central functions of framing in conflict mobilisation – the construction of a common identity and the legitimisation of action (which in this regard combines with other components of framing, e.g. alignment and resonance). Although it is generally recognised that frames often serve a combination of these and other functions, this distinction is still important to make, in order to understand the choice of social categorisations and their implications on conflict processes, as the above case demonstrates. These two functions serve the purpose of mobilisation in a mutually complementary manner, in that common identity construction creates in-group solidarity and builds a clear image of the self, whereas the legitimisation of action provides meaning for the conflict and the responsive action that has to be taken in a way that motivates the group to take up arms. It is also pertinent to mention that in a conflict situation a successfully constructed common identity might not always result in communal violence; hence, any framing process has to contain both aspects in order to enable mobilisation. These aspects can be reflected in one or more frames that are generated and selected by the conflict actors and the groups involved.

Conclusion

This chapter was driven by two intentions. First, I tried to illustrate that mobilisation processes in the conflict in Andarak can be analysed well by scrutinising the actors' framing, which, as shown above, shaped the resources and strategies used by them in the escalation of potential violence. Activists from both Kyrgyz and Tajik communities, belonging to two ethnically separate, adjacent villages, utilised ethnicity-based messages that built on the public reception of broader cognitive models and discourses for framing the conflict and thus organising support. Rumours and the memory of past violence, often founded and mediated on symbolic representations, proved to play an essential role in generating and enacting these frames.

One hypothesis that can be developed from the above discussion is that framing in mobilisation processes related to conflicts is, on the one hand, very complex because of the different frames generated and enacted by different actors and, on the other hand, is not an autonomous phenomenon. Rather, frames as well as mechanisms of frame generation and implementation make use of references that are available to actors in a given social and political setting. In the case of the conflict in Andarak, references and their suitable application were crucial for the resonance of a set of frames and the mobilisation processes based on it. Whereas Kyrgyz activists were able to activate ethnic framing with images of past violence, and Tajiks could build on *othering* based on blame displacement and victimisation, both communities mobilised ethnic solidarity due to the internalisation of broader political discourses relating to ethno-nationalism at the local level.

Second, I suggested that framing, as a theoretical approach, yields analytical value for understanding conflicts from a process perspective. In a nutshell, a framing perspective suggests that through the interpretation of an issue or skirmish, actors, while functioning as signifying agents, are involved in the production of meaning and "maintenance" of mobilising ideas contingent on the general social and political environment. The frames produced by conflict actors evolve within broader cognitive frames, discourses and worldviews persistent in society and their interaction in the conflict process. This shapes mobilisation processes in conflict. Hence, framing as a theoretical approach helps to comprehend the conflict better, along with its actors, phases of development and, most likely, its proximate causes (rather than seeking its root causes).

Last but not least, for the practical purpose of examining the conflict at hand, the analysis of framing in Andarak is not only able to capture the multiple narratives of the conflict, produced by one or the other party, but also determines the wider social and political setting of inter-communal relations in the Batken province of Kyrgyzstan. In this sense, the framing analysis discloses the ideational content of local order and public sentiment, pertinent beliefs and dominant discourses at the local level, and actual issues and structures of inter-communal relations that go far beyond the given incident. This makes the understanding of everyday inter-communal skirmishes no less essential than analysis of large-scale violent clashes, such as the June 2010 violence in Osh, in order to understand conflict dynamics in southern Kyrgyzstan.

REFERENCES

Bates, Robert H./De Figueiredo, Rui .J.P./Weingast, Barry (1998): "The politics of interpretation: rationality, culture and transition." In: Politics & Society 26/4, pp. 603–642.
Benford, Robert D./Snow, David A. (2000): "Framing processes and social movements: an overview and assessment." In: Annual Review of Sociology 26, pp. 611–639.
Bromlei, Yulian (1983): Очерки теории этноса *(Essay on theory of ethnos)*, Moscow, Nauka.
Cordell, Karl/Wolff, Stefan (2010): Ethnic conflict, Cambridge: Polity.
Cummings, Sally (ed.) (2009): Domestic and International Perspectives on Kyrgyzstan's "Tulip Revolution": Motives, Mobilisation and Meanings, London: Routledge.
Desrosiers, Marie-Eve (2011): "Reframing Frame Analysis: Key Contributions to Conflict Studies." In: Ethnopolitics, pp. 1-23.
Dzhuraev, Shairbek (2012 [2011]): Governance Challenges in Post-Soviet Kyrgyzstan: The Externalization and Parochialization of Political Legitimacy, Norwegian Institute of International Affairs, Regional Competence-Building for think-tanks in the South Caucasus and Central Asia.
Esser, Hartmut (1999): "Die Situationslogik ethnischer Konflikte." In: Zeitschrift für Soziologie 28/4, pp. 245-262.

Fearon, James D./Laitin, David D. (2000): "Violence and social construction of ethnic identity." In: International Organization 54/4, pp. 845–877.

Foundation for Tolerance International (2012): "Отчет по мониторингу инцидента в селе Андарак (Monitoring Report on events in v. Andarak)." (http://fti.org.kg/en/component/content/article/36-monitoring-reports/86-monitoring-in-andarak; accessed January 12, 2012).

Goffman, Erving (1974): Frame Analysis: An Essay on the Organization of Experience, Cambridge: Harvard University Press.

Halbwachs, Maurice, trans. Coser, Lewis A. (1992 [1950]): On Collective Memory, Chicago: The University of Chicago Press.

Horowitz, Donald L. (1998): "Structure and strategy in ethnic conflict: a few steps towards synthesis", Paper presented at the World Bank Conference on Development Economics, Washington, DC, World Bank.

Human Rights Watch (2010): "Where is the Justice? – Interethnic Violence in Southern Kyrgyzstan and its Aftermath." (www.hrw.org, accessed June 1, 2012).

International Crisis Group-ICG (2010): "The Pogroms in Kyrgyzstan", Asia Report 193.

Ismailbekova, Aksana (2012): "Coping Strategies: Public Avoidance, Migration and Marriage in the Aftermath of the Osh Conflict, Fergana Valley", Crossroads Asia Working Paper Series 04.

Ivashenko, Evgeniy (2010): "Interview with Kamchibek Tashiev." (http://www.fergananews.com/articles/6728; accessed July 1, 2012).

Juraev, Shairbek (2010): "Back on Track? Kyrgyz Authoritarianism after the Tulip Revolution." PONARS Eurasia Policy Memo 95.

Kyrgyzstan Inquiry Commission-KIC (2011): "Report of the independent international commission of inquiry into the events in southern Kyrgyzstan in June 2010."(http://reliefweb.int/sites/reliefweb.int/files/resources/FulltReport_490.pdf, accessed January 20, 2012).

Laruelle, Marlene (2012): "The paradigm of nationalism in Kyrgyzstan: Evolving narrative, sovereignty, and political agenda." In: Communist and Post-Communist Studies 45/1-2, pp. 39-49.

Leilek Danishmani (2012): Аналитический отчет о конфликтном инциденте в селе Андарак между кыргызами и таджиками (Сумбулинский АО, Лейлекский район, Баткенская область) (*Analytical report on conflict incident between Tajiks and Kyrgyz in v. An-*

darak, Sumbula vicinity, Leilek district of Batken province), Unpublished report.
Lepgold, Joseph/Lamborn, Alan C. (2001): "Connecting Research Agendas on Cognition and Strategic Choice." In: International Studies Review 3/3, pp. 3-29.
Matveeva, Anna (2010): "Kyrgyzstan in Crisis: Permanent Revolution and the Curse of Nationalism." Crisis States Working Papers Series.
Matveeva, Anna/Savin, Igor/Faizullaev, Bahrom (2012): "Kyrgyzstan: Tragedy in the South." In: Ethnopolitics Papers 7 (http://www.ethnopol itics.org/ethnopoliticspapers.htm, accessed January 13, 2013).
McGlinchey, Eric (2011): "Exploring Regime Instability and Ethnic Violence in Kyrgyzstan." In: Asia Policy 12, pp. 79-98.
Megoran, Nick (2012): "Averting Violence in Kyrgyzstan: Understanding and Responding to Nationalism." Russia and Eurasia Programme Paper 03. Chatham House.
Mielke, K./Schetter, C./Wilde, A. (2011): 'Dimensions of Social Order: Empirical Fact, Analytical Framework and Boundary Concept', ZEF Working Paper Series 78, April, Bonn.
Radnitz, Scott (2010): Weapons of the Wealthy. Predatory Regimes and Elite-Led Protests in Central Asia, Ithaca: Cornell University Press.
Rahmetov, Anvar (2011): The Kyrgyz Presidential Elections: A Historic Step Towards Exclusive Democracy? ISPI Analysis 80.
Reeves, Madeleine (2010): "The ethnicisation of violence in southern Kyrgyzstan." (http://www.opendemocracy.net/odrussia/madeleinereeve s/ethnicisation-of-violence-in-southern-kyrgyzstan-0, accessed June 12, 2012).
Schütz, Alfred/Luckmann, Thomas (1973): The structures of the Life-World. Translated from German by Richard M. Zaner and H. Tristram Engelhardt, Jr., Illinois: Northwestern University Press.
Snow, David/Benford, Robert (1992): "Master frames and cycles of protest". In: Morris, A.D., and Mueller, C.M. (eds), Frontiers in Social Movement Theory, Yale University Press, New Haven, CT, pp. 133–155.
Snow, David/Byrd, Scott.C (2007): "Ideology, Framing Processes and Islamic Terrorist Movements." In: Mobilisation 12/1, pp. 119-136.
Snow, David/Rochford, E. Burke/Worden, Steven.K./Benford, Robert D. (1986): "Frame Alignment Processes, Micromobilisation and Move-

ment Participation." In: American Sociological Review, 51/4, pp. 464-481.

Tishkov, Valeriy (1995): "'Don't Kill Me. I am a Kyrgyz': An Anthropological Analysis of Violence in the Osh Ethnic Conflict." In: Journal of Peace Research 32/2, pp. 133-149.

Wachtel, Andrew Baruch (2013): "Kyrgyzstan between democratization and ethnic intolerance." In: Nationalities Papers 1/16, pp. 971-986.

Wimmer, Andreas/Schetter, Conrad (2003): 'Ethnic Violence', in W. Heitmeyer/J.Hagan (eds.), International Handbook on Violence Research, Netherlands: Kluwer Academic Publishers, pp. 247-260.

Institution-Centred Conflict Research: A Methodological Approach and its Application in East Afghanistan

JAN KOEHLER

INTRODUCTION: THE PUZZLE OF SOCIAL ORDER AGAINST THE ODDS

The notion of conducting more systematic research into the relationship between institutions and conflict originates from an empirical conundrum I observed in the 1990s during fieldwork in the former Soviet Union. It was a dilemma relating to maintaining local social order against the backdrop of structural breakdown and institutional disintegration that accompanied the dissolution of the Soviet Union. With the collapse of Soviet statehood not everything that could go wrong went wrong, and what went wrong did not go wrong to the same degree. Local differences in this respect were particularly striking, since under similar structural conditions, violent conflict was contained successfully in some locations, while in other places it was only minimal, and yet in other regions the breakdown of the Soviet Union triggered all-out civil war (cf. Koehler/Zürcher 2003: 244). The research agenda that followed was once summarised by the late Georg Elwert in the following terms: "We want to investigate whether in conflict more institutions mean less violence". (Elwert 2003, personal conversation)

In this paper I first introduce the methodological approach to *institution-centred conflict research*, in order to investigate a specific aspect of social order theory, namely do institutionalised modes of conflict-processing reduce violence, foster social cohesion and enable adaptive change? I then use this approach for a multi-layered empirical study of local conflict dynamics in Eastern Afghanistan, while in the last section I return to the question of social order based on the empirical evidence provided.

CONFLICT, INSTITUTIONS AND THE DYNAMICS OF SOCIAL ORDER

Social order means social rules and structural conditions that reduce contingency over time in interactions between individual and collective social actors. Any concept of social order rests on a notion of stability with regard to human association and interaction, i.e. there is some sameness in terms of those constraints on contingent social action. If everything changes all the time, and according to no recognisable rules, there is nothing left to identify as social order. However, on the question of what it is that is constant, there is no agreement between what Alan Dawe called the two sociologies: the sociology of social action and the sociology of social systems (Dawe 1970).

One approach relates to the sameness of form or structure over time, while another relates to retaining core functions of social order through competition, conflict and resulting adaptive change. It is this latter, conflict-based model of social processes that I follow when I develop empirical conflict research as a heuristic instrument to assess the diversity and dynamics of social order.

Actors' Will and its Constraints

Interrelations between human beings are shaped and influenced by different variables: some – like biology and geography – are to a significant extent external to society, while others – like cultural representation and social rules – are creations of social interaction. Actors' will and what constraints it is my principle starting point into the investigation of variety in and the dynamics of social order. An actor, which is the smallest unit of analysis of social science, is an individual or collective unit capable of executing an action, i.e. an intentional deed as opposed to unintentional behaviour.

Goffman conceptualised the context in which interdependent actors define and constrain each other's options to act as 'fields of action' (Goffman 1971), while Norbert Elias referred to it as 'figurations' (Elias 1970). These are the structured interdependencies between social actors with specific interests and characteristic power differentials between them.

Even in the most basic strategic social situation two actors are constrained in their actions by the power of the other actor to interfere with this action. It is, however, not only real power that informs and shapes interaction. More importantly it is the *limited knowledge* actors have about each other, the *perception* of power differentials and, finally, the *interpretation* of information and perceptions they apply.

Hence, information is a resource vital to understanding actors' options and any subsequent choices taken. Other resources also matter, because, in general, resources are part of actors' incentives and constraints: resources are often what actors are after in conflicts, and resources are always needed to pursue one's interests when in conflict with other actors. In short, resources are material and immaterial means actors may acquire and use in order to progress their interests and secure their reproductive needs.

In order to understand the scope of action available to actors, and the strategies and tactics they apply, we need to analyse the way in which incentives and constraints informing their actions are organised in a more permanent way. In other words, we need to look beyond the more idiosyncratic, power-informed social situation and identify relevant institutions and analyse their impact on actors' choices. In an attempt to consolidate the individual decisions of actors with the systemic logic of super-structures detached from actors and their actions, the concept of institutions offers some form of middle ground.

Definitions of institutions are plentiful throughout the different social sciences disciplines that are interested in the predictable, rule-based part of human action (Esser 2000: 5-8). Most approaches, nonetheless, agree on two defining aspects of institutions: first, they are social rules, and second these rules are of some consequence to the groups to which they apply. In this paper I treat institutions as society-made constraints that shape social interaction (North 1990: 6).

Institutions, in essence, are implemented social rules. Hence, not all rules are institutions, i.e. private rules, laws of nature or rules of no consequence, if broken, do not qualify as institutions. Rules that do qualify must be known commonly as being imperative by those to whom they apply.

This knowledge does not necessarily require cognition, since institutional rules may be internalised and "known by heart".[1] Furthermore, compliance must be expected, and it must be backed up by some kind of positive or negative sanctions.

Institutions increase the likelihood of the sameness of social and organisational forms over time. They inform actors on how to act within a given social context and on how to interpret their own and others' actions within this context. Institutions thus provide the framework of rules accessible to cognition that help to reproduce organisational sameness over time.

Institutions, however, may also facilitate "controlled" breaks in the reproduction of sameness, in that they reduce the risks involved in "anything goes"-anomy and control the number of likely options available to actors (Elwert 2004). As trusted safeguards against the threat of anomy they may make possible otherwise unlikely innovations, differentiations and adaptations to the social order. Without institutional backup such changes would either not take place or would be disruptive.

Conflicts and Change

There are two reasons to turn to the concept of conflict in order to research the variety in and dynamics of social order. First, because conflict-processing is a universal and constitutive part of social order and is linked causally to social constraints at the heart of social order discussed above. Second, because focusing on conflict serves heuristic purposes in inductive research whereby actors, their interests and institutional constraints are simply more visible in conflicts than in day-to-day routine.

While institutions facilitate social order, conflicts have often been associated with a challenge to the established order. I will briefly introduce this approach, most pointedly associated with Ralf Dahrendorf's criticism of Lewis Coser's functionalist theory of social conflict.

---

[1] This is a key assumption in Elias's theory on the process of civilisation (Elias 1939); however, how the internalisation of norms works in practice is not explained by sociology but rather falls into the discipline of psychology.

I will first sum up some of Coser's main points. According to Coser,

"[c]onflict means the struggle over values and claims to scarce status, power and resources in which the aims of the opponents are to neutralise, injure or eliminate their rivals." (Coser 1956: 8)

This classic definition made by Lewis Coser, though some sixty years old now, is still helpful as a starting point to discussing the main aspects of the operational concept of conflict. It captures a wide range of issues relating to social conflicts and the forms they may take – from non-violent competition to violent destruction.

Coser's main achievement in relation to a theory of social conflict was not, however, the still widely used working definition of conflict he proposed. The main point he elaborated, drawing on Simmel's classic work on disputes (Simmel 1992 [1908]: 284-382), was how conflict can be both functional and dysfunctional for the social relationship in which it occurs. He found that the institutionalisation of conflict is necessary to maintain social relationships.

"One safeguard against conflict disrupting the consensual basis of the relationship [...] is contained in the social structure itself: it is provided by the institutionalization and tolerance of conflict." (Coser 1956: 152)

Hence, social conflict may contribute to the maintenance and adaptation of social relations and social structures. Nonetheless not all conflicts are functional in the maintenance of social relations, even if conflict is institutionalised as a tolerated form of pursuing one's interests. According to Coser, only conflicts over those interests, norms and values are functional that are not a defining or constituting part of the relationship itself. Otherwise, socially dysfunctional forms of conflict may occur in the form of withdrawal or destruction.

Coser contributed a convincing theoretical concept explaining the functional and dysfunctional impacts conflict may have on social relations. His approach, however, does have typical functional limits in explaining social processes, i.e. functionalist theory is ahistorical in the sense that it is unable to account for endogenous social change.

This was the main criticism Ralf Dahrendorf raised against the functionalist approach to conflict in particular, and against static structural-functionalist models of society in general (Dahrendorf 1986: 272). Dahrendorf brought back power, rule and, essentially, the competitive rule-making and rule-breaking human being into a theory of the conflict-driven differentiation of society.

To Dahrendorf the normal state of society was one of dispute over norms, competition for resources and conflict about the best organisational answers to existing problems, all rooted in one universal aspect of the human condition, namely the uncertainties of life. To him, sociology seeking to explain social cohesion in consensus and equilibrium was looking for an imaginary utopia. Dahrendorf therefore explicitly disregarded research into what keeps society together; rather, he was concerned with what drives society on (Dahrendorf 1979: 109).

Dahrendorf failed in his ambitious task of developing a consistent counter-theory of conflict-society (*Konfliktgesellschaft*) that would bring about a paradigmatic change in the research interests of social science: from consensus to conflict, from stability and equilibrium to innovation and change, from functional systems (back) to historic processes.[2]

A number of authors have picked up from where Coser and Dahrendorf ended the discussion on the universal function (Coser) or principle constitutive force (Dahrendorf) of conflict for society or, respectively, for the process of social change. A tendency in the social sciences has since been to move away from attempts to arrive at universal theoretical statements on social conflict and shift more towards explanations for the impact of specific types of conflicts under specific institutional conditions in different societies.

One line of thought seeks to place conflict firmly in the fabric of a very special type of politically constituted society, namely a modern, complex, rule of law-based liberal democracy. Authors such as Albert Hirschman, Helmut Dubiel and Marcel Gauchet share Dahrendorf's main concerns by questioning the functionality of normative or moral consensus as the social glue of democratic, liberal societies. Rather, they propose that through particular ways of institutionalising unavoidable social conflict as a constitutive part of the political and economic system, social cohesion is achieved and sustained (cf. Hirschman 1994; Dubiel 1992; Gauchet 1990).

---

2   For a critical account of Dahrendorf's achievements, and an attempted explanation of this failure from a contemporary viewpoint, see Lamla (2008: 226-27).

This proposition remains a theory-driven conclusion that these authors derive from the history of Western democracies. What they contribute is a focus on certain types of societies characterised by the way their fundamental institutions come to terms with social conflict.

What remain unanswered and opaque, however, are two crucial elements: first, the precise interdependencies of conflict and institutions and how they result under certain but not all political framework conditions, in social cohesion and the legitimacy of the political order; and second, whether cohesion as a result of specific ways of institutionalising social conflict is indeed unique to modern liberal and democratic societies.

A highly significant contribution to the question of what it takes to institutionalise conflicts in such a way that social cohesion and political legitimacy are likely outputs can be found in Niklas Luhmann's theoretical work on procedures.

Luhmann identified three defining characteristics that institutionalised conflict-processing must meet to qualify as a procedure (Luhmann 1983 [1969]: 38ff.). First, the procedure must create its own reality-realm and must take place in a social space that is set apart from the reality in which the conflict itself occurs. Second, the procedure must arrive at decisions that are not pre-determined by factors outside of the procedure, and the decisions reached must be implemented in the reality realm of the conflict. And third, some specific manifestations of 'real-life' power differentials between the conflicting parties must be excluded from the procedure.

The theoretical approaches to the interdependencies of institutions and social conflict introduced herein have been developed for what their authors see as *modern*, *complex*, industrialised and state-constituted (and constituting) societies. Nonetheless, theoretical discoveries on the interdependency of institutions and conflict in 'modern' societies should inform the analysis of conflictive social processes in *all* societies and should also stand the empirical test in volatile institutional settings not pacified and dominated by advanced statehood.

An institutional theory of conflict adds to the explanation of the general problem of social order, irrespective of the particular historical, cultural or economic conditions in which it occurs. Ultimately, investigating figurations of actors – their interests, power differentials, interdependencies and resource endowment – as well as the institutional constraints they face through the looking-glass of conflict analysis informs us about the quality, reach and dynamics of social order.

Institution-Centred Conflict Research

Based on conflict and institutional theory I develop assumptions on the nexus between conflicts and institutions (cf. Koehler 2013; Gunya et al. 2008; Koehler 2004). I treat conflicts and institutions as empirically observable social phenomena, in that all societies have to deal with conflicts and all societies are defined by the collective rules they establish and enforce. The relationship between conflict and institutions is plausible but inconsistent. Conflict can disrupt established relations and fragment society, while at the same time conflict can form and connect social units and enable the dynamic adaptation of social order. Institutional rules that inform social interaction can be followed or broken, and sets of institutional rules can contradict each other and cause conflict. Furthermore, institutions and their distributive consequences for actors, social groups and different strata of society can be questioned and contested (Knight 1992).

Hence, there is a strong and ambivalent relationship between these two social phenomena whereby conflicts make and break institutions, and institutions contain but also cause conflicts.

Institution-centred conflict theory predicts that specialised institutions, processing a wide range of conflicts via procedures, are conducive to dynamic social order, i.e. they make the institutional framework of society more reliable, thereby enabling selective change that is not disruptive and does not fragment society as a whole (cf. Eckert 2004; Zürcher 2004; Dubiel 1992).

According to this theoretical assumption, it is not the causes of conflict that explain the impact of conflict on social order, stability and change. Rather, it is a question of specialised institutions that are able to process conflicts from alternative confrontations (or zero sum games) and the denial of the right of the opponent to be party to the conflict, into more predictable, rule-based social action (Koehler 2013).

This rule-based mode of conflict-processing is what Elwert identified as 'procedure' (Elwert 2004), Luhmann demonstrated as generating legitimacy (Luhmann 1983 [1969]) and Hirschman called the more-or-less approach to conflict, arguing that it is at the heart of the cohesion observed in democratic liberal modern societies (Hirschman 1994).

Based on these predictions of institution-centred conflict theory I arrive at the following three general questions for empirical investigation.

1. How Are Conflicts Processed?

Conflict is a social process in which the interests of actors clash (cf. Bonacker 2008: 12-15). The conflict situation should be separated from the way with which a conflict is dealt. Dealing with a conflict can be more or less violent, and it can also be more or less embedded in rules and norms (Zürcher 2004).

Violence and institutional embedding are treated as conceptually separate variables that characterise different modes of conflict-processing. I use Georg Elwert's differentiation of four ideal types of what he called 'actors' conflict' (Elwert 2004). The most violent and non-embedded is the physical destruction of the opponent, the more embedded but still violent forms are warring and feuding, the non-violent but also non-embedded strategy is avoidance and, finally, the most embedded and least violent type of conflict-processing is procedure.

I modify Elwert's typology in three ways (Koehler 2013): First, I use this typology to describe modes of conflict-processing rather than ideal types of conflict situations. Furthermore, I use the degree to which conflict-processing follows institutional rules rather than the wider concepts of social embedding as criteria to assess the degree to which conflict-processing is integrated in social norms. Lastly, I suggest that the concepts of violence and institutional embedding are, while conceptually independent, correlated to each other, i.e. the more institutional embedding, the less violence. I treat this notion, however, not as an assumption but as a testable hypothesis.

2. What Role Do Institutions Play in Conflicts?

Institutions inform and constrain actors' choices in general – and in conflict in particular. Procedures are a special case of institutionalised conflict-processing. Hence, a dynamic conflict-processing model predicts that institutions may play a central role in conflicts, a role that tends to reduce the likelihood of violent self-help and guarantees the institutional embedding of conflict-processing.

However, the simple fact that institutions constrain actions, create path dependencies and prioritise certain actions in comparison with other actions has distributional consequences and privileges a specific social order over all alternatives. Here, distributional consequences and the exclusion of alternatives may be contested by actors, and hence institutions may cause conflicts.

3. Finally, I Ask What Impact Conflict-Processing Has on Social Order

The model of conflict-processing on which I draw, in order to approach the problem of social cohesion and change, predicts that acts of power manifesting in conflicts about the institutional order go a long way to explaining institutional change (breakdown, transformation and innovation), while the functional output of institutions (the problems they solve) is key to explaining institutional continuity.

On the one hand, expectation from the conflict-processing model is that if a wide range of conflicts is processed via specialised institutions – through procedures – then social cohesion and adaptive change are best served. As long as the core social process, i.e. disputes about the best, most appropriate social order, follows reliable and accepted rules, non-disruptive and adaptive institutional change is possible. On the other hand, the model predicts that dis-embedded conflicts about the institutional setup of social order will tend to veer towards disruption, fragmentation and violence.

So far I have sketched out a research methodology based on institution-centred conflict theory that assesses social order through the identification and analysis of conflicts. In the following I will apply this method to the subnational conflict dynamics in two Eastern Afghanistan provinces, recorded during fieldwork which took place in 2005. The method captures the conflicts in their case-specific chronological depth, which in this case means a time span of two generations, or forty years.

THE EMPIRICAL RESEARCH

The empirical research extracts presented hereafter follow the steps developed above, including context narrative, actor analysis, an analysis of relevant resources and institutional analysis. The results are based on field research I conducted during three field visits to Eastern Afghanistan in 2005 and a number of follow-up interviews since then.[3]

---

3   As a field supervisor I designed and implemented the research in a framework of cooperation between the Volkswagen Foundation-financed project "Accounting for State Building, Stability and Violent Conflict in the Caucasus and Central Asia" (development of the methodological approach and implementation) and

The field research was implemented in cooperation with a local partner organisation, namely what was known at that time as the research unit of the NGO Coordination of Afghan Relief (CoAR). It consisted of three components: first, context analysis based on literature as well as forty-five expert and key informant interviews second, twenty-five detailed conflict case studies based on qualitative interviews in the target districts and third, a household survey of 359 people in thirty villages in the target districts.

Fieldwork (Implementation)

We selected five districts in two eastern Afghan provinces, namely Laghman and Nangarhar. For this research the choice criteria related to accessibility and a minimum of security for multi-week field visits. The representativity of the whole province or region was not a criterion.

Two districts were chosen in the Laghman province (out of a total of five), and three districts in Nangarhar (out of a total of twenty-two districts; see Map 1). Within the districts a systematic sampling strategy was used. Two geographically distinct locations – village clusters – in each district (a *mantaqa* in Laghman, or *qaria* in Nangarhar) were chosen according to their known or expected relevancy in relation to conflict processes.

---

the European Union-financed Programme for Alternative Livelihoods in Eastern Afghanistan (PAL).

Map 1: Target Districts in the eastern Provinces of Nangarhar and Laghman

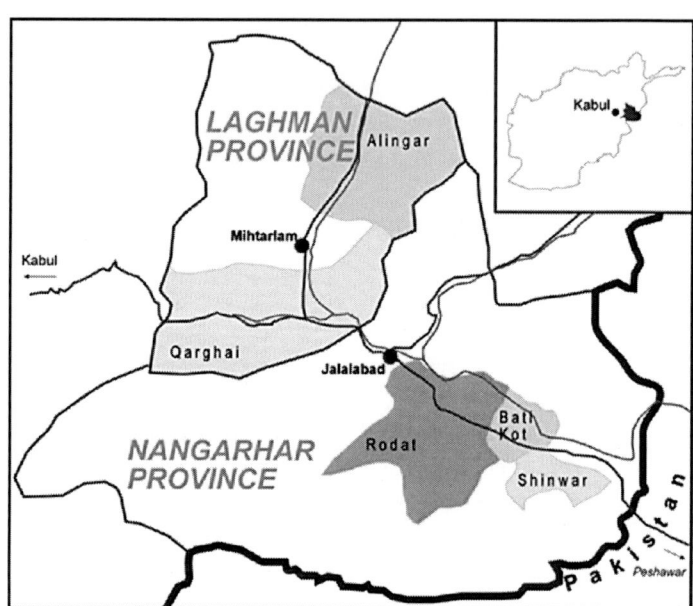

Source: Copyright by Jan Koehler

Context

Historical context is relevant for understanding the processes described in these case studies. Institution-centred conflict analysis, by definition, deals with dynamic social processes over time (conflicts) that are scrutinised for possible path dependencies (institutions).

The fieldwork itself took place in early 2005, i.e. three years after the US-led military intervention toppled the Taliban regime in late 2001 and the Bonn process of building principle state institutions had been initiated (cf. UN 2001). It was one year after the *Loya Jirga* had adopted a new constitution in January 2004, and a few months after the first ever elections for a head of state had taken place in Afghanistan in late 2004. No parliament had been elected at that point, but preparations for the elections, held in September 2005, were certainly underway (cf. Sedra/Middlebrook 2005).

The specific local socio-geographic context deserves an introduction of its own. Afghanistan cannot be treated as a homogenous society in which political, economic and cultural characteristics have been streamlined by the nation-building process.

The eastern provinces of Nangarhar and Laghman form the north-eastern part of the predominantly Pashtun-settled areas of Afghanistan that are sometimes referred to as the "Pashtun tribal belt" (cf. Grötzbach 1990: 68; Giustozzi 2009: 74). It is a part of the country where a sense of tribal belonging has historically been strong, both as an identity and as an institution of segmentary social organisation with implications for access to land and the local honour-based prestige economy (cf. Elphinstone 1972 [1842]: 149ff.; Barth 1965: 13ff.; Glatzer 2002). The main Pashtun tribes are the Mohmand, Shinwari and Khugyani, along with some settled as well as nomad Ghilzai and Ahmadzai groups.

Pashtun tribal areas in Laghman and northern Nangarhar border a region which is home to ethno-linguistically distinct groups of *kohistani* people (highlanders), such as the Pashai (a Dardic Indo-European language, spoken only in this part of Afghanistan) and some linguistically separate Nuristani groups.

Eastern Pashtun tribes were active in government during the Old Regime and were over-represented in one of the two principle wings of the Afghan Communist Party (the Kahlq wing of the PDPA, Rubin 2002: 93, 240). Successive governments in Kabul had strong direct control over Jalalabad and well-established patron-client relations with the *khans* and strongmen controlling the fertile Jalalabad plains along the Kabul River (cf. Rubin 2002: 242).

The tribes in the highlands around the plains, however, have been much less influenced by Kabul. Here, the state exerted, for the most part, indirect and negotiated influence when it did not intervene directly with military forces.

Despite the relatively strong and direct reach of the central state during the PDPA regime, the eastern provinces developed an active Mujahidin presence in the Jalalabad agricultural hinterlands. These were contested territories, though, and the fertile valleys around the Kabul River, and its main contributories on the plains, saw some of the worst fighting the Afghan countryside has experienced.

The closeness to the Pakistani border – and hence exposure to the direct interference of Pakistan's notorious secret service, the Inter-Service Intelligence (ISI), as well as competing Peshawar resistance parties in addition to the tribal makeup of local society – meant that resistance in the eastern provinces remained fragmented during the *jihad*, and violently competitive during the civil war, until the Taliban pacified the area in 1996 (Rubin 2002: 261f., 277; Giustozzi 2009: 74).

Following the downfall of the Taliban regime, three forces emerged from within the Eastern Shura (council of mujahidin commanders), initially competing with each other: the Hizb-e Khalis-affiliated Arsala clan consisting initially of four brothers[4], the Jamiat-affiliated Pashai commander Hazrat Ali and his relative Haji Musa, who came to dominate the emerging police force after the fall of the Taliban, and the worldly (drug) business-oriented Haji Zaman, a former commander of Hizb-e Khalis from the Qurgani tribe (cf. Weaver 2005; Giustozzi 2009: 87; Human Rights 2003: 6, 19; Rashid 2008: 87f., 98, 128).[5]

Cross-Case Overview

The fieldwork identified twenty-five conflicts for closer investigation in the ten community clusters of the two provinces under scrutiny. The table of conflict case studies (see Table 1) indicates the district in which the conflict evolved and the subjective ranking of the conflict in terms of disruptiveness for the communities involved, as understood from the interviews and observations within the communities (italic indicating disruptive conflicts). Bold font is used to show that a conflict involved physical violence. In the following section I present emerging patterns in relation to this cross-case analysis.

I coded the individual cases of conflict as being related primarily to (1) competition over natural resources (land, irrigation water, forest or pastures), (2) the opium poppy economy (OPE), (3) state emergence (4) NGO activity and (5) social and identity issues. If a case was related primarily to one of these five conflict fields but showed secondary relations with other

---

4   Abdul Haq, killed in 2001 by the Taliban, Haji Qadir, killed in Kabul in 2002, Haji Din Mohammad, who took over the position of governor of Nangarhar from his deceased younger brother, and Haji Nazrullah Barmaley, the civilian leader of a Shura of tribal elders from Nangarhar province.

5   Jamiat and Hizb-e Khalis are two influential politico-military parties that participated in the Jihad against the Soviet Union and subsequent civil war.

conflict fields, I coded this as a cross-relation. Secondary relations are given when resources, incentives, ideas or actions associated with one of the other conflict fields influence the conduct of the primary conflict identified.

Table 1: Conflict Coding Overview

	Field 1 Natural resources	Field 2 Opium Poppy Economy	Field 3 State emergence & power	Field 4 NGO activity; development	Field 5 Social/ Identity conflict
District I: Shinwar	*C01*	X	X		X
	C02	X			X
		C03	X		X
	C04	X	X		X
		X	X	*C05*	X
District II: Bati Kot	*C06*	X			X
	C07	X	X		
	C08		X		X
	C09	X	X		
	C10				
District III: Qarghayi	*C11*	X	X		X
			C12		
	X	X	X		*C13*
	C14	X		X	
			X		*C15*
District IV: Alingar	*C16*				X
		X		*C17*	
	X	X	X		C18
	X	X	X	*C19*	
			X	X	*C20*
District V: Rodat	*C21*	X	X		
	C22	X	X		X
	X	*C23*	X		X
		C24			X
	X			C25	
Total primary conflicts	13	3	1	4	4
Total cross relations	5	16	16	2	14

Source: Copyright by Jan Koehler

Though by no means a statistical assertion, some of the trends reflected in this table are relevant for the further analysis of the fieldwork.

The most relevant area of conflict by far is competition over natural resources. More specifically, conflict over agricultural land and, related to this, access to irrigation water come in first place, while pasture and forested areas play a role but figure less prominently in the research locations chosen.

Table 1 also alludes to the geographical concentration of issue areas, i.e. conflicts about social issues, discrimination and values figured more prominently in the two districts of Laghman than in the three districts in Nangarhar covered by the survey. This impression was confirmed by the quantitative results of the household interviews. In Laghman, roughly 25 per cent of the respondents considered social issues to be of pressing importance compared to an average of only 5 per cent in Nangarhar's districts. Conflict over natural resources, however, dominated across the board in all districts, with replies confirming its significance, ranging from 56 per cent in Rodat (Nangarhar Province) to 69 per cent in Alingar (Laghman Province).

The different sensitivity attached to social issues as causes of conflict, including value differences and matters of discrimination, might be explained as being related to ethnic minority belonging. Only in Laghman did the research capture a significant non-Pashtu-speaking ethnic minority, namely the Sharri Pashai (33 per cent of respondents in Alingar and 4 per cent in Qarghayi district). Amongst the Sharri Pashai, 58 per cent considered social issues highly relevant to conflict processes, and natural resource issues were significantly down to 46 per cent.

There was a high level of violence as part of conflict-processing in all of the identified fields. Violence may be an indication of disembedded conflict, i.e. conflict beyond social or other forms of institutional control in relation to conflict-processing. A constant degree of violence, however, may also simply show that certain forms of violent behaviour in conflicts is socially acceptable or even a social norm (as in honour killings or blood feuds).

During the household interviews, the respondents were asked how many conflicts occurred during 2004 that were of concern to the community, and how many of these conflicts did in fact include the use of violence. For the whole sample (359 interviews), 216 respondents identified one or more conflicts of concern to their community. One or more *violent* conflicts affecting the community were identified by 160 respondents. There was strong variance between districts. At roughly 50 per cent, Bati Kot, Rodat and Qarghayi scored equally high on the 'no violent conflict identified' scale, with Shinwar next at about 25 per cent and Alingar at the bottom with an astonishing 3 per cent.

A rather surprising result with regard to conflicts, which one would expect to affect local security seriously, is the absence of two fields I initially considered relevant: the activities of the ousted Taliban and their local allies, on the one hand, and direct pressure meted out by local commanders on the population, on the other hand.

The Taliban were hardly mentioned at all in the interviews, neither as a contemporary threat nor as an asset or as a corporate actor in conflicts. The respondents discussed them when explaining how conflicts occurred while the Taliban were in power, but at the time of the fieldwork, the post-Taliban period appeared also to be truly post-Taliban from the local perspective.

Likewise, responses to the question as to who was responsible for security in the community overwhelmingly indicated that there was no clear responsibility. Only 6 per cent pointed to the representative of the district governor and, surprisingly, only 2 per cent pointed to the local commander. Local security, of course, was the principle strategy used by local commanders after the *jihad* ended, to seek legitimacy (referring to themselves often as *qumandon-e amniat*, i.e. security commanders).

Hence, at the time of the fieldwork, the Taliban insurgency and US-led counter-insurgency measures, which would soon dominate insecurity in the provinces, had not yet developed into a relevant conflict field from a local perspective.

Foreign-driven enforcement, however, was a hotly debated and very relevant issue. Most explicitly in the interviews with community leaders, notables and government officials, many people took issue with the drastic escalation of counter-narcotics operations (crop eradication and interdiction measures) that started in late 2004. These measures effected the population through military operations, as well as the operations of special Afghan police under foreign command and supported by private foreign contractors.

The opium poppy economy (OPE) itself, however, was not identified as the most relevant conflict field. Up until February 2005, when this fieldwork was conducted, conflict within the OPE appears not to have been a major concern for the communities. Most observed conflicts did, however, show a strong indirect link to the OPE. This secondary link related predominantly to the resources generated in the OPE (extra money to bribe, to acquire land or to buy weapons) or the impact of the OPE on other resources, such as the value of agricultural land and water.

I will scrutinise these issues in the next section, in which I apply an institution-centred conflict analysis to a specific case involving resource conflict.

Case Example: Land Grabbing in Nangarhar, Rodat District, the Mazina Village Cluster

Rodat is located in the central Nangarhar province southeast of Jalalabad. To the northeast the district meets the Kabul River. Halfway between the river and the district centre (Shahi Kot) crosses the Jalalabad-Torkham main road. Rodat has irrigated land along Khazar Naw Creek in the Char-Qala Dasht and a *karez* system[6] connected to it. North of the Jalalabad-Torkham road can be found irrigated land with orchards. At the time of the fieldwork, Kot Valley, along with the Kotkhvar Creek, still belonged to Rodat. In 2005, this area was established as a separate district.

The village cluster of Mazina is located in the south of the district in the Hazar Naw valley, bordering Dehbala district. According to a group interview in Rangrezan Village's shura, the Mazina village cluster (*qaria*) consists of eight villages and is home to about 11.100 inhabitants. There are three main tribes, namely the Mohmand, Shinwari and some Durrani, and ten subtribes present.

Case Narrative: Land Dispute between a Commander and a Landlord[7]

In the village of Rangrezan, within the *qaria* of Mazina, a conflict had been ongoing since 1990 between the clan of Sayed Kateb Pacha, consisting of

---

6   A karez system is a traditional irrigation system consisting of vertical wells and a combination of underground and surface channels.

7   Based on: C22 case interviews by A., February 22, 2005 with Malek Sameullah and Sayed Kateb Pacha in Rangrezan; references: p-010 (Malek Samiullah, landless shura assistant, explained the position of Qumandon Mullah Jan, who was not available for an interview); debriefing discussion and notes March 18.-23., 2005 in Jalalabad; timeline, profile and actors' mapping.

four families of the Sadat descent group (in the following the 'Pachayan clan'), and the *Mujaheddin* commander, Mullah Jan (of the Shinwari tribe), over the ownership of 4.5 jeribs[8] of agricultural land. Before Taliban rule, Mullah Jan, who is affiliated to the mujahidin party Hizb-e Islami, was a leading representative of Gulbuddin Hekmatyar in Nangarhar.

In 1990, land belonging to Sayed Kateb Pacha's cousin, who resided in Germany at that time, was taken over by *Qumandon* Mullah Jan (*'qumandon'* is the Dari and Pashtu term for 'commander'). The commander claims that this was done in agreement with Sayed Kateb Pacha, who had asked the commander to help him forcefully remove some thirty houses built by neighbouring villagers on land owned by the cousin of Sayed Kateb Pacha.

The background to this action by Sayed Kateb Pacha involves a dispute over social obligations. The Pachayan clan was the dominant local landlord family (*khan*) in the past. After the communist coup in 1979, Sayed Kateb Pacha and one of his brothers secured a position in the administration of the communist regime and eventually moved to the provincial centre of Jalalabad. Before moving to Jalalabad, Sayed Kateb Pacha had promised one of his daughters to Zabiullah, a neighbouring villager of considerable social standing. After moving to Jalalabad, though, Sayed Kateb Pacha changed his mind and married his daughter to someone in the city. Zabiullah felt that his honour had been tainted and unsuccessfully demanded *bad*.[9]

At this time, landless villagers started to settle on land belonging to the Pachayan clan. Allegedly, at least Sayed Kateb Pacha's cousin initially agreed to this, possibly in order not to aggravate relations with the neighbouring villagers further. The situation in the 1980s was delicate for rural people seeking careers in the communist system: according to Sayed Kateb Pacha, they left for Jalalabad because the mujahidin took control over his village. They left their land with a trusted long-term share-cropper, Zafari, to look after it in their absence. Zafari, however, enrolled with the mujahidin of Qumandon Mullah Jan, and instead of paying the due share of annual yield to the Pachayan clan he claimed that the mujahidin demanded that share instead. After the fall of the Najibullah government and the rise to power of the mujahidin, the Pachayan clan returned to the village; they felt

---

8   Jerib is a traditional unit of land measurement in the Middle East and south-western Asia. One Afghan Jerib is 2000 sqare metres or 0.2 hectare.

9   *Bad* is revenge or satisfaction for moral injury that recovers the damage done to someone's honour.

safe, to some extent, because one of their brothers had been a classmate of Mullah Jan and managed to negotiate security guarantees with the commander. This was the time at which Kateb Pacha and the commander cooperated in clearing the clan land of thirty squatters' houses (1990).

In return for his services, i.e. forcefully clearing the land and thus creating additional agricultural ground for the clan, the commander claimed half of the land – on which he wanted to build a house. Kateb Pacha claims that the commander had been pushing his clan for some time to sell some land to him, in order to establish himself in their community.

In 1993, Mullah Jan recommended that the Pachayan clan flee to Pakistan for the sake of their own security, as he feared that other mujahidin commanders not under his control might attack them. Retrospectively, however, Kateb Pacha is of the opinion that Mullah Jan's actions were not those of a benevolent patron but that they were staged by the commander in order to take control over their land and secure himself a foothold in the Pachayan community.

In 1994, the clan fell out with the commander over who in actual fact held the title to the land in question. Qumandon Mullah Jan arrested Kateb Pacha and his brother, and, allegedly at gunpoint and threat of death, forced them to officially sign over the transfer of the 4.5 jeribs of land to him.

When the Taliban came to power, the commander fled the area and the clan reclaimed the 4.5 jeribs, cultivating it with opium poppy and making good profit from the venture.

In 2001, the fortunes of the parties changed yet again. With the ousting of the Taliban and the arrival of coalition forces, Mullah Jan was appointed commander of the border troops (or customs office – the information here is contradictory), and he reclaimed the land. Additionally, the commander demanded compensation in the form of a share in the profit for the time the clan had used the land in his absence. To enforce this claim he kidnapped one of Kateb Pacha's brothers and transferred him to his village, Mullah Jan Kalay, in the remote Dehbala district, where he ran a private jail. This community of loyal Shinwari tribesmen had specialised in handling kidnapping cases as a strategy used in conflict-processing. The elders of the Shinwari community held a *jirga* that decided in favour of the commander and imposed a penalty of 80.000 Pakistani Rupees (about 1300 USD) on the clan and gave Mullah Jan a right of pre-emption, in case they wanted to sell their land. After both parties accepted the ruling, Mullah Jan released Kateb Pacha's brother on bail. When the payment did not come through,

Mullah Jan abducted one of the clan's sharecroppers, took 70 kg of opium from his house and, before releasing him, instructed him to pay the landlord's usual sharecropping fee, due to him, since he mortgaged the land (*giraw*).

In 2002, however, Mullah Jan lost his position as border commander, and both Sayed Kateb Pacha and his brother secured jobs with the post-Taliban security structure (i.e. the militia) of the eastern provinces. One of them enrolled with the then security commander of the eastern provinces, Hazrat Ali, and one as bodyguard of Hajji Musa, the brother-in-law of Hazrat Ali, who was considered one of the most powerful people in the province at that time. With the support of these powerful patrons, the clan reclaimed the land. Commander Mullah Jan was warned by Gul Karim, then security commander of Nangarhar province and allegedly a distant relative of Hazrat Ali, not to push his claim on the land anymore. Allegedly, the new commanders in charge also issued a warning to Meer Za Ahmad, district governor (*woliswol*) of Rodat and (formerly subordinate) fellow commander to Mullah Jan in the politico-military party structure of Hekmatyar's Hizb-e Islami. At the time of the fieldwork, the conflict was power-locked and frozen.

Analysis: Actors, Resources and Institutions

In this conflict the constellation of main actors is rather straightforward: the Pachayan clan holds a possession that the commander is trying to wrest from their grasp and secure in a legally binding way. The relationship between the main actors has changed significantly over time: first, there was the classmate relationship before Mullah Jan joined the mujahidin resistance while the Pachayan entered official state structures. Then there was the indirect relationship via the sharecropper/caretaker of the clan's land during the period of anti-Soviet resistance, when in the absence of the four Pachayan brothers the landlord's sharecropping dues were in fact delivered to Qumandon Mullah Jan and his mujahidin. When the mujahidin rose to power after the collapse of the Najibullah government and took over the administrative centres of the country, the relationship changed again, whereby Mullah Jan acted as patron and guardian to the Pachayan clan, who had fallen from grace in the eyes of the mujahidin because of their active collaboration with the communist government. This patronage went as far as actively helping the clan in removing thirty households that had settled on clan land in the absence of the landlords. During this time, the commander established informal control over part of the clan land and the surplus it produced.

This asymmetrical – though mutually beneficial – patron-client relationship was disrupted and escalated into open conflict when the commander increased the pressure to finally formalise his control over the land in the form of a written title deed. Ever since the forced transfer took place, the relationship has been characterised by open confrontation in which real power and external parameters beyond the control of the actors have determined the conduct of the conflict. First, the commander de facto expelled the clan (had them move to Pakistan) and grabbed the land from the clan. Then the commander had to flee himself to Pakistan, when the Taliban took control of the eastern provinces and the Pachayan clan was able to reclaim its land.

After the fall of the Taliban and the re-emergence of mujahidin power under the umbrella of OEF (*Operation Enduring Freedom*), Mullah Jan not only managed to reclaim the land (by force, persuasion and the manipulation of accepted procedures), but also received compensation for past profits lost during the Taliban period. Finally, the commander fell out with the dominant commanders of the eastern provinces and was forced to flee yet again to Pakistan.[10] At the same time, two brothers from the Pachayan clan managed to establish formal relations with these commanders by entering their security operation.

There are, however, different nuances to this conflict. The picture is incomplete and the dynamics of this conflict will be misunderstood if further actors are not considered. These actors are connected to the two protagonists, either via side conflicts or via existing networks of trust, mutual obligations or other forms of reciprocal exchange. Most importantly there are official power holders using the power of their office to protect the interests of their patron (in the case of Mullah Jan's relationship with the district governor, Meer Za Ahmad) or of their clients (in the case of the security commanders' protection of Pachayan clans' interests).

Aside from patronage, mujahidin-party connections, and a shared work or education history, indicate a further, more complex fault line between

---

10 The mujahedin faction under Gulbuddin Hekmatyar, to which Mullah Jan as well as the woliswol of that time belonged, broke off relations with the US-backed Karzai government and joined forces with the Taliban insurrection in 2002.

social strata that merge to some extent with identity groups constructed around the notion of kinship. The Pachayan clan was referred to by the interviewed villagers as the original (or principle) lineage of Rangrezan village, and has been traditionally part of the landowning elite of *khans*. The standing of these landholding elite changed with the communist revolution, albeit in the given case in a very different way than planned by the central government. While governmental attempts to enforce land reform in favour of landless and petty land-holding peasants met with stiff resistance in Rangrezan, mostly from the local sharecropping population, the landlords decided to pursue careers in the communist administration of the provincial centre. Their sharecroppers took up arms with the mujahidin and utilised the land of their former landlords as they deemed appropriate. In other words, in Rangrezan the *'kulaks' (khans)* followed the communists' call, while the peasantry joined the resistance. As such, the landlords (temporarily) lost their land not to the communists but to the mujahidin.

The mujahidin finally won and left the resistance struggle, in order to establish their own government – an endeavour that famously failed and led to the destructive civil war during the early 1990s. The first task of the de facto, though not de jure, dispossessed landlords was to retake control of the land they lost to those who stayed in the villages and established relations with the mujahidin groups dominating the countryside, even during the Soviet occupation. This is precisely what Kateb Pacha did for his clan when he negotiated the patronage of Commander Hajji Mullah Jan and convinced him to evict the landless villagers who had settled on clan-owned land.

In terms of *resources* this conflict is primarily about 4.5 jerib, or 1 hectare, of irrigated agricultural land, a resource which means very different things to those parties competing for its ownership.

First, there are the landlords and initially undisputed legal owners of the land. They needed the power to re-establish control over the land that de facto had been taken over by their sharecroppers (with the blessing of mujahidin commanders). This power, to secure their property in the long run, did not so much depend on the external patronage they managed to gain from a temporarily influential commander but was related much more to their standing within the community. Since they had already lost considerable prestige by leaving the village, breaking their pledge to marry a daughter to a fellow villager and joining the communist regime, regaining the image of a clan capable of defending their honour was vital. In the prestige economy of local landowning Pashtun tribesmen, losing one's land is shameful, particularly if it is lost under pressure. Seen in this light, the (unsuccessful) resistance to Mullah Jan's approaches to formally secure the 4.5 jeribs of land makes more sense.

For Mullah Jan, with his traditional powerbase in a remote highland district, the main motivation for taking legal possession of the land in question was to establish himself physically in a strategic location. The meaning this plot of land had to him appears to have been related more to the prospect of establishing himself in a lowland community (building a house, binding sharecroppers to him) than to economic gains from the sharecropped agricultural land. By taking over or demanding profits from the land, he put pressure on the landlords to officially sell their land to him.

The last group with a vested interest in the disputed 4.5 jeribs were the sharecroppers, who took possession of the land and its profit crop during the years of mujahidin resistance. While thirty houses were constructed on this territory, there is no evidence that any fight was put up when Mullah Jan sent in a tractor to pull down the houses in 1990.

In institutional terms, three types of *institutions* compete with the raw power of potentially violent action over influencing the course of conflict-processing between the parties involved: land tenure, formalised in land titles, tribal or community *jirgas* and codes of conduct in the application of self-help. All three differ in their degree of formalisation, in their autonomy from the power of actors in conflict and in the impact they have on the course of action within a conflict. I shall focus on the more formal institutions herein.

The most startling observation is the sustained bearing that formal land tenure has in this conflict, unimpressed by changing political tides. Even when actors have (and use) the power to actually ignore this institution, they nonetheless seek the legitimacy of accepted rules in the long run. Mullah Jan enjoyed control over some of the Pachayans' land for years, but still he spared no effort in securing legal ownership, even at the height of his power as the representative of the then prime minister, Hekmatyar, in Nangarhar province.

This principle status of formal land tenure is supported by the quantitative data collected at district, *qaria* and village levels. Seventy-five per cent of valid responses in Rodat district considered an official land title as the most important source of land tenure security, compared to only 25 per cent who opted for reference to time or tradition.

The widely accepted prevalence of formal entitlements over informal agreements in terms of land tenure is confirmed by the reaction of the thirty households that were evicted by force from the Pachayan land: while the sharecroppers complained that Sayed Kateb Pacha broke a promise given to them by his cousin, nobody questioned the principle right of the landlord to re-take full control of his land.

The social acceptance of land tenure institutionalised via official certification, however, excludes most state-sponsored arrangements made during the communist reign, for example the expropriation of private and common property, the redistribution of access to land and forms of collectivisation. As the case of the Pachayan and Mullah Jan shows, the legitimacy of formal documentation can also be called into question when there is suspicion that this documentation is the result of foul play, as in the case of forced decisions or corrupt administrative procedures.

While the principles of land tenure rights are widely accepted, the enforcement of those rights requires self-help (the commander kidnapping the Pachayan brother and the sharecropper) or access to external power (Sayed Kateb Pacha drawing on the violent services of Mullah Jan to clear his land of squatters, and the Pachayan brothers seeking protection from the commanders Hazrat Ali and Hajji Musa).

Both strategies – self-help and external patronage – involve a degree of arbitrariness, lack legitimacy and are sustainable only as long as the configuration of relative power between actors does not change. Hence, actors successfully enforcing what they see as their tenure rights may still feel compelled to legitimise their action by employing socially accepted procedures. In the present case study, Mullah Jan called for a tribal *jirga* after kidnapping and imprisoning one of his opponents.

Jirgas are time-honoured and well-tested conflict-processing institutions that operate in an environment devoid of core functions usually found in the modern state – common peace, by virtue of a widely enforced monopoly of violence, and the rule of state law as a fall-back position when local social institutions fail to process emerging conflicts.

In some types of *jirgas* safeguards have been integrated into procedures to deal with their general vulnerability in light of the real power parties may apply to influence conflict-processing. First, there is the public and formal acceptance of the authority of the *jirga* by all parties, prior to convening the respected representatives of the parties and uninvolved mediators. Second, there is the principle of free and open speech within the time and space of the *jirga*. Then there is the *machlega* payment, or bail, that conflicting parties may be required to pay prior to the *Jirga*, in order to safeguard their commitment to the process and to ensure that they will stick to the ruling of the *jirga*. Finally, there is the option that rulings must be consensual, and this consensus is publicly declared and formalised (usually by fingerprinting a document of agreement).

All of these factors make it difficult for actors to control fully the proceedings and outcomes of a *jirga* once it convenes. However, the *jirga* has no monitoring and sanctioning apparatus of its own; hence, there is no guarantee that parties will stick to decisions and agreements reached, other than what the loss of reputation or even shame disregarding the ruling of the *jirga* might entail for the involved individuals or groups. For weak parties that depend on their social embedding in networks of kinship and neighbourhood solidarity, sanctions on reputation can be a formidable threat. For the likely transgressors, the more powerful party in a conflict, the threat may be less substantial and more a matter of consideration.

This is precisely the risk Mullah Jan faced when he decided to seek the ruling of a respected *jirga* led by Shinwari tribesmen specialising in kidnapping cases. Despite the fact that he himself belonged to the Shinwari tribe, he could not be completely sure that the decision of the *jirga* would fully satisfy his ambitions. If the decision had not satisfied his requirements, nobody could have forced him to drop his claims or release the hostage, but it is important to note that the main intention of calling the *jirga* would have failed publicly, i.e. legitimising a situation created by acts of power. The *jirga*, however, did decide in his favour, and according to neutral observers there was hardly anything the dignitaries could do, since both the land title and the brother of the opponent were in the hands of Mullah Jan. This is also the reason why the Pachayan clan accepted the ruling of the *Jirga*, to compensate Mullah Jan for profits lost during the Taliban period.

CONCLUSIONS

I return to the three guiding questions on institution-centred conflict research developed above (p. 88 ff.): How are conflicts processed, what role do institutions play and is there evidence for adaptive institutional change?

The cross-case summary and individual case study presented above demonstrate one thing very clearly: with regard to conflicts, even in times of the violent breakdown of statehood and the fragmentation of society, not everything is acceptable. Actors in conflict stick to certain rules and do not apply all means at their disposal to further their interests or to win. The physical destruction of the opponent, even if possible, remains an exception in this respect.

The theoretical expectation developed in the first part of this paper was that actors' deeds in conflict are constrained by the distribution of power between involved parties, by resources sought or utilised in the conflict and by institutions setting the rules of engagement and informing actors of the consequences of breaking those rules. All three constraints – relative power, available resources and institutional rules – figure prominently in the conflicts researched herein. Crucially, the quality and mix of constraints changes to various extents as the conflict moves on over three decades. This change can be attributed to shifts in outside parameters (the governance context), although some changes can best be explained by interaction between outside parameters and patterns of local conflict processes.

Three ordering principles are at work in the case study of local conflict presented: corporate core group self-help, relations of power emerging from the constellation of actors in conflict and the remnants of institutional constraints applying to conflict. Based on the case evidence provided herein, my conclusion is that local conflict-processing institutions survive war and social fragmentation. They are, however, marked by limitations in terms of scope and the sustainability of any decisions taken.

Nevertheless, do I find evidence for institutional change in the case studies? And specifically, do institutions adapt to changing framework conditions? Moreover, do some break down and do other institutions emerge as a reaction to pressure placed on society by arbitrary rule and civil war? And finally, does conflict itself create and change institutions?

The expectation from the theoretical discussion on causal links between institutions and conflict was that the ability of actors to challenge the distributive consequences of institutional rules would be a driving force for endogenous institutional change. Whether this change takes the form of institutional breakdown, institutional adaptation or innovation, I argue, may depend on the degree to which this dispute or challenge is itself institutionalised. In other words, I expect that institutionalised conflict-processing prefers adaptation and innovation over the disruption and breakdown of institutional order.

Against this backdrop of theory-guided expectations, I find that local institutional continuity is surprising. Nonetheless, it is the continuity of informal institutions with some systemic weaknesses in their ability to process conflicts conclusively. People seem to rely on power, not improving or inventing institutions, in times of uncertainty. They return to the institutions they know when a degree of security returns. The endogenous emergence of institutions appears to require a more sophisticated degree of security.

I have no evidence of institutions emerging as a reaction to the pressure of insecurity, arbitrariness and violence. Existing institutions are used, however, as a fall-back option if direct access to power (self-help, patronage) fails. Without external protection, i.e. without manifest or latent enforcement that keeps power away from procedure and guarantees that non-compliance does come with consequences, the reliability and the effect of such institutions remains low.

This finding does not exclude the possibility that institutions emerge as part of the coping strategy employed by people trying to come to terms with Hobbesian pressure and that this results ultimately in a new social contract. It is possible that the time needed for such dynamics to unfold is simply not given in between the series of external interventions Afghanistan faced during the time of observation (Soviet, Taliban and US-lead interventions). However, the lack of institutional innovation as an act of adaptation is most likely also linked to the absence of a social space protected from arbitrary violence that facilitates adaptive institutional change. This space is most explicitly provided through rule of law-based democratic states.

Hence, what does the empirical evidence provided herein tell us about the more basic starting point of this research – the puzzle as to whether procedures as specialised institutions reduce the potential deadliness of conflicts, and whether they do so only under specific political framework conditions, i.e. liberal democracies governed by the rule of law? The evidence indicates that violence is constrained even in conflicts marked by stark power differentials, if the long term goals of the more powerful party can only be secured within an accepted institutional context. In Eastern Afghanistan, this is the case with land titles; it is not the case for violent competition between commanders over territorial control or political power. In a social space open to violent action, institutions still matter; however, procedures like *jirgas* are used to legitimise claims rather than to contain violence by institutionalising conflict and providing a proper alternative to the power of direct action. In other words, procedures as an alternative to more violent or disruptive forms of conflict-processing are an option for the powerful, rather than a condition constraining the powerful.

REFERENCES

Barth, Fredrik (1965): Political Leadership among Swat Pathans, London: The Athlone Press.
Bonacker, Thorsten (2008): "Sozialwissenschaftliche Konflikttheorien – Einleitung und Überblick. " In: Thorsten Bonacker (ed.), Friedens- und Konfliktforschung, Wiesbaden: VS, Verl. für Sozialwiss., pp. 9-29.
Coser, Lewis A. (1956): The Functions of Social Conflict, London: Routledge & Kegan Paul.
Dahrendorf, Ralf (1979): "Zu einer Theorie des sozialen Konflikts." In: Wolfang Zapf (ed.), Theorien des sozialen Wandels, Königstein, pp. 108-123.
Dahrendorf, Ralf (1986): Pfade aus Utopia, München: Serie Piper.
Dawe, Alan (1970): "The Two Sociologies." In: British Journal of Sociology 21/ 2, pp. 207-218 (http://www.fphil.uniba.sk/uploads/media/Dawe-2Sociologies.pdf; accessed February 2, 2013).
Dubiel, Helmut (1992): "Konsens oder Konflikt? Die normative Integration des demokratischen Staates." In: Beate Kohler-Koch (ed.), Staat und Demokratie in Europa, Obladen: Leske und Budrich, pp. 130-137.
Eckert, Julia M. (2004): "Einleitung: Gewalt, Meidung und Verfahren: zur Konflikttheorie Georg Elwerts. " In: Julia M. Eckert (ed.), Anthropologie der Konflikte. Georg Elwerts konflikttheoretische Thesen in der Diskussion, Bielefeld: transcript, pp. 7-25.
Elias, Norbert (1939): Über den Prozeß der Zivilisation. Soziogenetische und psychogenetische Untersuchungen. Wandlungen der Gesellschaft. Entwurf zu einer Theorie der Zivilisation. Band II, Basel: Verlag Haus zum Falken.
Elias, Norbert (1970): Was ist Soziologie? München: Juventa.
Elphinstone, Mountstuart (1972 [1842]): An Account of the Kingdom of Caubul [Volume II], vol. 2, London, New York [Karachi]: Oxford University Press.

Elwert, Georg (2004): "Anthropologische Perspektiven auf Konflikt." In: Julia M. Eckert (ed.), Anthropologie der Konflikte. Georg Elwerts konflikttheoretische Thesen in der Diskussion, Bielefeld: transcript, pp. 26-38.

Esser, Hartmut (2000): Soziologie. Spezielle Grundlagen, Fankfurt/M. and New York: Campus Verlag.

Gauchet, Marcel (1990): "Tocqueville, Amerika und wir. Über die Entstehung der demokratischen Gesellschaften." In: Ulrich Rödel (ed.), Autonome Gesellschaft und libertäre Demokratie, Frankfurt a.M.:Suhrkamp, pp. 123-207.

Giustozzi, Antonio (2009): Empires of mud: wars and warlords in Afghanistan, London: Hurst.

Glatzer, Bernt (2002): "The Pashtun Tribal System." In: G.Pfeffer/ D.K. Behera (eds.), Concept of Tribal Society, vol. 5, New Delhi: Concept Publishers, pp. 265-282 (http://liportal.giz.de/fileadmin/user_upload/oe ffentlich/afghanistan/40_gesellschaft/glatzer_pashtun_tribal_system.pdf, accessed February 16, 2013).

Goffman, Erving (1971): Interaktionsrituale. Über Verhalten in direkter Kommunikation, Frankfurt/M.: stw.

Grötzbach, Erwin (1990): Afghanistan: Eine geographische Landeskunde, Darmstadt: Wissenschaftliche Buchgesellschaft.

Gunya, Aleksey/Koehler, Jan/Zürcher, Christoph (2008): Empiricheskie issledovaniya lokal'nykh konfliktov: Vvedenie v metodologyu i metody polevykh issledovanii, Moskva: Media-Press.

Hirschman, Albert O. (1994): "Wieviel Gemeinsinn braucht die liberale Gesellschaft?" In: Leviathan 2, pp. 293-304.

Human Rights Watch (2003): "'Killing You is a Very Easy Thing For Us': Human Rights Abuses in South-East Afghanistan." In: Human Rights Watch 15/5 (http://www.hrw.org/reports/2003/afghanistan0703/; accessed February 19, 2013).

Knight, Jack (1992): Institutions and Social Conflict, Cambridge: Cambridge University Press.

Koehler, Jan (2004): "Institutionalisierte Konfliktaustragung, Kohäsion und Wandel. Theoriegeleiteter Praxischeck auf Gemeindeebene." In: Julia M. Eckert (ed.), Anthropologie der Konflikte; Georg Elwerts konflikttheoretische These in der Diskussion, Bielefeld: transcript, pp. 273-297.

Koehler, Jan (2013): Institution-centred conflict research. The methodology and its application in Afghanistan (Freie Universität Berlin: Doctoral Thesis), Berlin.

Koehler, Jan/Zürcher, Christoph (2003): "Institutions and the organisation of stability and violence." In: Jan Koehler/Christoph Zürcher (eds.), Potentials of Disorder, Manchester, New York: Manchester UP, pp. 243-265.

Lamla, Jörn (2008): "Die Konflikttheorie als Gesellschaftstheorie." In: Thorsten Bonacker (ed.), Sozialwissenschaftliche Konflikttheorien: eine Einführung, Wiesbaden: VS, Verl. für Sozialwiss., pp. 207-229.

Luhmann, Niklas (1983 [1969]): Legitimation durch Verfahren, Frankfurt/M.: stw.

North, Douglas (1990): Institutions, Institutional Change and Economic Performance, Cambridge: CUP.

Rashid, Ahmed (2008): Descent into chaos: How the war against Islamic extremism is being lost in Pakistan, Afghanistan and Central Asia, London: Allen Lane.

Rubin, Barnett R. (2002): The Fragmentation of Afghanistan: State formation and collapse in the international system, New Haven: Yale Univ. Press.

Sedra, Mark/Middlebrook, Peter (2005): "Revisioning the International Compact for Afghanistan: Beyond Bonn." (http://www.fpif.org/pdf/papers/0511beyondbonn.pdf; accessed June 26, 2006).

Simmel, Georg (1992 [1908]): Soziologie: Untersuchungen über die Formen der Vergesellschaftung, Frankfurt a.M.: Suhrkamp.

UN (2001): "Agreement on Provisional Arrangements in Afghanistan Pending the Re-Establishment of Permanent Government Institutions (UNIC)." (http://www.afghangovernment.com/AfghanAgreementBonn.htm; accessed February 19, 2013).

Weaver, Mary Anne (2005): "Lost at Tora Bora." In: New York Times Magazine (http://www.nytimes.com/2005/09/11/magazine/11TORABORA.html?pagewanted=all; accessed January 11, 2013).

Zürcher, Christoph (2004): "Einbettung und Entbettung: Empirische institutionenzentrierte Konfliktanalyse." In: Julia M. Eckert (ed.), Anthropologie der Konflikte; Georg Elwerts konflikttheoretische These in der Diskussion, Bielefeld: transcript, pp. 102-120.

Table of Figures:

Map 1: author's original, copyright by Jan Koehler.
Table 1: author's original, copyright by Jan Koehler.

Land-based Conflict in Afghanistan: On the Right of Pre-emption (shuf'a) as 'Back-Channel' Diplomacy and a Show of Indignation

NICK MISZAK

Photo 1

Source: Copyright by Casey Johnson

INTRODUCTION

In Afghan society, tensions related to access to land are a privileged entry point from which to study spaces of conflict in everyday life. Land is the main economic resource for the majority of people practicing subsistence agriculture, and land ownership is also a social factor crucial in defining people's social status and in shaping political arenas and power relations at different levels.

As Shipton stated,

"[...] people seek in land not just material satisfaction but also power, wealth and meaning – their aims, that is, can be political, economic and cultural... people relate to land not just as individuals, but also as members of groups, networks and categories." (1994: 348)

Among Pashtuns, more particularly, land is linked to the idea of *namus* which, besides female members of the household and weapons, signifies "properties (especially his home, lands, and tribal homeland) that a man must defend in order to preserve his honor" (Edwards 1996: 240). In his description of the Pashtunwali, the Pashtuns' code of honour, Bernt Glatzer (2000) pointed out that a person who jeopardises even an inch of his land risks losing everything else.[1] Conflicts over land ownership and access to land are thus central to the sovereignty and status of individuals and communities, and because of this centrality, conflict, warfare and violence in Afghanistan are frequently entangled with conflicts over land.

Since the onset, in late 2001, of the US-led military and international peacebuilding and reconstruction intervention in Afghanistan, land-related conflicts have been linked to the massive transformation of the Afghan political economy, and access to land has become a crucial political issue (e.g. Abdelkhah 2013; Baczko 2013; Miszak/Monsutti 2013). Between 2002 and 2012, an estimated six million Afghan refugees returned to their country, many moving to the rapidly urbanising centres (UNHCR Website 2014). In addition, thousands of international ex-patriates working for humanitarian aid and development organisations, as well as the armed forces of the international military coalition, poured into the country, thus affecting, among other things, the levels of land rent. At the same time, massive amounts of money spent on combined international aid, security and the military flood-

---

1 "Das Pashtunwali setzt die Unantastbarkeit von Frauen und Heimat gleich; man sagt, wer die Integrität der Familie und der Frauen nicht schützt, verliert bald auch Land und Existenz, und wer auch nur eine Handbreit seines Landes preisgibt, bei dem hat bald jeder Zutritt zu den Frauen. Angriffe auf das namus sind die häufigsten Ursachen von Gewalttaten. Als kurz nach dem Linksputsch 1978 die neue Regierung versuchte, Frauen und Mädchen auf den Dörfern unter Zwang einzuschulen, empfanden dies viele Paschtunen als Verletzung ihres namus und reagierten gewalttätig" (Glatzer 2000).

ed a country which had been devastated by decades of war and affected people whose lives were based largely on agricultural subsistence. The Costs of War Project, run by Brown University, estimates that US$4 trillion was spent, and aligned and with little other absorption capacity, the combined effect of the influx of enormous amounts of people and money in such a short time period saw a massive boom in the construction sector, with the expansion of cities and settlements in rural areas driven by soaring land prices and real estate as the new central theatre of accumulation (Sexton 2012; Miszak/Monsutti 2014). In areas of central Kabul, where many offices of NGOs, government development agencies, and private contracting firms are located, real estate prices soared. In some cases, prices for a *jerib* (0.2 hectare) of land increased by 1.900 per cent, from US$60.000 to US$80.000 during the Taliban regime (1996-2001) to peak prices of US$1.2 million in February 2012 (Miszak/Monsutti 2014). In anticipation of post-conflict boom conditions, the capture of Kabul in late 2001 was followed immediately by large-scale land appropriation (Nathan 2009).

The return of six million people over a span of ten years, to a country devastated by decades of war, would have presented any government with serious problems. Furthermore, previous regimes had allocated land to their own supporters as a way of building political constituency support, with many cadastres storing property title or tax records (based on land) which had been destroyed and returnees seeking restitution for property appropriated by their neighbours in their absence. Consequently, situations regarding access without rights and rights without access (Ribot/Peluso 2003; Lund/Sikor 2009) were frequent. However, there is a widespread consensus that neither the Afghan government nor the international community adequately addressed land-related problems, and they have rarely been described in a positive light in relation to managing these processes. Some authors suggest that, generally speaking, government officials pay little or selective attention to "the proper procedures, the relevant policies or the laws" (Mumtaz 2013: 173). Consequently, authorities and institutions officially charged to manage land affairs have been widely characterised as having failed to live up to their mandate (e.g. Wily 2003, 2012, and 2013; Majidi 2011 and 2013; Mumtaz 2013, Scalettaris 2013).

In Afghanistan, state courts are not the only institutions solving disputes. In addition, there are jirgas, councils of elders, commander *shuras* or Taliban courts (Barfield/Nojumi/Thier 2006). Cases can also meander from one arena of conflict resolution to another in a process of forum-shopping.

However, the case presented herein does not involve any of these sites of conflict resolution but instead encompasses 'back-channel diplomacy' with government officials as well as shows of indignation, such as roadblocks and demonstrations staged for media, in an attempt to shape the opinions potential conflict mediators (e.g. government officials, tribal and religious elders) have of a conflict. Back-channel diplomacy refers to the petitioning of government officials (frequently members of the executive, such as provincial and district governors and chiefs of police) or Members of Parliament. Conflict actors also display a sophisticated understanding of the use of Afghan and international media to construct land-related problems in the public arena. Through publically visible forms of contention which attract the attention of the media, conflict actors may stage performances which Kriesi, in his discussion of Tilly (2008), "[came] to call *protest events* – demonstrations, petitions, strikes – ... episodes, where people make claims, and then disperse" (2009: 342). In such performances outside the plurality of conflict resolution systems, conflict actors construct paradigms of arguments based on normative referents (Comaroff/Roberts 1981), in order to justify their own actions and frame the actions of others as illegitimate. Building on the insights of Mumtaz (2013), I argue that recourse to and the right of pre-emption, or *shuf'a*, is central to these paradigms of arguments. *Shuf'a* is used to deduce legitimate, pre-emptive rights to land, even if, and this is frequently the case, the act of taking possession is an appropriation of state or public property (Mumtaz 2013).

The structure of this chapter is as follows. First, I will describe the context of a conflict over access to land in the district of Mohmandara, in eastern Afghanistan's Nangarhar province. I will then narrate the events that triggered the confrontation between the conflict parties and explain the legal status of the conflicted land. In a next step, I will discuss the right of pre-emption as it is used by conflict actors, "... to convey a coherent picture of relevant events and actions in terms of one or more (implicit or explicit) normative referents" (Comaroff/Roberts 1977: 86), to construct legitimacy for their own actions and claims and to render the arguments and actions of others illegitimate. I will finish with some considerations of the right of pre-emption in relation to the idea of a tribal homeland, before finishing with some concluding remarks. The data presented herein are part of the fieldwork for my doctoral dissertation and were produced in January and February 2013 in Jalalabad. They also build on research conducted in 2010 and 2011 in Nangarhar province for The Liaison Office (TLO Afghanistan Website 2015). The methods used included individual in-depth interviews and focus group discussions.

CONTEXT

Between 2002 and 2012, an estimated six million Afghan refugees returned to their country, many moving to the rapidly urbanising centres. An estimated 20 per cent of them moved to Nangarhar province (Author's interview Kabul, January 2013). Even if these figures are overly high, the population of the province increased massively, and access to land for housing – and as a source of livelihoods – became a crucial issue. The flipside of these processes was that conflicts over access to land became very much a feature of everyday life. The United States Institute for Peace pointed out that in 2010 more than half of all disputes were about land, leading some authors to conclude that in the Afghan context talking about land automatically involves talking about conflict (Wily 2013).

The conflict discussed in this paper emerged in 2002 in the Daka area of the Mohmandara district of Nangarhar province, the main economic, political and cultural centre of eastern Afghanistan. Mohmandara shares a border with the Khyber Agency of Pakistan's Federally Administered Tribal Areas (FATA). The Torkham border crossing, located only three kilometres from the conflict land, is the most important port of entry for goods coming from Pakistan. Between 2002 and 2014, it was also the main passage for ferrying supplies to NATO forces stationed in Afghanistan, making the province crucial also from a strategic point of view. Nangarhar province, and especially the border districts, is tightly linked to the cross-border smuggling economy related to the Afghanistan-Pakistan Transit Trade Agreement (APTTA). The APTTA agreement gives landlocked Afghanistan the right to import commodities tax-free from the seaports in Karachi, Pakistan, in sealed containers to Afghanistan (Dorronsoro 1996). Since these same goods, such as cars, car spare parts, electronics, cooking oils, etc., carry high import taxes in Pakistan, they are unloaded and stored immediately just over the border (for example at a site which is at the centre of this land conflict) and subsequently smuggled back into Pakistan. Considering the larger illegal smuggling economy flourishing on import tax differentials between the two countries, there are important economic interests at stake.

The importance of the Daka area and its location close to the border with Pakistan's Khyber Agency increased significantly after the US-led intervention in Afghanistan in 2001. During the decades of war (since 1978, with several waves of migration and return), many people from Nangarhar, most of whom are Pashtuns, migrated to nearby areas in Pakistan and established businesses which they continue to run to this day. After the 2001 US-led intervention and the subsequent voluntary or forced (closing of refugee camps) return of Afghan refugees from Pakistan, many of the returnees had an interest in settling in areas such as Daka, which were close to their businesses and families on the Pakistani side of the border.

CONFLICT BREAKS OUT

The conflict discussed herein broke out in 2002, shortly after the beginning of the US-led intervention in Afghanistan, after rumours had spread among the local people that a township would be constructed in a desert area of the Mohmand Dara district called Daka. In Afghanistan, the term 'township' (or *khargota* in Pashto and *shahrak* in Dari) designates a constructed space which can include residential housing, warehouses, storage facilities or factories. The idea of constructing a township in the Daka area was not new. The former Afghan president Daud Khan's (1973-1978) master plan for the development of Nangarhar province had already foreseen the construction of a township in this area, which included a fruit-processing factory and housing for the factory workers. As in other areas of Afghanistan, the local population still remembered these master plans very well and pressured the government to implement them accordingly.

Shortly after rumours about the construction of the township started to circulate, locals began to speculate about increasing land prices. As a reference point, the land for one shop next to the main road (three metres wide and six metres long) in the Torkham bazaar cost (in 2012) between 900.000 and 1 Million PKR (US$10.429 to 11.588), whereas in Hazarnaw, an area in the same district some twenty kilometres away, the same unit located along the main road cost 150.000 PKR (US$1740), which this shows that there were significant economic factors at stake in the conflict.

In a daring nighttime action, a group of people known as the Pekhawal (literally 'from Pekha') took construction materials and equipment to the area and started to install warehouses and shelters. Anticipating the development of the township, the Pekhawal had acted pre-emptively to install themselves in the Daka area, knowing that for reasons linked to custom or social norms, forced evictions from a piece of land were very difficult once labour had been invested in construction, even if the initial occupation of the land was illegal.

The following day, a Mohmandara (the term 'Mohmandara' is used both to refer to the district and its residents) delegation went to the area and attempted to stop construction work, claiming that the Pekhawal were illegally occupying the land. To prevent an escalation of conflict, the district governor and the chief of police of the Mohmandara intervened and, with the help of six tribal elders from each side, negotiated a ceasefire. At the same time, the Mohmandara sent another delegation to the deputy provincial governor of Nangarhar province, asking him to act in his capacity as deputy governor and use his leverage to evict the Pekhawal from the area. The position of the Mohmandara was clear: they wanted the government to evict the Pekhawal and implement the township as part of Daud Khan's master plan. As *shuf'adar*, meaning neighbours owning adjacent land, they reserved the right to benefit from the future township for themselves. As a tribal elder of Mohmandara explained, "First, it is the right of the local people, then of others" (*Awal de dzai khalqu haq da au beya de nuru*).

However, the Mohmandara faced an unfavourable power hierarchy. After the collapse of the Taliban regime, Haji Din Mohammad had become provincial governor of Nangarhar. While the governor was not related to the Pekhawal by tribal affiliation, he had been their ally during the war – as members of the Hizb-e Islami of Mawlawi Khales, they had fought together against the Soviets and the Afghan communist regime of the People's Democratic Party of Afghanistan. On the other hand, some of the Mohmandara elders had worked with the Afghan communist government and during the government of Dr. Najibullah (1986-1992), while a pro-PDPA militia assured continued access of the communist government to Mohmandara and the border region. Respondents suggested that, consequently, the governor saw no reason why he should intervene against his war-time allies in favour of his war-time enemies.

Hence, the Mohmandara found themselves in an unfavourable constellation of power and, for the time being, were forced to accept the presence of the Pekhawal. The Mohmandara chose to bide their time until 2005, one year after Hamid Karzai was inaugurated as President of Afghanistan, when a series of political appointments reshuffled the country's political landscape. Haji Din Mohammad was transferred from Nangarhar to Kabul, while Gul Agha Sherzai, the former governor of Kandahar, was appointed to Nangarhar.

For the Mohmandara and the Pekhawal, political rotation at provincial government level brought not only its own dangers, but also opportunities to reverse or maintain the status quo over the conflict in the Daka desert. The Mohmandara seized the moment and started a campaign to influence the new provincial governor, Sherzai, and shape his perception of the conflict and of the legitimacy of their claims. In numerous gatherings held in *hujras* (guesthouses of tribal elders), the Mohmandara elders began to construct a case and develop detailed arguments to support their claims to the Daka desert – and for the eviction of the Pekhawal. Then, as interlocutors from Mohmandara explained, the Mohmandara sought a meeting with Provincial Governor Sherzai: "We presented a complaint to him and told him the entire story." The Mohmandara also contacted members of parliament in Kabul, asking them to pressure the governor into helping their case. As the respondents explained, central to the argument of the Mohmandara was a particular interpretation of the *right of pre-emption*, or *shuf'a*. Before turning to the right of pre-emption in more detail, a few words are in order to explain why neither conflict party sought a resolution to the conflict in the courts or *jirgas*.

Courts and *Jirgas* as 'Non-Sites'

The conflict actors did not go to the state courts for several reasons: first, neither the Mohmandara nor the Pekhawal had any formal (government origin) or customary title (registered and validated by the government) to the conflicted land. Without such title, there was no basis for the court to make a decision. Furthermore, the interpretation of the respondents was that the land occupied by the Pekhawal was either state property belonging to the Afghan government (the Ministry of Agriculture, Irrigation and Livestock) or public property.

In Afghan law, state and public property are distinguished (Sadeghi 2013: 83), and both types of property preclude settlement of the land and its exclusive use by a private party.

"Both sides will lose the case if they go to court, because none of them has any documents. Only those people who have official or even traditional documents go to courts, so the Shinwari and Mohmand are not going to go to the court." (Local analyst and outside observer of the conflict, Jalalabad, February 2013)

"From a legal point of view the issue is quite clear and all land adjacent to streets is state land." (Elder from Kunar province, Jalalabad, February 2013)

Furthermore, both sides in the conflict agreed that the occupied land was either the property of the state or public property.

"It is public land, because there aren't any governmental infrastructures. Those lands where there are no governmental buildings we can call public land." (Elder from the Mohmand tribe of Mohmandara, Jalalabad, February 2013)

"Concerning the Daka dasht conflict, we want to highlight that the mentioned land belongs solely to the government, because neither tribe has any legal documents regarding the land." (Shinwari maliks from Dur Baba, Jalalabad, February 2013)

Considering that neither the Mohmandara nor the Pekhawal had a solid base on which to demonstrate ownership through government or customary title, the situation could be described as access without rights (Ribot/Peluso 2003).

An estimated 80 per cent of land conflicts are resolved outside the state court system by local actors (Sadeghi 2013) who do not hold government positions – referred to in the literature as 'informal', 'customary community governance', also known as *jirgas* (Stanfield et al. 2013). However, in this case the *jirga*, or council of village elders, played no role in the matter, because *they* work on the basis that both conflict parties, in this case the Mohmandara and the Pekhawal, agree to a resolution of the conflict by giving *wak* (literally authority) to a group of elders charged with resolving the conflict. There are in fact different degrees of *wak*, or authority, given out, but the main idea is that you consent to accepting the decision taken by the *jirga*. To assure compliance, both conflict parties give a sum of guarantee, known as *baramta*, usually in the form of money, prior to agreeing to a *jirga*. In this case, however, the Pekhawal were simply not interested in a compromise. The Taliban courts were not involved either, although it is not entirely clear why this was the case. This author assumes that either the conflict parties did not expect a favourable decision from a Taliban court or, stated differently, the expectation was that a Taliban court would rule the land as state property, or the conflict parties did not want to vex the government by seeking a solution in a Taliban court. At the same time, the Taliban were not yet strong enough in the area to force the conflict parties to seek a solution to the conflict in their own court. Hence, the Mohmandara sought a resolution from the executive branch of government, i.e. the provincial governor, in their favour. In order to sway the government, they resorted to the abovementioned repertoire of contention in the form of demonstrations and roadblocks as events which attracted the attention of the media, and where the Mohamandara could voice their claims in an attempt to shape public opinion, the opinion of the provincial governor and the opinion of other third parties (elders, Members of Parliament) who would potentially be agents of a future conflict resolution commission. A centre piece of the Mohmandaras' argument was the right of pre-emption, to which we will turn now.

The Right of Pre-Emption

In Islamic property law the right of pre-emption or *shuf'a* is described as:

"[...] the right which the owner of certain immovable property possesses to acquire by purchase certain other immovable property which has been sold to another person. The following three classes of persons, and no others, are entitled to claim pre-emption, namely, (1) co-sharers; (2) 'participators in the appendages'; and (3) owners of adjoining immovable property; but not tenants (j) nor persons in possession of such property without any lawful title. The first class excludes the second, and the second excludes the third. The right of pre-emption, on the ground of vicinage, does not extend to estates of large magnitude [such as villages and zamindaris] but only to houses, gardens, and small parcels of land. The reasons why the right of pre-emption cannot be claimed when the contiguous estates are of large magnitude is that the law of pre-emption was intended to prevent vexation to holders of small plots of land who might be annoyed by the introduction of a stranger among them." (Mulla 1905: 143; Schacht 1964)

From a sharia perspective large estates are excluded from the right of pre-emption, and furthermore, claimants need to be able to document ownership of adjacent land:

"If a person wants to claim a piece of land based on shafa, he or she should prove his her status as shafdar (legal neighbour of the claimed land) and should possess all relevant legal documents such as a qawala (a land ownership document registered with the government land registration department, AMLAK) or an urfi khat (a written piece of paper to show his or her ownership...)." (Mumtaz 2013: 172)

Neither condition applied in this, as well as many other, land-grabbing case, which is the reason why Mumtaz (2013) speaks in such cases, which are very frequent in Nangarhar (and elsewhere), of the misuse of *shuf'a*.

Lacking the strict rights linked to *shuf'a* in the sense of Islamic property law, both conflict actors turned to *shuf'a* as a normative referent to justify their claims as legitimate. There are two (related) aspects to the right of pre-emption which should be highlighted.

One of the crucial notions is the idea of adjacency (Mumtaz 2013). Hence, the Mohmandara argue that in order to have a right of pre-emption (to be a *shuf'adar*), the Pekhawal would have to own land adjacent to the conflicted area in Daka, i.e. they would have to own property which shares a border or boundary with the conflicted land. Their framing of the Pekhawal's actions as illegal is thus based on the presumed lack of such a border:

"The Pekhawal have no right to this land. It was our right to take it, because it is our shafa. The Pekhawal are being cruel, because they crossed three districts and grabbed the Daka land." (Shinwari maliks from Dur Baba district; February 2013)

"It should also be mentioned that only Mohmandara and the Dur Baba district have a border with the grabbed land in Daka; other districts do not." (Mohmand elders from Mohmandara district; February 2013)

The Mohmandara thus claim that the Pekhawal do not have a boundary with the conflicted land; they transgressed the norm of pre-emption, since they had to cross three districts, leading the Mohmnadara to conclude that the claim of the Pekhawal to the land was weak. Glatzer (2001), among others, has highlighted the important role played in Afghan society by the production of spatial boundaries, while Favre (2005) insisted on their centrality for governance and reconstruction. Some of the relevant local terms in this respect are "*manteqah* (area), *jay* or *dzay*, (place) *mamlakat* (territory of a state), *watan* (home area, *Heimat*), *hadud* (boundary, limits, end, transition) or *sarhad* (frontier)" (Glatzer 2001: 380).

At the same time, boundaries and territories are not given but are instead reproduced by maintenance, transgressions and struggles (Raffestin 2012). Hence, the Pekhawal resorted to questioning the legitimacy of the district boundaries themselves and introducing a historical dimension to their argument. Furthermore, they argued that the entire Shinwari tribe, of which they are a faction, had had an agreement with Ahmad Shah Baba, the founder of the Sadozai dynasty (1747-1818) and commonly considered the first ruler of Afghanistan. In this agreement the Shinwari appear to be the protectors of the royal way of Khyber (*Mahapiz-e Sahi Rah-e Khyber*), which led through the area which was now being disputed between the Mohmandara and the Pekhawal. This past agreement charged the Shinwari with maintaining security for the king's military convoys and trade caravans, on their way to what later became British India, in exchange for three privileges: exemption from taxes (on landholdings), exemption from military service, a salary for some elders and the provision of grain (as aid) (Yapp 1983: 156). Such agreements between tribes in eastern and southeastern Afghanistan and the Afghan rulers of Kabul are not unusual. Many brokered or imposed, these agreements depended on the strength of the respective ruler and government, contracts to obligate tribes to protect the king's caravans and supplies on major routes (Poullada 1973; TLO 2009).

The Pekhawal were thus trying to legitimise their land occupation and township construction vis-à-vis the Mohmandara through a right of preemption based on prior possession. By invoking Ahmad Shah Baba, the founding figure of the Afghan polity, the legitimacy of a past ruler in Kabul was mobilised in order to add legitimacy to the current right of preemption, functioning like an *argumentum ad auctoritate*. But the Pekhawal did not stop there, as they also tried to delegitimise the relations the Mohmandara had with other, later, Afghan rulers, in particular Amir Abdur Rahman, who had ruled from 1880 to 1901 and transferred responsibility to the Mohmandara for the area in which the currently conflicted area lies.

What the Pekhawal argued is that Amir Abdur Rahman had essentially been a tyrant:

"During the time of the Shinwari rebellion, Amir Abdur Rahman beheaded 200 men and stacked their heads as a gate; we only reconciled with the government once we got the bodies back to bury them." (Interview with a Shinwari tribal elder from Ghanikhel district; February 2013)

An important element of constructing social legitimacy for claims to land, then, is based on past relations with Afghan rulers. In this case, if Amir Abdur Rahman was a tyrant, then his decision to give responsibility over the now conflicted land to the Mohmandara could not possibly have been a very good decision; hence, by delegitimising the past ruler, the claims of the Mohmandara were also rendered less legitimate. Furthermore, the actions of the Pekhawal rectified a past injustice. In referencing past Afghan rulers and making a judgment on them, conflict actors mobilise different temporal points of departure and epochs (Jacob/Le Meur 2010; Hagberg 2001), and they use selective memories of the past (Comaroff/Comaroff 2012: 35) to construct the social legitimacy of their current claims.

In the introduction to this paper, reference was made to the ways that land conflicts are bound to everyday life through the idea of property (especially the home, land and tribal homeland) as *namus* (Edwards 1996; Glatzer 2001), and hence what a man must defend in order to preserve his honour. In the context of the conflict discussed above, this is significant because what the Mohmandara claim is that

"The mentioned land belongs to Mohmandara district, and there are no legitimate claims of the Pekhawal on that land. It was our right to take it, because it is our *shafa*." (Mohmand elders from Mohmandara; February 2013)

The important idea here is that the Mohmandara equate the district boundary with their tribal homeland; the latter as *namus* implies an *obligation*, not a possibility, to mobilise for conflict and defend the tribal homeland. As Mumtaz pointed out in a similar land-based conflict in Nangarhar, people argued that

"if they did not take any action, [against land-grabbing on what they considered their tribal homeland] this would represent a permanent stigma for their tribe... People also commented that it was shameful for a person from another province [Governor Sherzai from Kandahar] to be distributing land located in their *shafa*."(Mumtaz 2013: 176).

The stigma is important in itself – a way of exerting symbolic violence on others – but it is also problematic, because not defending the tribal homeland might encourage others to grab even more land, and this is dangerous because, in the words of an interlocutor, "They might become a despotic ruler or your malik, and hence rule you in the future." Mobilising the community through normative referents such as the right of pre-emption thus also serves to prevent potential, future political domination by another tribe. We come back to the idea which was expressed so concisely by Bernt Glatzer and which I paraphrased in the introduction, namely that a person who jeopardises even an inch of his land risks losing everything else.

Mohmandara respondents maintained that in their discussions with the governor, he accepted their position, since *shuf'a* is an accepted argument among Pashtuns (see also Mumtaz 2013) and Sherzai is a Pashtun from Kandahar. However, despite the governor's assurances, by 2013, the issue remained unresolved and the Pekhawal were still in control of the land in the Daka desert. The authorities had not evicted the Pekhawal and neither had they implemented the formal township as specified in Daud Khan's 'Master Plan for the Development of Nangarhar Province'. Mohmand elders stated that they had lost faith in this government and were simply biding their time and waiting for a new government which, the hoped, would apply the law in their favour.

Shaping Perceptions of a Future Government and Conflict Mediators

Until 2011, the Mohmandara had been working discretely through meetings in the space controlled by the provincial governor. Faced with government inaction, and having lost faith that the current government would intervene, the Mohmandara changed strategy. They opted for a different repertoire of action altogether which centred on shows of indignation (Tilly 2008) in the form of direct action, including roadblocks and demonstrations, with local and national media as amplifiers.

At 8 am on January 29, 2012, the people of Mohmandara and Lal Pura districts took direct action in a show of force and attracted the attention of journalists and government officials by blocking the Torkham-Jalalabad highway (Hashmi 2012). Shortly after the roadblock started, word reached the local police, and soon media and a delegation of government officials appeared on the scene. The Mohmandara protestors voiced their indignation "against strongmen from Achin and Speen Ghar districts who had grabbed 300 acres land… adding they would continue their protest until the government returned their land" (Hasmi 2012).They also announced to the media and government officials present that "although blocking the highway was not a wise act, if the problem was not resolved, they would close it again" (Hashmi 2012). Furthermore, they shut down all public schools and clinics, symbols of government presence, in the Mohmand Dara and Lal Pura districts. Only after high-level provincial government officials assured the "hundreds of local elders that they would resolve the problem by Monday evening" (Hashmi 2012) was the roadblock lifted. However, the government remained inactive, and in April 2012, the Mohmand blocked the Jalalabad-Torkham highway again. In subsequent interviews the Mohmandara elders explained that they considered this land their *shuf'a* (adjoining land) and hence that it was their right to build houses and buildings there.

Again, months passed without visible progress until eventually Mohmandara elders decided not to use force against the Shinwari and maintained that the government should resolve the issue through negotiations. As the respondents explained, they had lost hope that their new course of action would induce the current governor to intervene in their favour. However, they hoped that their actions would shape the perception of the new government (expected to take office in 2014) and induce this new regime to intervene in favour of the Mohmandara.

Conclusion

A study of conflict in everyday life in Afghanistan is undeniably an account of land-based conflict. This is linked to the central status that land ownership holds for Afghans, not only as an economic resource, but also as a social relation central to defining people's social status and in shaping local political arenas. Land-related conflict has arguably intensified since the start of the US-led military and international peacebuilding and reconstruction intervention in Afghanistan in late 2001, alongside the massive transformation of the Afghan political economy. While any country would have had difficulties in managing these processes, there is widespread consensus that neither the Afghan government nor the international community has effectively addressed land-related problems. Unfortunately, land-related problems have become synonymous with what many Afghans consider to be wrong with their government. Land-grabbing has come to reify the common description of Afghanistan as a place characterised by the twin dynamic of lacking a rule of law and the prevalence of warlords and local mafia. Situations relating to access to land, without rights and rights without access, are frequent reminders of the images of "kleptocracy, neopatrimonialism, clientelism, prebandalism' and the thesis of the "criminalization of politics" (Comaroff/Comaroff 2006: 6–7) attached to postcolonial states.

The conflict over land in the Daka desert in Mohmandara, Nangarhar province, shows that despite such characterisations, Afghanistan is by no means lawless, and violence is not necessarily the preferred option. While threats of violence and force are always present in land-based conflict, they do not overrule legitimacy, and people make great efforts in justifying their own actions and framing the actions of their opponents as illegitimate, as well as shaping the opinions of potential mediators (e.g. government officials and tribal and religious elders) and a wider public in relation to conflicts. This paper has argued that the right of pre-emption, or *shuf'a*, is an important normative referent used in the construction of argument paradigms (Comaroff/Roberts 1977) to legitimise own actions. The right of pre-emption is used by conflict actors in a variety of situations in which people make claims to land, including meetings with government officials and protest events where shows of indignation are staged.

REFERENCES

Abdelkhah, Fariba (2013): "Guerre et Terre En Afghanistan." In: Revue Des Mondes Musulmans et de La Méditerranée 133, pp.19–41.

Baczko, Adam (2013): "Les Conflits Fonciers Comme Analyseurs Des Guerres Civiles : Chefs de Guerre, Militaires Américains et Juges Taliban Dans La Kunar." In: Revue Du Monde Musulman et de La Méditerrané 133, pp.115–32.

Barfield, Thomas/Nojumi. N./Thier, A.J. (2006): The Clash of Two Goods: State and Non-State Dispute Resolution in Afghanistan, Washington, D.C.: United States Institute of Peace (USIP).

Comaroff, John L./Comaroff, Jean (2006): "Law and Disorder in the Postcolony: An Introduction." In: Jean Comaroff/John Comaroff (eds.), Law and Disorder in the Post-colony, Chicago: University of Chicago Press, pp.1–56.

Comaroff, John L./Comaroff, Jean (2012): Theory From The South. Or, How Euro-America Is Evolving Towards Africa, Boulder/CO and London: Paradigm Publishers.

Comaroff, John/Roberts, Simon (1977): "The Invocation of Norms in Dispute Settlement: The Tswana Case." In: Ian Hamnett (ed.) Social Anthropology and Law, A.S.A. Monograph 14, London, New York, and San Francisco: Academic Press, pp. 77–112.

Comaroff, John L./Roberts, Simon (1981): Rules and Processes. The Cultural Logic of Dispute in an African Context, Chicago and London: Chicago University Press.

Dorronsoro, Gilles (1996): "Afghanistan: Des Réseaux de Solidarité Aux Espeaces Régionaux." In: François Jean/Jean-Christophe Rufin (eds.), In Économie Des Guerres Civiles, Paris: Hachette, pp.147-188.

Edwards, David (1996): Heroes of the Age, Berkeley, Los Angeles, and London: University of California Press.

Favre, Raphy (2005): Interface between State and Society in Afghanistan. Discussion on Key Social Features Affecting Governance, Reconciliation and Reconstruction, Addis Abbeba: Aizon.

Glatzer, Bernt (2000): "Zum Pashtunwali Als Ethnischem Selbstportrait." In: Günter Best/Reinhart Kössler (eds.), Subjekte Und Systeme: Soziologische Und Anthropologische Annäherungen. Festschrift Für Christian Sigrist Zum 65 Geburtstag, Frankfurt a.M.: IKO-Verlag, pp. 93–102.

Glatzer, Bernt (2001): "War and Boundaries in Afghanistan: Significance and Relativity of Local and Social Boundaries." In: Welt Des Islams 41/3, pp. 379–99.

Hagberg, Sten (2001): "À L'ombre Du Conflit Violent. Règlement et Gestion Des Conflits Entre Agriculteurs et Agro-pasteurs Peul Au Burkina Faso." In: Cahiers d'Études Africaines 161 (XLI-1), pp. 45–72.

Hashmi, Abdul Moeed (2012): "Kabul-Jalalabad highway reopens." (http://www.pajhwok.com/en/2012/01/29/kabul-jalalabad-highway-reopens; accessed February 3, 2015).

Jacob, Jean-Pierre/Le Meur, Pierre-Yves (2010): "Citoyenneté Locale, Foncier, Appartenance et Reconnaissance Dans Les Sociétés Du Sud." In: Politique de La Terre et de L'appartenance. Droits Fonciers et Citoyenneté Locale Dans Les Sociétés Du Sud. Édition Scientifique, Paris: Karthala, pp. 5–57.

Kriesi, Hanspeter (2009): "Charles Tilly: Contentious Performances, Campaigns and Social Movements." In: Swiss Political Science Review 15/2, pp. 341–49.

Lund, Christian/Sikor, Thomas (2009): "Access and Property: A Question of Power and Authority." In: Development and Change 40, pp. 1–22.

Majidi, Nassim (2011): Urban Returnees and Internally Displacement persons in Afghanistan, The Middle East Institute Pour la research stratégique (MEI-FRS(c).

Majidi, Nassim (2013): "Home sweet home! Repatriation, reintegration and land allocation in Afghanistan." In: Revue des mondes musulmans et de la Méditerranée 133, pp. 207–225.

Miszak, Nick/Monsutti, Alessandro (2013): "La Terre Du Pouvoir, Le Pouvoir de La Terre. Conflits Fonciers et Jeux Politiques En Afghanistan." In: Revue Des Mondes Musulmans et de La Méditerranée 133 (forthcoming), pp.151–68.

Miszak, Nick/Monsutti, Alessandro (2014): "Landscapes of Power: Local Struggles and National Stakes at the Rural-urban Fringe of Kabul, Afghanistan." In: Journal of Peasant Studies 41/2, pp. 183–98.

Mulla, D.F.S. (1905): Principles of Mahomedan Law, Bombay: Thacker.

Mumtaz, Wamiqullah (2013): "Three Faces of Shafa. Land Ownership on Trial in Ningarhar." In: Revue Des Mondes Musulmans et de La Méditerranée 133 (June), pp. 169–85.

Nathan, Joanna (2009): "Land Grab in Sherpur: Monuments to Powerlessness, Impunity, and Inaction." In: Middle East Institute (Washington D.C.) (ed.), Afghanistan, 1979-2009: In the Grip of Conflict, Washington, D.C.: Middle East Institute, pp. 71–75.

Poullada, Leon B. (1973): Reform and Rebellion in Afghanistan, 1919-1929. King Amanullah's Failure to Modernize a Tribal Society, Ithaca and London: Cornell University Press.

Raffestin, Claude (2012): "Space, Territory, and Territoriality." In: Environment and Planning D: Society and Space 30, pp. 121–41.

Ribot, J.C./Peluso Nancy Lee (2003): "A Theory of Access." In: Rural Sociology 68/2, pp. 153–81.

Sadeghi, Ahmad Reza (2013): "La Protection de La Propriété Terrienne Entre Loi et Arbitrages." In: Revue Des Mondes Musulmans et de La Méditerranée, Guerre et terre en Afghanistan 133, pp. 83–91.

Scalettaris, G. (2013): "Would-be places for displaced Afghans – The UNHCR, landless returnees and the enforcement of the national order." In: Revue des mondes musulmans et de la Méditerranée 133, pp. 189–206.

Schacht, Joseph (1964): An Introduction to Islamic Law, Oxford: Clarendon Press.

Sexton, Renard (2012): Natural Resources and Conflict in Afghanistan. Seven Case Studies, Major Trends and Implications for the Transition, Kabul: Afghanistan Watch.

Shipton, Parker (1994): "Land and Culture in Tropical Africa: Soils, Symbols, and the Metaphysics of the Mundane." In: Annual Review of Anthropology 23, pp. 347–77.

Stanfield, J.D./Murtazashvili, Brick, J./Safar, M.Y./ Salam, A. (2013): Community documentation of land tenure and its contribution to state building in Afghanistan." In: Jon Darrel Unruh/Rhodri Williams (eds.), Land and Post-conflict Peace-building, London and New York: Earthscan, pp. 265–292.

Tilly, Charles (2008): Contentious Performances, Cambridge: Cambridge University Press.

TLO Afghanistan Website (2015): (http://www.tloafghanistan.org/; accessed June 1, 2015).

TLO. 2009. "Tribal Jurisdiction and Agreements. The Key to Sub-National Governance in Southeastern Afghanistan." Policy Brief 1. TLO Policy Brief, Kabul: TLO.

UNHCR Website (2014): (http://www.unhcr.org, accessed July12, 2014).

Wily, Liz Alden (2003): Land Rights in Crisis: Restoring Tenure Security in Afghanistan, Kabul: Afghan Research and Evaluation Unit.

Wily, Liz Alden (2012): Land Governance at the Crossroads. A Review of Afghanistan's Proposed New Land Management Law. Briefing Paper Series, Kabul: AREU.

Wily, Liz Alden (2013): Land, People and the State in Afghanistan: 2002-2012, Kabul: Afghanistan Research and Evaluation Unit.

Yapp, Malcolm (1983): "Tribes and States in the Khyber, 1838-1842." In: Richard Tapper (ed.), The Conflict of Tribe and State in Iran and Afghanistan, New York: St. Martin's Press, pp. 150–91.

Table of Figures:
Photo 1: Copyright by Casey Johnson

Not in in the Master Plan: Dimensions of Exclusion in Kabul

KATJA MIELKE

INTRODUCTION

Kabul, the capital city of Afghanistan, and thus a place and symbol which is deemed the epitome of all post-invasion reconstruction and state-building efforts in the country (Esser 2013), has become the fifth fastest-growing city in the world (cf. City Mayor's Statistics, n.d.). It has grown from its previous 290.000 inhabitants, at the time of the only census in 1965 (Grötzbach 1979: 46), to approximately five million residents today. The 1978 'Master Plan' projected 800.000 people for 2003 (Arez/Dittmann 2005: 64); however the city's population was already estimated at 1.6 million by 1995 (UN Habitat 2010: 258) – a year which marked the end of the so-called Civil War period, during which Kabul was mostly raised to the ground and most of its inhabitants had fled. In the decade up to 2005, the city's population grew by an average of 6.17 per cent annually, until it reached roughly three million inhabitants (ibid: 65). While official sources today largely underestimate the capital's population at 3.3 million for 2012-13 (CSO 2013: 4), other, still rather conservative estimates, speak of Kabul housing presently around five million people (roughly a sixth of the country's estimated overall population), and the city is assumed to be home to about six million by 2020 (UN Habitat 2010: 258). Given the legacy of war and its large-scale destruction, the post-2001 economic boom and the unprecedented and ongoing influx of people, not least as a result of newly increased violence throughout the country since 2006 (Calogero 2011: 71), the urban landscape experienced a visible overhaul. The international military and civil presence in the capital, from where overall reconstruction and aid efforts were launched countrywide, attracted rural unemployed, returnees and those fleeing political violence elsewhere. Thirty per cent of all internally displaced and secondary displaced, as well as repatriates, ended up settling in Kabul throughout the first post-Taliban decade, because they could find no comparable destination to earn a living (UN Habitat 2010: 53). Given the speed and the numbers of those arriving, Kabul's consequent urban growth has been largely unregulated and uncontrolled.

Urban planning was neither one of the 'development' or 'reconstruction' priorities over the past decade, nor could it have kept pace with the speed and intensity of changes in Kabul due to the high and rapid influx of people and capital (Esser 2013). Thus, with hindsight, over the last decade urban development in the sense of infrastructure establishment or improvement and access to services-provision has taken place spontaneously, according to perceived necessities in individual neighbourhoods. In addition, entirely new townships and settlement areas have been established with amazing speed – catering, on the one hand, to rural migrants, repatriates and the internally displaced looking for livelihoods, jobs and/or education in the city, and, on the other hand, to moneyed elites seeking fortunes through the forceful appropriation of land and through investing in the set-up of townships (*shahrak*). As a result, the contemporary city is largely constituted by unauthorised and unplanned settlements: 70 per cent of the urban area is said to have been built up 'informally', i.e. without official sanctioning and a plan (*ghair-e naqsha*). Accordingly, between 65 per cent and 80 per cent of Kabul's inhabitants reside in these informal settlements.[1] Moreover, settlement patterns reflect a high level of ethnically motivated spatial concentration according to the major population groups.

This chapter employs Elias and Scotson's figurational 'established and outsiders' paradigm (Elias/Scotson 1993), in order to facilitate a process analysis of how urban development is negotiated, practiced and thus implemented in one of Kabul's contemporary municipal districts, namely District 13 (abbreviated: D13, vernacular: *nāhiya sezdah*). Of the current twenty-two capital municipal districts, District 13 is among the three with the

---

1 Estimate according to an urban planner, interview November 4, 2013. A UNHCR/World Bank study from 2011 evaluated the share of the population living 'informally' throughout Kabul at 70 per cent (UNHCR/World Bank 2011: 12).

highest level of rapid unplanned urbanisation and is largely underserviced. Its residents and representatives are taken as protagonists who negotiate urban development within district limits, meaning at street *(kucha)*, neighbourhood *(guzar)* and administrative, i.e. municipal district *(nāhiya)*, levels. However, as the chapter will show, it is regularly necessary to jump administrative levels beyond the municipal district's stakeholders, in order to access resources in the form of services, information, protection and patronage. That said, District 13 is viewed as a figurational arena or platform ('core figuration') which is part of the larger figuration at city-scale and can even branch out beyond these limits – spatially and time-wise. And besides its more obvious exclusion from official urban development measures, which manifests in the under-provision of urban infrastructure, the perceptions of exclusion, neglect and social inequality go much deeper. At the administrative level (district administration), for instance, they find articulation in the notion of not being honoured or not being assigned authority *(salāhiyat)* by the municipality *(shahrwāli)*. In the everyday context of ordinary life-worlds, discrimination is experienced as inhibited mobility manifested in the absence of link roads and infrastructure, such as an electricity grid, education and health institutions.

Against this background I subsequently analyse urban politics in Kabul as the various attempts and processes undertaken by residents and administrators of District 13 to mitigate these perceived discriminations in local 'urban being', i.e. at the ordinary, everyday practices level and at the planning level – what I refer to as 'urban becoming'. For this purpose, after sketching out the conceptual background assumptions guiding the analysis, the case study will decipher the positionalities of the main stakeholders involved in local urban development and politics. The consideration of associated motility factors (socio-cognitive identities, endowment with resources and imaginations about the future) as dispositional dimensions or traits of positionality provides several conclusions.

CONCEPTUAL PREMISES

Elias and Scotson (1993 [1965]: 265), in their seminal study on Winston Parva, argued that municipal districts, neighbourhoods or townships can be treated as one special type of figuration. The figurational paradigm of established and outsiders revolves around conflict[2] as the manifestation of power imbalances.[3] In this chapter, the differences – and thereby generated tensions – between D13 and the Kabul municipality over the (non-) provision of services and the perceived deprivation of *salāhiyat* (with all minor differences over social status, practices, interests, values, etc. that feed in to this perception) constitute the main point of contention, which results in the exclusion of D13 from urban development projects and reveals itself in perceptions of the active production of social inequalities through systematic disadvantaging. Besides the technical argument of being outside the Master Plan, and thus not eligible for urban development measures, the impression of exclusion is amplified according to the historical experience of discrimination and harassment of the Hazara as D13's currently dominant population group throughout Afghanistan's history.

According to Elias and Scotson (1993: 249), it is typical for an established-outsider figuration that newcomers aim to improve their position while the established group is interested in maintaining and – if necessary – defending its privileged position. Thus, the advent of conflicts rests on the existence of unevenly distributed power resources, and from a policy perspective the challenge is to manage or countervail these imbalances. From the process perspective of a figurational approach, the main question is how

---

2   Conflict is understood here according to the broader sociological assumption as universal and omnipresent phenomenon (Coser 1956; Dahrendorf 1979, 1994) that manifest as differences over interests, resources, values and beliefs, social status or practices once they are perceived as such by the involved actors (Imbusch 2006). Cf. Crossroads Asia Working Group Conflict (2012/2014) for further elaboration of the notion of conflict guiding the research of the network "Crossroads Asia".

3   Elias and Scotson (1993: 16) show how differences in internal cohesion and control determine the rate of power of one group vs. another group. Assumed primordial identity factors like ethnicity are thus not taken to be decisive determinants of power differentials. Thus, contrary to the popular ethnic connotation of the urban figuration around D13, with power differentials predominantly framed as ethnic discrimination against the Hazara, the paper supports the idea that what appears to be and often is classified as ethnic conflict should be investigated beyond the ethnic connotation to gain a deeper understanding of the conflict figuration.

this negotiation of power imbalances is taking place in everyday practice.[4] This process of negotiating dissent is inherently political. Urban politics, thus, is understood to comprise a variety of interests and efforts pertinent to different types of actors organising or achieving improvements in urban settings or situations. In this case, it refers to negotiations over access to urban infrastructure (urban being) and over the municipality's assigning of legitimate authority (*salāhiyat*) to the district administration and subsequent inclusion of D13 in transformative urban planning ('becoming').

In this chapter, the location of D13 within a paradigmatic established-outsider figuration is analysed with the help of the auxiliary assumption of one larger 'meta'-figuration which makes up the city of Kabul – which itself is assumed to be situated in a wider figurational context imagined as the 'figuration of figurations'. Subsequently, D13 is viewed as a core figuration, with its residents and local stakeholders entering all kinds of figurations and forming nodes in the web of entangled interdependencies within district boundaries, albeit also branching out beyond and across different spatial and social scales. The multiple entanglements of elements at the core with the other figurational forms imply that a thorough understanding of processes and outcomes in the core figuration can only be achieved by considering the broader figurational context. Connected to this notion, this chapter draws distinctions between the spatial delimitations of figurations at the city scale versus national state boundaries, while imagined and actual links and social connections that spatially transgress and contract the latter are taken into account.[5] Whilst it might seem odd that D13 as a core figuration is sometimes deemed a totality but which again is also emphasised to consist of individual actors, Manderscheid's work on the nexus of mobility and social inequalities supports partial non-differentiation, thereby suggest-

---

4   This is especially interesting if it is considered that the real beginning or end of a conflict can hardly ever be traced and that most of the time individuals find themselves in a conflict setting without having chosen to be there and without much choice of escaping and much less of steering (completely free of) it (Elias/Scotson 1993: 246, 310). It is in this context that Elias and Scotson pointed to the possibility that figuration(s) can come to dominate or constrain their constituents' freedom and scope of agency (ibid: 267).

5   I deem social scales (and the networking and entangling of interdependencies across these) as equally important as spatial scales (cp. Mielke/Hornidge 2014: 25; Sheppard 2002).

ing that the role of mobilities in reproducing social inequalities would otherwise be invisible (Manderscheid 2009: 15). Extending her thoughts, I assume that the establishment and perpetuation of social inequalities, and of the perception of exclusion, can likewise only be drawn out if the analysis considers both individuals as constituents of a core figuration and a core figuration as collective in relation to other figurative formations.

In line with Elias (1978: 74), figurations are conceptualised as manifestations of power relations, and power is taken as a relational force. As such, it can only be traced in the interdependencies or web-like relations of individuals and groups.[6] Underlying power resources can be analysed as dispositional traits of individuals which determine these actors' positionalities, which shall be understood herein as the sum of the socio-spatial dispositions or assets of individuals (within the core figuration) and collectives, such as D13, as totality versus other figurational forms in the wider figurational context. As differently situated subjects, individuals are determined by dispositions in terms of space, time, social-economic status, socio-cognitive identity traits ('race', nationality, age, gender, sexuality, etc., institutional and ideological dispositions) and the disposal of additional (material, cognitive, etc.) assets. In this regard, grievances or perceptions relating to exclusion arise from perceived power imbalances, in particular the disposition of an inferior bundle of power resources[7] that could be mobilised to improve one's own position and overall context-dependent situation – in this case access to urban infrastructure, authority (*salāhiyat*) and, consequently, inclusion in transformative urban planning ('becoming').

With regard to investigating practices of exclusion and social inequality as consequences of inhibited or enabled mobilities, the respective dispositions could be grasped as motility factors, i.e. those factors which enable a person or a group to become socially, but possibly as a precondition to the former also spatially, mobile, for example, and most simply to improve

---

6   The understanding of power as relational, context-specific and being fuelled not solely by economic resources follows the elaborations on power by Foucault (2005), Bourdieu (2005), Lukes (2005) and Elias (1978).

7   Cp. the concept of bundle(s) of power resources elaborated by Mielke (2012) is based on Ribot and Peluso's article (2009), which stresses a bundle of powers perspective.

one's situation in the sense of becoming included and acknowledged.[8] From this perspective, motility can be taken to bridge the gap between spatial and social forms of mobility. Put differently, motility stratifies social relations and is stratified by them at the same time (Manderscheid 2009: 18). While conventionally positionality is often seen to manifest spatially (Leitner/Sheppard/Sziarto 2008), that is at different geographical scales and through relations of proximity and distance, I suggest building the analysis of positionalities on three additional pillars: first, the place-based material resource endowment, secondly, socio-cognitive traits connected to experiential knowledge, habitus and conscience and, thirdly, future imaginaries as explicit temporal dimensions. All three aspects, in addition to spatial positioning, constitute each other mutually and thus form a kind of motility capital which yields implications for the negotiation of social (and even spatial) exclusion and social mobility.

By connecting power and mobility in the analysis below, this article goes beyond a conventional governmentality perspective (Foucault 2006) which emphasizes the disciplining effects of urban space and underlying positionalities and dispositions. In addition, the more subtle workings of power can be traced when modes of power which are connected to practicing, imagining and sensing mobility are accounted for equally. Jensen (2011) highlights the potential role of embodied aspects of movements and flows, such as the unfolding of a certain atmosphere, moods or the feel of urban spaces, as an important factor in shaping perceptions and socio-cognitive attitudes such as experiences and imaginaries. Similarly, Willems (2010: 256) differentiates between a bodily-emotional and a cognitive-mental dimension of social practice, both of which act as a habitus generator and regenerator[9] and constitute positionalities which might generate, mitigate or perpetuate social inequalities.

Finally, then, through bringing in social inequality, conceptual elaborations come full circle in demonstrating how figurations actually work on

---

8   For derivations on the concept of motility, cp. Kaufmann, Bergman & Joye (2004: 750). Resources which are assumed to underlie the ability to move socially and physically could also be termed sorts of capital in Bourdieu's sense (cf. Bourdieu 1998).

9   Cp. Willems 2010: 256. Any actor is thus both a product as well as a co-producer of social figurations. Accordingly, the scope of agency available to each single actor depends on the peculiarity of his/her respective habitus.

the basis of the triangle of time-power-space. Following Urry's idea (2007: 185ff, cf. Manderscheid 2009: 19) that social inequalities are being enacted continuously within space through mobility mechanisms, social inequalities are understood to be constituted in different social spaces which consist of power relations and imbalances generated by power differentials. For the example of Kabul, exclusion at the city level is thus seen as being enacted on multiple scales (in the social and the spatial senses) through practical interrelations between people with certain dispositions in different places and via (non-)flows and social (non-)interaction.

In the following, empirical material will be presented in three steps.[10] First, District 13 will be introduced in more detail, to provide the background for the two analytical sections which trace the political processes that mark practices of everyday urban 'being' and efforts undertaken with the aspiration of 'becoming' – meant here as becoming included in urban development at the city scale. The second section is concerned with intra-D13 politics and the core-figuration, while the third section goes beyond the latter and contextualises local processes in the wider political and social environments.

INTRODUCING D13

Administratively, D13 has existed since 2003, or 1382, according to the Afghan calendar. It was established as a new municipal district after reforms and reshuffles in the Kabul municipality during the early Karzai transition government. Located in the western part of the city, and covering an area of 46.6 sqare kilometres (Gebremedhin 2005: 9), D13 was allotted part of District 6 (now on its eastern border) and otherwise comprised areas which up to that point had belonged to Kabul Province's rural districts in the west of the capital. Nevertheless, the area was most likely already peri-urban by 2003; several interviewees reported having bought land and settled there with their families from the 1960s onwards.

The area saw pushes in development in 1985-86, when the first electricity grid was extended to the area, and further expansion and construction

---

10 The empirical data presented in the following were collected during two fieldwork stays in Kabul in 2012 and 2013, amounting to five weeks in total. All names of people have been anonymised.

set in from 2003-04. Since the end of the Taliban regime, D13 ranks among the three most rapidly urbanising municipal districts of Kabul. Ethnic Hazara, i.e. both post-2001 returnees from Iran and Quetta in Pakistan and those who fled from Afghanistan's provinces in search of employment, constitute the bulk of the settlers and residents in the district. Official numbers for the population size are not available, but while Gebremedhin gives a number of 10.000 households as officially registered by the administration ten years ago, current estimates made by the district administration speak of 700.000 residents. My own calculations amount to roughly 780.000 inhabitants (see footnote 14).

A few words are in order to shed light on the historical background of D13, or 'Dasht-e Barchi' as the area is often designated locally. Given the once rural layout of the area up to the 1960s and 1970s, which was located some distance away from Kabul city at that time, the initial settlement pattern featured a few rural compounds (*qala*) with surrounding fields and gardens. The land was sparsely populated by Tajik and Pashtun settler-agriculturalist and landowner families. Due to population dynamics as a result of political conflict, war and civil war, only fractions of the original landowners still live in the district; many have sold their land and moved during the last decades. As a result of the civil war – during which increasingly ethnically-shaped mujahedin factions fought for control of Kabul, allied, dis-allied and re-allied in several guises until the capture of the city by the Taliban in September 1996 (Arez/Dittmann 2005: 113-135) – settlement structures existing in Dasht-e Barchi at the time were completely destroyed. Those initial residents who did not have to move mostly started selling to investors in the post-2001 decade; a few sold to ordinary, less well-off and less moneyed migrant arrivals or repatriates, of which Hazara made up the majority in this part of the city. Ethnic concentration, according to the self-perception of the Hazara, in D13 is more or less 100 per cent exclusively Hazara; however, as my interviews showed, Tajik, Turkmen as well as Kuchi[11] households exist throughout the municipal district, and their

---

11 The term 'Kuchi' – while traditionally signifying all kinds of nomadic and semi-nomadic pastoralists and traders originating in Afghanistan from any ethnic background – is used herein in its political connotation, which relates to the strong political identity of Kuchi representatives and their leaders, the majority of whom are Pashtuns. Kuchi are commonly subsumed as 'nomads', but they are also ascribed the status of an ethnic group. They have been granted ten re-

presence contradicts the common view of ethnic exclusiveness. The obvious reason for the concentrated settlement and respective perception of Hazara – besides the comfort of having like-minded people in terms of religious and legalistic (Shia) motives around – is the relative geographic connectedness in terms of proximity to Bamiyan (province) and the Behsud District of Maidan Wardak, which constitute significant parts of the traditional Hazara settlement areas (Hazarajat) in Afghanistan.

By late 2013, Dasht-e Barchi had expanded vastly, and with its integration into the municipal administrative set-up as a municipal district (D13), settlement and private construction activities saw another boom. The 1978 Master Plan for twenty-five years had terminated by design by 2003, although the municipality insisted on it being valid for future development. A newly developed Master Plan had been forwarded to the Presidential Office and was said to be in the process of signing in the last quarter of 2013; however, as it was only one of three city development plans existing at the time, its robustness and legitimacy were contested even before its official launching and endorsement by the President. Partly underlying this competition between plans (and donors) has been a conflict between the Kabul municipality (i.e. the Mayor's office) and the Ministry of Urban Development Affairs. While the latter is mandated to take care of all planning for urban areas throughout Afghanistan, including the capital city, and the Kabul municipality would accordingly be merely in charge of implementing the plan, the municipality has actively rejected this set-up. Based on its direct subordination to the President, it has traditionally claimed ministry status for itself and has pursued its own Master plan. As a result of these defensive tussles, more than a decade passed during which urban development in D13 was largely ignored on the grounds that it was not in this Master Plan.

Land was sold, grabbed, plotted out, partially developed in some cases, resold and grabbed again – leading to increased stringency in relation to available land and the intensified occupation of hillside settlements, such as in the Chehel Duxtarān area. In contrast, and catering to a different sort of clientele, considerable numbers of new residential townships (*shahrak*) were established. Only around 2 per cent of the inhabitants of D13 were said to hold legal title deeds in 2005 (Gebremedhin 2005: 10), and while

---

served seats in the Lower House of Parliament by government decree. Cf. Foschini 2013.

this indicates the high prevalence of customary (*urufi*) deeds, it apparently also invited opportunities for fraudulent dealings around land and properties. An investigative newspaper article of January 2013 (Rostami 2013), which lists the largest land grabbers in Afghanistan, disclosed that at least 1098 hectares of land had been grabbed in D13 alone. This amounts to eleven sqare kilometres and thus more than a quarter out of the total district size of 46.6 sqare kilometres. The same article reported on thirteen (illegal) townships in D13, the most prominent of which, Shahrak-e Umid-e Sabz (literally 'Township Green Hope'), is owned by Haji Nabi Khalili, the brother of the former Vice-President Mohammad Karim Khalili (2002-2014). Interestingly, and already offering a taste of dispositions and power relations, the same article suggested that Haji Nabi had merely bought approximately 62 hectares from land grabbers who had expropriated the area next to the first phase of the Haji Nabi Khalili township. Furthermore, the report quotes from a D13 letter stating that Haji Nabi was the only one among the thirteen *shahrak* which had "applied for processing," and "[w]hile the Kabul Municipality views Haji Nabi township as illegal, the Ministry of Urban Development has recognized it as one of the six top townships in the country" (ibid).

In terms of infrastructure development and services provision, investor-established townships in D13 usually offer most essential amenities (sewage tanks, water connection, although less so acceptable roads) and cater to small moneyed elites – mostly families where at least one member has earned a 'Western' salary for some time at least; otherwise, they are respected families, the heads of which traditionally play or have played some role in local politics, relatives and clients of local strongmen and whoever has access to illicit money flows. Needless to say, the majority of D13 inhabitants cannot afford to live in these different types of township residences. The sprawl of houses up to the highest points in the hills and on the fringes of the district, as well as the fact that most compounds (*haweli*) do not house just one extended family but are rented out to co-residents (*hamsāya*) who live in separate rooms and parts of traditional courtyards, are cases in point. Nevertheless, the analysis below, focusing on the dimensions of social exclusion in the core figuration and the wider context, is not meant to be economically anchored, thereby alluding to the suggested poverty of inhabitants and thus invoking a 'victims' perspective. The point of departure is exclusion from official urban development based on the municipality's argument of being *ghair-e naqsha*, i.e. not included in the Master Plan.

URBAN BEING

The regular characterisation of 'under-serviced' residential areas implies a lack of safe drinking water, functioning drains, household sanitation and electricity, unreliable or absent waste collection services and possibly difficult pedestrian and/or vehicular access for residents. The realities in D13 match this description quite closely, yet they nevertheless vary to extremes, depending on the location within the district and on the particular 'service' in question. According to the head of all D13 neighbourhood representatives, it is a significant achievement that 65 per cent of the residents have electricity.[12] Then again, according to another interviewee, only one public (i.e. government-run) hospital is working in the entire district.[13] D13 is subdivided into nine different zones and officially thirty-six neighbourhoods (*guzar*). In contrast, a total of seventy-eight neighbourhood representatives (*wakil-e guzar,* abbr. WG) are registered with the D13 administration. As individual representatives only get registered and officially acknowledged by the local district administration if they can prove they can represent a minimum of 500 houses, the contrast between officially existing neighbourhoods and locally endorsed neighbourhood representatives points once more to the rapid population growth and expansion of the district.[14]

Within neighbourhoods, neighbourhood representatives, who themselves are appointed by the residents in their constituency (*guzar*), in turn

---

12 Interview: October 23, 2013.
13 Interview: October 27, 2013.
14 In a quick survey with the WGs of D13, I found that one traditional compound, or house, enclosed within four walls (*haweli*) is on average home to twenty people. With 500 *haweli* heads needed as a minimum constituency for one WG, it can be concluded that the overall number of people who make up the minimum constituency of one WG amounts to 10.000 people. Note that the maximum number of followers is 2500 (thus adding up to 50.000 people in total in a large neighbourhood). Given that seventy-eight WGs were registered with the D13 administration at the time of the fieldwork, the minimum population figure of D13 can be estimated at 780.000 people.

appoint street representatives (*namoyenda-ye kucha*) as their local contacts with whom to exchange information. These street deputies are clearly subordinated to the neighbourhood representative and obliged to submit requested information, e.g. in conflict cases or to act as witnesses to prove somebody's residence or tenure history in the local quarter (*mahalla*). As a rule, only the neighbourhood representatives are linked to the district administration. The seventy-eight neighbourhood representatives form a council (*shurā-ye wakil-e guzar*) with different functionaries, e.g. an executive head, a deputy, a secretary. Given the relatively recent establishment of D13, and its rapid growth and expansion as a destination for rural-urban migrants and repatriates from Iran, a considerably higher share of neighbourhood representatives are young (30 per cent) as compared to the representatives of other, more established, municipal districts (10 per cent share of young WGs). The thought of taking up a WG position might seem unpopular and wasteful given the responsibilities, hassle and time that needs to be invested; however, fieldwork showed that, on the contrary, it is a much sought-after position, and regular contestations over constituencies occur because many of the relatively young and mostly educated WGs consider the position a springboard to higher office, such as the Provincial Council, the Lower House of Parliament or the Senate. That said, some interviewees suggested that most of the WGs are also party workers – in the case of D13, mainly for the two major Wahdat parties, i.e. Hezb-e Wahdat-e Islami-ye Afghanistan, led by Khalili, and Hezb-e Wahdat-e Islami-ye Mardom-e Afghanistan, led by Mohammad Mohaqeq – and thus they are part of special patron-client chains. Eventually, even though not compensated or paid any official salary, the position nevertheless also seems to be financially quite lucrative. Several respondents indicated that WGs take money for their services (i.e. issuing documents, linking people to others, intervening and getting involved in dispute resolution cases and organising access to and managing the provision of certain services, such as connection to the electricity grid; see next paragraph), which they feel is justified but also a kind of extortion money.

Regardless of the heterogeneous attitudes of WGs towards their constituencies, the helplessness and lack of capacities of the district administration when, for example, it has to implement the municipality's order to collect a sanitation tax, puts the WGs between a rock and a hard place, in that they are squeezed between the expectations of their constituencies, on the one hand, and the expectations, requests and orders of the municipality, on the other hand. This leaves the WG balancing the risk of losing his constituency because of non-delivery and thus declining legitimacy, while he also has to come up with some viable arrangement to satisfy at the very least his 'clients' in his *guzar*. In this respect, the narrative of WG Mohammad Ali on how he arranged for electricity in his neighbourhood is insightful: it took him almost five years, three and a half years of which were spent lobbying, and once the deal was agreed with officials of Brishna, the semi-governmental electricity supply company, it took another one and a half years to construct the poles and connect the wires. According to Mohammad Ali, nothing throughout the whole process went according to the legal or formal process, either in accessing Brishna or the installation on a local level. Electricians, for instance, would postpone work if people did not pay the three construction crew members 500 Afghani ($10) per head per day, phone credits for the supervisor and the additional provision of lunch. An attempt to complain about such behaviour to the electricians' superiors resulted in the construction halting for three months. The local parliamentarian was called upon, but in was all in vein. By that stage Mohammad Ali had already collected a first payment from each household, to facilitate the process with Brishna representatives, but increasingly he noticed that he would not be able to satisfy people's expectations. As a result he was intimidated and faced accusations that he was delaying the work on purpose, to satisfy his own interests. On the flipside, the electricians pursued their policy of earning extra money, and in line with the Brishna supervisor's demand for $1000, Mohammad Ali was able to collect and pay $200 on behalf of his constituency. The installation of metres cost extra.

A major point of contention in D13 was the lack of (sealed) link roads. Besides the main road artery from Shahid Mazari Square towards Paghman – a road which cuts through the main settlement area that came to be Dasht-e Barchi and D13 and which changes into an unpaved dirt road – only a few other road sections were gravelled, let alone paved. From the main artery, differently sized roads (in terms of width, e.g. forty or twenty metres wide) led away into densely settled neighbourhoods or new townships. Given the townships' rather planned layout despite their largely unauthorised nature, the bumpy dirt roads were comparatively spacious. In contrast, the roads leading into certain organically grown neighbourhoods, and those linking with other municipal districts, became narrow alleys. Settlement in the western part of Kabul is likely to have occurred first along these link ways and intensified from there, thereby encroaching upon the initial road space, because during the unplanned settlement process nobody observed minimum widths or even thought about urbanisation effects and the future need for wider roads to facilitate Barchi residents' spatial mobility. Burgeoning immobility constitutes a major grievance today. For example, the link road from the area known as Qabrstan (graveyard) to Shahid Mazari Road, or the Barchi connection to Pul-e Kampani area, where the major bus stand to Kandahar is located, is difficult to travel on because it takes time and needs suitable cars. In rainy weather the dirt roads become almost impassable for both pedestrians and traffic.

Reportedly, a single road project the municipality has implemented in the last few years in D13 is the 4.2 kilometres road between Qalai Naw and Argandeh, yet it took three years before a stretch of only 1.2 kilometres was completed.[15] The reason why the municipality became involved in road construction in this case at all was most probably connected to the fact that locals had managed to gain the international military force's (ISAF) support in gravelling the road (see below). The district administration regularly included other road projects in annual planning and budgets, but most of them were rejected by the municipality. Moreover, even in a few exceptional cases where road projects were granted, such as the road to Maidan Wardak, construction works stopped or did not even start despite an approved budget. In some cases the reason for this lay in the resistance of local residents whose houses were at risk of being destroyed for the road projects. A previous administrator of the district is said to have had a very strict understanding of development and would not compromise in such situations. Reportedly he even sacrificed a big market to start a road project – which eventually was stopped by the municipality and cost him his job, because of the interests he touched upon by taking down the market. Other examples of haggling with the municipality over road projects include the Mayor's offer continuing construction of the Darulaman Road if the municipality could get the budget allocated by the Turkish government for the construction of five secondary roads in D13. After district representatives rejected this proposal, construction was stopped and the budget for the five secondary roads was temporarily also lost – because of the Mayor's refusal

---

15 Interview: October 23, 2013.

to sanction the proposed constructions, the money was returned to its Turkish donor.[16]

Among the residents of D13, complaints about being under-serviced were amplified after the recent establishment of Kuchiābād, a township for Kuchi, by international donors under the aegis of the United Nations High Commissariat for Refugees (UNHCR) and championed by the Ministry of Repatriation and Refugees. A five kilometres 'thickly paved' link road with solar street lighting, from Dasht-e Barchi's main road artery to the settlement in Chāhar Asiyāb, was constructed in no time by an international donor. The model repatriation project[17] also featured support for the establishment of individual compounds (houses and protective walls), a water supply and sanitation infrastructure and a school building. In the eyes of the regular residents, this disproportionate development effort for only a 'few' (thirty-seven/forty-five) houses instead highlighted their own neglect and the dire needs of a purported half a million Hazara. The move invoked envy and irritation, to put it mildly, especially because many D13 settlers were secondary displaced returnees and repatriates. Against the backdrop that a small Kuchi elite at the national level had gained significant political influence through patronage and affiliations with specific political groups, Kuchi were reportedly granted large areas of land across the country, which was also the case in D13 (Gebremedhin 2005: 10). The subsequently settled Hedokhel Kuchi legitimated their claim to the land by referring to the traditional livestock grazing routes they used before the outbreak of war in 1979

---

16 The road towards Darulaman was in the meantime completed and inaugurated on the occasion of the visit of the Turkish President, Recep Tayyip Erdoğan, in Kabul in October 2014. However, a new conflict evolved about the designation of the road after the municipality removed street signs approved by the Council of Ministers, naming the road after Afghanistan's famous historian Faiz Mohammad Kāteb Hazara.

17 This recent construction, in what is labelled in UNHCR-terminology a 'high return area', is by no means comparable with the above described townships set up by private investors. Kuchiābād is instead very rural in outlook, despite consisting of 350 houses as part of the already mentioned infrastructure, except that the fully equipped school building lacks teachers (Interviews October 29, 2013). In the framework of its Voluntary Return & Reintegration Programme, the UN Refugee Agency plans to establish forty-eight priority sites across the country (cp. UNHCR 2012).

and the connected possession of a decree *(farmān)* over grazing rights issued by the first Afghan King Amir Abdur Rahman Khan (1880-1901).

The establishing of Kuchiābād in D13 provoked several clashes which have been interpreted as being mainly ethnically motivated. For example, several days-long fighting between Hazara and Kuchi, with reportedly 'dozens of casualties on each side', the burning of the Kuchi homes and their subsequent relocation to the Darulaman area by 2010, was reported (Bezhan 2012). Local rumours have it that the violence was provoked by the apparent attempt of some Kuchi to occupy the land around a Hazara graveyard. Adding to this, and to some extent in contrast, a letter (*'ariza*) issued by the Kuchi leaders to the D13 administration, referring to the conflict, stated that the Kuchi had been targeted by followers of a Kuchi MP (Member of Parliament) hailing from Maidan Wardak, a rival of their own patrons' MPs, who had tried to grab their land after they had previously rejected more peaceful advances made by the same MP to take over their plots. Even though this indicates that the violence was motivated primarily by competing interests among different Kuchi groups, the general perception remained captioned by the framing of the conflict between Hazara and Kuchi. This follows the logic of the grievance narrative connected to the nomad-settler conflict at the national level (Behsud clashes etc.) and the killing of twelve Hazara in the events of 2010. Against this backdrop, a proposal to start the construction of another, more sophisticated and fully-fledged Kuchi township, based on international standards, in the Kuchiābād area was reportedly 'prevented' in 2013.[18] The underlying rationale was the fear of D13 representatives and the administration of further provocation and violent escalations, but the main argument against the Kuchi township was based on a lack of robustness in relation to the ownership claims of the Kuchi. In this reading, the earlier agreement of the local administration and local representatives to settle Kuchi in D13, and to allocate government land for this purpose, was based simply on humanitarian grounds. However, in the meantime, D13 residents and representatives came to feel strongly about the government's favourable treatment of the Kuchi population, the apparent neglect of their own issues and the rejected jurisdiction and facili-

---

18 Interviews with district administration and neighbourhood representatives throughout October 2013. The violence in 2010 erupted at the same time as governmental decrees supporting Kuchi's sedentarisation by distributing land to Kuchi families were issued (cp. Wily 2013: 79f).

tation of Hazara returnees and repatriates. Consequently, they were not ready to tolerate a second Kuchiābād in their area.

The narrative of perceived material neglect could be taken even further, but the relatively detailed depiction of arrangements for electricity supply and link roads, plus the contrast with the development of Kuchiābād, is already ample evidence of this neglect. The processes underlying this figurational outcome are complex: in the case of roads and geographic mobility, the everyday experiences of gridlocked traffic jams and not having the right means of transport to get from one point to another in all weather conditions generate the perception of discrimination and physical immobility and cause residents to assert that they would be ready to contribute to any road gravelling project with their own labour and finances, if only construction would start and leadership were provided. The example of electricity provision illustrates that, actually, in many interactions it is not service (non-)provision as such that is at stake and accounts for (dis-)satisfaction in D13, but the degree, quality as well as timing of service provision – in short, the 'how'. Related to this is the observed preference for permanent urban development measures rather than temporary constructions (electricity wires, above surface water pipelines). There is an implicit distinction between the provision of services which are reversible and can be undone, if necessary, i.e. to fit a future planning framework, and those creating hard facts on the ground, for example the construction of hospitals, schools and roads.

The second storyline of this case study, namely the experience of inferiority and unequal treatment in a socio-cognitive sense (neglect in terms of *salāhiyat*), has so far been touched upon only indirectly, most clearly in the discussion of Kuchiābād. In this respect the relationship of the district administration and its head (*rais*) with the municipality, on the one hand, and with neighbourhood representatives, on the other hand, yields significant insights.

The administrative head of D13 finds himself in a moral dilemma which is similar to the dilemma of the neighbourhood representatives (WGs) as pointed out above, because he depends on their cooperation and is caught between their expectations and a municipality that does not extend much support to the district administration. Thus, for example, the recent launching of sanitation taxes, and the insistence by the municipality that they had to be collected retrospectively, is in stark contrast with what the latter actually delivers. The obvious disconnect and lack of legitimacy arising from this issue has to be balanced by the D13 administration – and most importantly by its head – with the help of the WGs who cannot escape the pressure that is being passed down to them. The grievances generated by this type of municipal behaviour were summed up by one *wakil*: "The government treats people like a sixth finger."[19] This dissatisfaction is amplified by the perception that the Mayor actively avoids meeting with representatives of D13. The commonly heard conclusion, "You don't work for us, because we are not suicide bombers," uttered by ordinary residents and local leaders alike, fuses with the popular perception throughout Afghanistan that the government and international donors only invest in volatile areas. Of forty-eight projects proposed by D13 for inclusion in the annual development plan of 2013, only four or five have reportedly been granted.[20] It is not rare that the centralistic policymaking of the municipality administration results in new rules which are not communicated down to the districts' staff. This leaves local administrators clueless and apparently unprofessional in the eyes of their constituents, because they are not aware of their administration's own regulations.

While it is hard in these circumstances to avoid a sense of hopelessness, the district chief is further intimidated by pressure from various sides. For example, I was present in his office when two residents from Chehel Duxtarān area visited his office to report new incidences of land-grabbing. They told him that during the previous night three houses had been erected on land belonging to the public school in their neighbourhood. The police post, which had been notified by local residents first, reportedly said that it was not able to help, since the land-grabbers were related to people from the Ministry of Defence. The only action available to the head of the district administration was limited to reporting the incident to the Mayor's office (*shahrwāli*) and the D13 police precinct (*hawza*). Although they were reported by locals and mentioned in the discussion, the proper names of the encroachers were not stated in the report. Asked for the reason, the head of the D13 administration explained that the last time he had disclosed land-grabbers' names he had been called in by the parliamentary investigation committee on three consecutive days, while the culprits had been released on the very first day of their initial arrest.[21] Moreover, personal intimidation and bullying of the district head increased dramatically when the refusal of

---

19 Interview with a neighbourhood representative: October 27, 2013.
20 Interview in a district administration: November 3, 2013.
21 Ibid.

the D13 administration to recognise the Kuchi's land titles for the establishment of a new township became public.

URBAN BECOMING

The previous section indicated that it is not possible to take into view dynamics in the core figuration in an isolated manner. Against this backdrop, in the ensuing paragraphs I adopt a broader viewpoint for understanding how D13 is envisaged as being developed – against some of the described odds – via linkages beyond its borders. While these actions and processes reflect attempts to mitigate the perceived exclusion, the examples indicate that social boundaries instead become perpetuated and social exclusion is sustained, if not actually amplified.

Who, then, is reaching out to whom and from 'where' (positionality)? Typical local actors working in D13 on local urban development are the street and neighbourhood representatives as well as the head of the WG council and the chief district administrator, all introduced in the previous section. While the street and neighbourhood representatives mostly confine their activities to lobbying the D13 administration as the extended arm of the municipality, and given that the dilemma of the D13 district chief has been discussed already, the interesting point of departure for this section is the case of the head of the council of the seventy-eight neighbourhood representatives (brief: WG head). He stands for attempts and partial successes in increasing both service coverage and *salāhiyat*, i.e. he gives attention to the needs of D13 in general, but of course also to his own immediate constituency (*guzar*). Several dispositions enable his impressive record in neighbourhood development in terms of the number of projects that he has been able to realise. Moreover, attracting other donors and obtaining more funding did seem somewhat easier once he had established relations with a few crucial donors and attracted the Mayor's attention at the annual meeting of district and municipal office bearers.

A few words about his background: at the time I met him, the WG head was thirty-nine years of age. Hailing from Jaghori District in Ghazni, and having lived in exile in Iran for several years, where he served a two-month prison term, he emphasised his own experiences through deprivation. He explained that leading a life of poverty, and having been prosecuted in Iran on racial grounds, motivated him to 'work for the people'. He originally started working as a shopkeeper and teacher during the Taliban years, after his return to Afghanistan. Employed by an international NGO as a teacher, he established two girls' education centres in the second half of the 1990s and subsequently founded his own NGO with foreign assistance. The network of young people educated in these educational centres over the course of three years is apparently very strong and bears great potential, as many of his former students went on to study in further education institutions, receiving university degrees and subsequently obtaining influential positions. Also in the 1990s he was embroiled in a Hazara party network, and he only decided, in the late 1990s, to live in Kabul after the Kabul-Jaghori Road had become too dangerous to travel. Between 2001 and 2004, he served in the police service. His brother, who had emigrated earlier to Italy, and whose contacts that had already facilitated the establishment of the girls' education centres helped him to set up a clinic in the neighbourhood. This was all before he became a regular WG in 2007-08. By the end of 2013, he had been serving as the WG of his neighbourhood for six years. His main occupation was the management of the health centre. With the help of his brother's connections in Italy – he had reportedly become the representative of all exiled Afghans in Italy – he managed to win funding from ISAF to gravel one of the major roads in his area, and as a consequence of which the mayor's office was pushed to take notice. At the time of the fieldwork, he was in his second one-year term as WG head.

Having set up residence and infrastructure in a previously vacant area of D13, he was furthermore able to reach agreement amongst the residents to allocate plots for a school, a mosque and the aforementioned clinic. While the usual way would be that the local community would allocate the land and the government develop it, his experiences over the previous decade reportedly meant that he was unable to count on the government (municipal departments, e.g. for public health or education), and so he would 'just develop' without official permission. The examples he recounted referred to the construction of the school and the mosque, for which he had secured a donor. Once construction was finished he informed the municipality and arranged to pay the teachers' salaries via the Education Department. In another example, when he needed the green light to go ahead with the clinic construction but the Ministry of Public Health remained inactive for more than a year, he lobbied via Mohaqeq, the prominent leader of one of the Hezb-e Wahdat branches and a challenger to the then Vice-President Khalili. The clinic was opened in October 2008. Among the WG head's multiple achievements is an additional NGO-financed road of two kilometres in length, arranging electricity connections within three years and tackling the waste management problem in his neighbourhood.

What all of this shows is not only the importance of connections, but also that they depend to a great extent on a person's background and character traits, which likely evolved on the basis of past experiences and sociohistorised, sedimented cognitive features (habitus). While the WG head's development successes and ability to attract foreign funding for his projects were based largely on these traits alone, other exceptional WGs who lacked international links additionally disposed of certain material or status endowments. For example, several WGs hailed from traditionally influential and resourceful families and used their political and financial clout to campaign for projects or to become self-made entrepreneurs. In this way, many *shahrak* and their services, most prominently water provision, were realised locally. There is no denying that all the projects mentioned so far are most likely also very good business ventures for the initiators. However, given the neglect of the municipality, and its blocking of funds and the activities of international donors in the area via municipal offices since 2011, the entrepreneurial abilities of different representatives and other investors constitute the only pathways for local development. That said, it was remarkable to note that many of the WGs also ran a property business, and as such they benefited additionally from their office. Moreover, given that the majority of WGs are said to be active party workers, there is indication that the idea of accountability to the local community (and the dilemmas linked therewith), as well as some degree of politicisation, is very much present throughout the neighbourhoods of D13.

Besides connections to foreign organisations and capital, links with politicians at different administrative levels were observed to be a very crucial determinant for locals' positionalities, including relations with MPs and government bodies, Senators, party leaders, Members of the Provincial Council and the former Vice-President Khalili or his family. This is particularly apparent when D13 is compared with D6, because D13 is home to one Senator and two MPs whereas thirteen MPs and one Minister live in D6, which makes access to government resources and funding much easier for D6, although the district has also traditionally been part of the 1978 Master Plan. However, in terms of access and scale-jumping, in order to circumvent the municipal administration or to access the Mayor directly, D13 residents experience the additional disadvantage of being Hazara and thus having to cope with the heterogeneous interests that determine their different levels of identity (Ibrahimi 2012). For example, several representatives complained that despite the Hazara of Kabul Province, who live as a concentrated cohort in D13, electing fourteen Hazara onto the twenty-nine-member provincial council, this does not translate into any particular advantage for the district.[22] Given the widespread prevalence of racial prejudices, internal rivalries, a culture of disrespect and power politics driven mainly by powerful strongmen, even lobbying with the Vice-President has not helped the cause of individual D13 neighbourhoods. For example, some interviewees reported that a vice-presidential order requesting the municipality to take action in a road construction project landed in the bin, just like the $10 million designated to D13 after Mohaqeq's lobbying tour in India was never released by the municipality.

Thus, the municipality appears to be a major bottleneck for the implementation of official projects in D13. Even if the right connections could be activated, the legal-bureaucratic process involving the Mayor's office or municipal departments is deemed too time-consuming. As a result, ways to circumvent government involvement are more popular, albeit they push unplanned development further. Moreover, they add to resident and representatives' estrangement from the municipality and the government in general, which might not bode well for future cooperation. However, what is interesting is the respondents' overall attitude, which indicates that their own identity is very much adapting to the overall situation as being 'othered', racially discriminated against, disadvantaged and – specifically in the case of D13 – socially excluded, because of not being part of the Master Plan. What was noticeable during the interviews was how this identity is substantiated by repeated references to past conflicts in the Hazara collective memory. King Abdur Rahman Khan's conquest of the Hazarajat in the last decade of the 19th century (Ibrahimi 2012: 3-6), the massacres and destruction in the fight for Kabul during the Civil War between 1992 and 1996, the subsequent renewed large-scale persecution of Hazara by the Taliban in the Hazarajat and finally the violent escalation of the conflict over grazing grounds with the Kuchi in the last years can all be interpreted to have trickled down and settled into the socio-cognitive being of Hazara and D13 as a collectivity. Forming the particular habitus of local residents, representa-

---

22 Interviews with neighbourhood representatives of D13: October 23 and 29, 2013.

tives and administrators, the motivation of one WG is indicative of a broader behavioural pattern: "This is the first time in history we can do well and prove it in a peaceful environment."[23] Others formulated similar motivations to improve their living conditions by all possible means.

While the last paragraph might seem to draw a very naïve picture of D13 residents' aspirations and underlying motivations in terms of consciousness etc., the fragile livelihood situation, and particularly the dependence on other external factors such as international politics and aspirations for the future, was found to be extremely crucial for D13 prospects. For example, in several interviews the respondents first spoke at length about their commitment to work for local 'development' and their businesses but towards the end started to mention their desire to emigrate abroad and leave D13 and Afghanistan behind. Australia, but also secondary migration back to Iran and Pakistan, was mentioned as a way of circumventing the absence of jobs and development in Kabul. Likewise, the prospect of the 2014 withdrawal of the greater part of the international forces in Afghanistan loomed at the time of the fieldwork, and many interviewees indicated that the uncertainty connected to the 2014 events, such as the presidential and provincial council elections as well as the continued withdrawal of international forces and its economic as well as security impacts, would keep them from investing, constructing, buying and engaging themselves locally. As a result of these future imaginaries, property dealers' businesses in D13 suffered especially, and many had been or were in the process of closing down their offices for an undetermined length of time, if not for good.[24]

Conclusion

Kabul represents itself to the contemporary observer as an ethnically divided city space. However, following Elias's assumption that fundamental power imbalances are never purely based on dimensions such as race or ethnicity, the present chapter has tried to analyse Kabul as an agglomeration of neighbourhoods and city districts whose residents enter figurations. The residents of District 13 and their interdependencies across scales have been identified as part of a wider figurational web, in order to understand

---

23 Interview: October 23, 2013.
24 Interviews with property dealers in D13: October 14 and 27, 2013.

how they negotiate their being and becoming urban through attempts to improve their current situation as newcomers to the city. The underlying forms of interdependence were found to be determined by three dimensions of motility or individual dispositional factors that form part of D13's positionality: socio-cognitive identities, endowment with resources and imaginations about the future. Urban politics as the negotiation of 'development' is studied from a conflict perspective, by taking account of disposition-determined power imbalances, both historically and in the future.

Empirically, the article highlighted that basic service provision and recognition or assigned authority, taken here to correspond to the emic notion of *salāhiyat*, depend on individuals' assets and not on regulations or grand designs such as standard rules of procedure or master plans. This suggests the significance of jumping levels to make ends meet in urban development processes and politics. However, the data also point out that jumping administrative levels does not work equally for everybody; instead, attempts at level-jumping by various D13 residents regularly fail without sufficient backing or the right connections. Moreover, social immobility seems to become reinforced by the provision of temporary services vs. the establishment of more permanent structures. The consideration of the socio-cognitive dimension of positionalities, and of a historical perspective in the analysis, yields an understanding about how and why exclusion is also being reconfirmed and reproduced among stakeholders. Theoretically, the empirical evidence of individuals' limited scope in negotiating for urban development suggests that figurations can indeed exert influence over their constituent parts and constrain their freedom of action (Elias/Scotson 1993: 267). This means that agency is fundamentally dependent on motility factors as part of individuals' positionalities in figurations of wider figurational contexts and entangled interdependencies contextualised spatially, in terms of mobility, and cognisant of a temporal perspective. Thus, the data presented herein provide ample evidence that processes in or of the core figuration do not make sense if the wider figurational context – the social, spatial and temporal interdependencies extending to 'figuration of figuration constellations' – is ignored.

Acknowledgements

I would like to express my deep appreciation and thanks to Ali Y. Adili, who assisted me in conducting this research. Furthermore, I am indebted to the chief administrator and all the neighbourhood representatives and ordinary residents of D13 I was able to interview in the course of my field research in 2013. Without their time and dedication this chapter could not have been written. This research was made possible by a post-doctoral grant within the framework of the research network Crossroads Asia, funded by the German Federal Ministry of Education and Research (BMBF).

REFERENCES

Arez, Ghulam Jailani/Dittmann, Andreas (2005): Kabul: Aspects of Urban Geography, Peshawar.
Bezhan, Frud (2012): "Afghan Nomads Fend Off Authorities In Kabul Land Dispute." (http://www.rferl.org/content/afghan-nomads-fend-off-authorities-kabul-land-dispute/24798956.html; accessed December 14, 2012).
Bourdieu, Pierre (1998): Praktische Vernunft: Zur Theorie des Handelns, Frankfurt: Suhrkamp.
Bourdieu, Pierre (2005 [1992]): Die verborgenen Mechanismen der Macht, Hamburg: VSA-Verlag.
Calogero, Pietro (2011): "Kabul cosmopolitan: Geopolitical empire from the planner's viewpoint." In: Planning Theory 10/1, pp. 66–78.
City Mayors Statistics (n.d.): "The world's fastest growing cities and urban areas from 2006 to 2020." (http://www.citymayors.com/statistics/urban_growth1.html; accessed October 1, 2012).
Coser, Lewis A. (1956): The Functions of Social Conflict, London: Routledge & Paul.
Crossroads Asia Working Group Conflict (2012/2014): Conflict Research on Crossroads Asia: A Conceptual Approach [with Postscript to the Concept Paper of the Conflict Research Group]. In: Crossroads Asia Concept Paper Series, No.01.
CSO/Central Statistics Organization (2013 [1392]): "Afghanistan Statistical Yearbook 2013-14/1392, Kabul: Government of Afghanistan.

Dahrendorf, Ralf (1979): "Zu einer Theorie des sozialen Konflikts." In: Wolfang Zapf (ed.), Theorien des sozialen Wandels, Königstein, pp. 108-123.
Dahrendorf, Ralf (1994): Der moderne soziale Konflikt, München: Piper.
Elias, Norbert (1978): What is Sociology? New York: Columbia University Press.
Elias, Norbert/Scotson, John L. (1993 [1965]): Etablierte und Außenseiter, Frankfurt: Suhrkamp.
Esser, Daniel (2013): "The Political Economy of Post-invasion Kabul, Afghanistan: Urban Restructuring beyond the North-South Divide." In: Urban Studies 50/15, pp. 3084-3098.
Foschini, Fabrizio (2013): The Social Wandering of the Afghan Kuchis. AAN Thematic Report 04/2013, Kabul: Afghanistan Analysts Network.
Foucault, Michel (2005): Analytik der Macht, Frankfurt: Suhrkamp.
Foucault, Michel (2006): Geschichte der Gouvernementalität II: Die Geburt der Biopolitik, Frankfurt: Suhrkamp.
Gebremedhin, Yohannes (2005): Preliminary Assessment of Informal Settlements in Kabul City. Report, USAID/LTERA Project Kabul, Kabul: USAID/Emerging Markets Group.
Grötzbach, Erwin (1979): Städte und Basare in Afghanistan: Eine stadtgeographische Untersuchung, Wiesbaden: Reichert.
Ibrahimi, Niamatullah (2012): Shift and Drift in Hazara Ethnic Consciousness. The Impact of Conflict and Migration. In: Crossroads Asia Working Paper Series, No. 5.
Imbusch, Peter (2006): "Sozialwissenschaftliche Konflikttheorien: Ein Überblick." In: Peter Imbusch/Ralf Zoll (eds.), Friedens- und Konfliktforschung: Eine Einführung, Wiesbaden: Verlag für Sozialwissenschaften, pp. 143-178.
Jensen, Anne (2011): "Mobility, Space and Power: On the Multiplicities of Seeing Mobility." In: Mobilities 6/2, pp. 255-271.
Kaufmann, Vincent/Bergman, Manfred M./Joye, Dominique (2004): "Motility: Mobility as Capital." In: International Journal of Urban and Regional Research 28/4, pp. 745-756.
Leitner, Helga/Sheppard, Eric/Sziarto, Kristin M. (2008): "The Spatialities of Contentious Politics." In: Transactions of the Institute of British Geographers 33, pp. 157-172.
Lukes, Steven (2005): Power: A Radical View. The original text with two major new chapters (Second Edition), New York: Palgrave Macmillan.

Manderscheid, Katharina (2009): "Integrating Space and Mobility into the Analysis of Social Inequality." In: Distinktion 18, pp. 7-27.

Mielke, Katja (2012): (Re-)Constructing Afghanistan? Rewriting Rural Afghans' *Lebenswelten* into Recent Development- and State-making Processes: An Analysis of Local Governance and Social Order, PhD-Dissertation, University of Bonn.

Mielke, Katja/Hornidge, Anna-Katharina (2014): Crossroads Studies – From Spatial Containers to Interactions in Differentiated Spatialities. In: Crossroads Asia Working Paper Series, No. 15.

Ribot, Jesse C./Peluso, Nancy Lee (2003): "A Theory of Access." In: Rural Sociology 68/2, pp. 153-181.

Rostami, Akbar (2013): "Disclosure of Big Land Grabbers." In: 8am Daily (Hasht-e Sobh), January 16, 2013 [Jadi 27, 1391].

Sheppard, Eric (2002): "The Spaces and Times of Globalization: Place, Scale, Networks, and Positionality." In: Economic Geography 78/3, pp. 307-330.

UN Habitat (2010): The State of Asian Cities 2010/11, Fukuoka: United Nations Human Settlements Programme.

UNHCR/World Bank (2011): "Research Study on IDPs in Urban Settings: Afghanistan." May 2011 (http://siteresources.worldbank.org/EXT SOCIALDEVELOPMENT/Resources/244362-1265299949041/6766328-1265299960363/WB-UNHCR-IDP_Full-Report.pdf; accessed December 5, 2014).

UNHCR (2012): "Programme Outline: The Voluntary Return & Reintegration Programme." July 2012 (http://www.unhcr.org/4fedc64b9.pdf; accessed November 3, 2013).

Urry, John (2007): Mobilities, Cambridge: Polity.

Willems, Herbert (2010): "Figurationssoziologie und Netzwerkansätze". In: Christian Stegbauer/Roger Häußling (eds.), Handbuch Netzwerkforschung, Wiesbaden: VS Verlag für Sozialwissenschaften, pp. 255-268.

Wily, Liz Alden (2013): Land, People, and the State in Afghanistan 2002-2012. AREU Case Study Series, Kabul: AREU.

Negotiating Space in the Conflict Zone of Kashmir: The Borderlanders' Perspective

DEBIDATTA AUROBINDA MAHAPATRA

> No borders existed in Kashmir prior to the war of 1947-48. Everything changed so abruptly... the tragedy happened... it is hard to believe, even though decades have passed. All of a sudden we became borderlanders. Our suffering has become eternal.
> SABINA, KARGIL/MAY 24, 2007

India and Pakistan have addressed the Kashmir conflict from a perspective informed mostly by concerns regarding state security and national identity, and wars between the two nations have led to the drawing and redrawing of the border in this highly contested geographical space. The militancy that started in the late 1980s, in the Indian part of Kashmir, led to increased stringency at border points, which became more violent as a result of the increasing number of security personnel, the planting of mines to check cross-border infiltration, electrified fencing and observation towers. The border as a territorial fact and marker of state sovereignty became sacrosanct, while for the borderlanders, their identity and perspectives remained subsumed under the state-led discourse on the border and security. State actors – the dividers – remained in focus while the borderlanders, who lived in the contested space and experienced the consequences of the division –

the divided, remained neglected.[1] Pushed to the edge of power contestation between India and Pakistan, these borderlanders (particularly those living within five to seven kilometres of the border) had to negotiate with conflict on an everyday basis.

Borderlanders in Kashmir continuously have to consider the violent border area when negotiating their safety and survival, but their narratives are not part of the mainstream discourse. Kashmir as a 'dangerous place in the world' has often been highlighted, but the borderlanders and their perspectives remain in the shadows.

This chapter, based on my surveys in border areas on the Indian side of Kashmir, from 2005 to 2012, aims at widening the discourse by centrally engaging the borderlanders and their perspectives. One of the key arguments of the chapter is that the 'borderlander' identity has been imposed on people living along the dividing line in Kashmir, and this identity has been erected on the pedestal of contested territorial claims between India and Pakistan. Unlike borders established with the consent of adjoining states or under international agreements – in short, settled borders – the border in Kashmir is highly contested, which has created enduring anxiety and uncertainty in the lives of the borderlanders, further accentuated by the protracted conflict situation. The forced nature of the border has contributed to the intensity of violent conflict in the region in a cyclical fashion. The border dispute characterised by continuing tensions, as reflected in cross-border

---

1   The term 'borderland' does not have an exact definition, it is used by scholars in different ways. The Merriam-Webster Dictionary provides two definitions. It can imply "the land on either side of a border between countries" or "a vague intermediate state or region" (http://www.merriam-webster.com/dictionary/borderland; accessed January 12, 2015). Similarly, the Oxford English Dictionary provides two definitions: "A district near the line separating two countries or areas" or "an area of overlap between two things" (http://www.oxforddictionaries.com/definition/english/borderland; accessed January 12, 2015). Even if one applies a geographical definition, which this chapter does, there is ambiguity about an exact definition, as there are differences between the terms 'border' and 'frontier'; while 'border' denotes "a formally demarked line" between sovereign states, 'frontier' denotes a "zone of influence along the line" (Kutsche 1983: 16). For the purpose of this chapter, the term 'borderland' implies "the area adjacent to a political border" between two sovereign countries (Stoddard, Nostrand and West 1983: 6).

gunfire and shelling, has made the lives of the people living on the border an unending ordeal.

By questioning the state-centric approach based on traditional notions of border, security and territorial integrity, and by positioning the people at the centre of the analysis, this chapter seeks to rescue the humane space from the state-dominated territorial discourse on the border conflict in Kashmir.

A NOTE ON THE METHODOLOGY

The chapter is based mainly on my field studies in the Indian state of Jammu and Kashmir since 2005. I was in the charge of a project on Kashmir[2] for the University of Jammu from January 2005 to May 2007, and during this period I visited the border areas frequently. By using participant observation, informal interviews and semi-structured interviews, I studied the lives and experiences of the borderlanders.

I conducted surveys in border displacee camps, located on the outskirts of Jammu City, in 2006. In 2007, I conducted research in the border areas of the Kargil region in relation to divided families, and then later in 2007 I joined the University of Mumbai and hence moved out of the region. Since then I have visited the region almost every year, to collect data from the field.

This study is confined to the Indian side of Kashmir, though I am aware that similar conditions prevail on the other side of the border. For the purpose of this chapter, the term 'Kashmir' implies the princely state of Jammu and Kashmir before its division, 'Jammu and Kashmir' (J&K) implies the part of Kashmir on the Indian side of the border and 'Line of Control' (LOC) implies the de facto border between India and Pakistan in Kashmir.

---

2   The project's focus areas included socio-economic developments in the Pakistani side of Kashmir, as well as analysing developments in both parts of Kashmir in a comparative framework, and it was headquartered in the Center for Strategic and Regional Studies at the university.

MAKING OF THE BORDER IN KASHMIR

The princely state of Kashmir became a source of contention between India and Pakistan in 1947. As per the Indian Independence Act 1947, the rulers of the princely states had the option to merge with either of the independent states while taking into account the wishes of their people. While the ruler of the princely state of Kashmir, Maharaja Hari Singh, was exploring the idea of remaining independent, the states of India and Pakistan staked separate claims over Kashmir and started pressuring the king, who in turn requested a standstill agreement with both nations. Pakistan accepted the agreement while India asked for further negotiations. Uprising in Poonch and the infiltration of armed groups from Pakistan in the undivided Kashmir created instability and violence in the region. The infiltrators succeeded in taking control of Muzaffarabad, in Kashmir, on 22 October 1947, and then they advanced towards the capital, Srinagar. The Maharaja requested help from India, for which India sought Kashmir's accession. Hari Singh signed the Instrument of Accession with India on 26 October 1947. The legality of the accession was contested by Pakistan, and a full-scale war broke out between India and Pakistan. On January 1, 1949, a ceasefire negotiated by the United Nations created the line of division in Kashmir based on factual position of the security forces of the two protagonists, which led to the drawing of the forced border.[3]

The division led to a major portion of the princely state remaining with India, leaving a smaller part in the possession of Pakistan,[4] but this did not settle the issue. In the following decades, the forced border was redrawn in the aftermath of the 1965 and 1971 wars, and what was known earlier as the 'ceasefire line' was rechristened the 'Line of Control' (LOC), with some alterations based on actual possession of territory at the time of the

---

3   The literature on the inter-state dimensions of the Kashmir conflict is vast. See, for instance, Ganguly (2002), Dasgupta (2002), Gupta (1966), Lamb (1966), Khan (1975), Schofield (2004), Dixit (2002) and Wirsing (1994).

4   The total area of the Kashmir region is 222.236 sqare kilometres, including 101.387 sqare kilometres with India, 78.114 sqare kilometres under the control of Pakistan and 42.735 sqare kilometres under Chinese control, 5130 sqare kilometres of which was handed over by Pakistan in 1963. Pakistan has divided Kashmir under its control into 'Azad Jammu and Kashmir' and 'Gilgit-Baltistan'.

ceasefire following the 1971 war. The redrawn forced border remained sacrosanct until the Pakistani intrusion into Kargil in 1999, but this skirmish ended without any redrawing of the border.

India and Pakistan share about 1126 kilometres of border in Kashmir. While the international border (IB), extending from Kathua to Akhnoor, is recognised internationally, the LOC, extending from Akhnoor to the Siachen Glacier, is a de facto border.[5] As per India's Ministry of Home Affairs, of the 3323 kilometres land border that India shares with Pakistan, about one-third runs through this state (Ministry of Home Affairs 2012: 49). Of this, 210 kilometres is the IB, around 150 kilometres is the actual ground position line (AGPL) and about 788 kilometres is the LOC.

In Kashmir, the realist paradigm of inter-state relations in terms of sacrosanct borders, as markers of the sovereignty and independence of India and Pakistan, have remained largely intact, even after more than six decades. The all-pervasive security apparatus in terms of observation towers, strict border surveillance, landmines and electrified fencing is testament to the borderlands being a 'site and symbol' of state power and the extremely unfavourable conditions prevailing in this contested space (Mahapatra 2013). Pushed to the edge by power contestation, the ordeals of the people living around the forced border are multifaceted, ranging from recurring displacement to frequently dodging gunfire and shelling.

FORCED BORDERS AND STATE SECURITY

In his pioneering work on African borderlands, Asiwaju argues that borders separate states and regulate, marginalise and constrict cross-border movement (Asiwaju 1984). The regulation of borders is considered one of the most essential duties of a state. Borders particularly "are viewed as constituting a given territorial fact, a static, unchanging feature, rather than one which has its own internal dynamics and which influences, and is influenced by the patterns of social, economic and political development which take place in the surrounding landscapes — the frontier regions and/or borderlands" (Kilot/Newman 2000: 9). Traditionally, these 'symbols of power' were perceived as "markers of the limits of 'national'... to be defended... not to be negotiable or flexible," and "domains of contested power, in

---

5   The chapter uses the terms 'border' and 'LOC' interchangeably.

which local, national, and international groups negotiate relations of subordination and control" (Wilson/Donnan 1998: 10).

Van Schendel notes, "The state's pursuit of territoriality – its strategy to exert complete authority and control over social life in its territory – produces borders and makes them into crucial markers of the success and limitations of that strategy" (Schendel 2005: 3).

Johnson and Graybill argue that

"National borders represent the territorial embodiment of a bundle of ideas that modern states have propagated and enforced. They tell us that all of humanity is divided up among discrete nation-states; that these nations have sovereign powers over particular territory to the exclusion of other nations; and that, collectively, nations exercise this sovereignty over all the earth." (Johnson/Graybill 2010: 2)

In international relations theory, this narrow definition of what constitutes a border is attributed to realism, one among many contending theories that are at the core of the discipline. Realists consider states to be at the hub of international relations, and they view international politics as being competitive and conflictual wherein the Darwinian theory of survival of the fittest and the 'psychology of egoism' govern relations between states (Boucher 1998). The actions of states are governed by the narrow definition of security in relation to gaining power, survival and the pursuit of national interests in an international system that continues to remain anarchic and hierarchical (Waltz 2000). Here, borders are forced upon people, with scant consideration for the concerns of those living along these dividing lines and little attention paid to their identity, group relationships and shared culture. This was done abundantly during colonial times across the globe, with South Asia being no exception. Many of the borders remained unsettled and led to a number of inter- and intra-state conflicts, the case of undivided Kashmir being a major example in this respect.

Though border studies as a discipline gained currency in the post-Cold War era, they were prevalent after the Second World War, too. The discourse on borders and borderlands has witnessed significant changes over time.

Oscar Martinez, who did considerable work on the US-Mexico border, argues that

"As frontline zones of contact, borderlands encountered opportunities previously unavailable to them. Their functions underwent substantial redefinition, from frequently ignored wastelands to dynamic centers of trade, commerce, and even industrialization. Many closed borders became open, allowing capital, people, and products to move from country to country in search of new opportunities. Borderlands that were enmeshed in this process developed economic activity sufficient to spur the growth of existing population centers and the emergence of new ones. Borderlanders affected by such trends, especially borderlanders from developed nations, found a new place in the world, playing roles long denied to them by an international system driven by the ideology of national sovereignty." (Martinez 1994: 3)

However, the borderlanders of many developing countries, including those living in the region of Kashmir, remain largely deprived of such crucial opportunities.

In the past two decades, the border discourse has been widened to include habitations around the markers of territorial state integrity. The borderlander-centric approach has emerged as a crucial component of the border discourse. Scholars have interrogated the traditional notion of security that considers borders sacrosanct, pointing out the asymmetry of attention accorded to states at the cost of the people in border and security discourses (Donnan/Wilson 2010; Newman 2001). People's input is essential for making the concept of security inclusive and relevant to existing realities (Buzan 1992), and state security and human security cannot be mutually exclusive, as they are interlinked. Edward Newman argues, the notion of human security does not "exclude the importance of traditional ideas of security, but it does suggest that it may be more effective to reorient the provision of security around people – wherever the threat comes from. Traditional conceptions of state security – based on the military defence of territory – are an important but not a sufficient condition of human welfare" (Newman/Selm 2003: 8). The security and welfare of people need to be given as much importance as that currently accorded to territory. Hence, opening borders to allow free flow of goods and people is crucial. This awareness has to reach South Asia. In consonance with this emerging global discourse, this study argues that border and borderlander security cannot remain mutually exclusive; the border in Kashmir needs to be problematised, interrogated and humanised, for which it is quite crucial that the perspectives of the borderlanders become the centre of analysis.

THE ALIENATED BORDERLAND

Kashmir provides a classic case of an 'alienated borderland', characterised by violence and instability. Martinez argues that alienated borderlands are characterised by "extremely unfavourable conditions," including "warfare, political disputes, intense nationalism and ideological animosity," thereby leading to "militarization and establishment of rigid controls...," thus making the lives of the people living in the region extremely difficult. He further contends that "such a tension-filled climate seriously interferes with the efforts of local populations to lead normal lives...The ever-present possibility of large-scale violence keeps these areas sparsely populated and underdeveloped" (Martinez 1994: 6).

Martinez classifies borderlands into four types, on the basis of "different degrees of cross-border interaction and prevailing tendencies in a borderland." Irrespective of the level of interaction that defines a particular borderland, i.e. alienated, coexistent, interdependent or integrated, Martinez argues that "as the peripheries of nations, borderlands are subject to frontier forces and international influences that mold the unique way of life of borderlanders, prompting them to confront myriad challenges stemming from the paradoxical nature of the setting in which they live" (Martinez 1994: 25). The alienated border of Kashmir is one of the most violent, and most fortified, boundary lines in the world, earning it the sobriquet 'the most dangerous place in the world'.[6] In many ways the forced border in this region continues to adversely impact the lives of the borderlanders, making it *abnormal*.

---

6 Former US President, Bill Clinton, had referred to Kashmir as the most dangerous place in the world. In a statement on 10 March 2000, Clinton said, "The most dangerous place in the world today, I think you could argue, is the Indian subcontinent and the line of control in Kashmir" (http://news.bbc.co.uk/2/hi/south_asia/687021.stm; accessed September 10, 2014). I argue that the conditions that motivated Clinton to call Kashmir the most dangerous place have not totally abated, and the border remains in a state of conflict. The intense violence on the border in 2014 is a case in point.

Forced Identity

The borderland in Kashmir is underdeveloped and sparsely populated. A significant percentage of population reside on the edges of violent battlegrounds created by India and Pakistan, and they continue to bear the brunt of being a borderlander, an identity the people living in these regions never chose. As one borderlander in Kargil confided,

"Initially we were not borderlanders, we were mainlanders, and it was the abrupt division of our state between India and Pakistan that forced on us this identity of being a borderlander. Our forefathers lived here for centuries; they were not borderlanders, we became... we did not choose this identity... one day we were told this line drawn amidst our houses and fields is a border, and we are borderlanders."
(Personal Interview January 21, 2012)

People are not able to come to terms with this forced identity, even after decades of living along the division.

Bufon's idea pertaining to the 'liability of political partition', which he developed in the context of the Italian-Slovene border, is relevant in the context of Kashmir. Bufon argues that when a region is partitioned, its border people try to reproduce a traditional territory, or rather traditional territorial behaviour, even in the changed territorial context (Bufon 1993: 235). In Kashmir, the constant effort of the borderlanders is visible in their daily behaviours and activities, in the way they go about reinforcing their traditions and integrated identity, which transcends the forced border. The more intense the forced partition, the more willingness of the people to return to traditions of past living. The partition of Kashmir, as discussed above, did not happen within the confines of a smooth political framework; rather, the region was torn asunder due to the conflict between India and Pakistan which escalated into war, separating the people, destroying their integrated identity and eventually paving the way for one of the most intractable territorial conflicts in the world. However, the continued longing of the borderlanders to regain their integrated identity from pre-partition times positions them in a constant war with their state. Their attempts to retain pre-partition ties are viewed with suspicion, leading to their further marginalisation.

Gunfire and Shelling

Borderlanders living within five to seven kilometres of the forced border have to face frequent gunfire and shelling from across the border. A small trigger, such as a belligerent statement made by a political leader from either side, leads to gunfire and shelling. There are occasions when the exchange of heavy gunfire, including artillery and mortar attacks, takes place without apparent reason. No reliable data are available on the exact number of casualties caused by gunfire and shelling on the borders, though it is commonly agreed that hundreds of people have lost their lives besides material losses in terms of destruction of houses and other immovable property as well as livestock. The nature and extent of the devastation can be gauged from a local newspaper, which reported the killing of seventy-two people in cross-border gunfire between May 2001-2003 (Daily Excelsior: May 10, 2003). As per another report, between January and May 15, 2003, firing took place as many as 1007 times, claiming the lives of twenty-nine people and many cattle, and damaging forty-nine houses (Daily Excelsior: May 22, 2003). The paper quoted Garoo Ram, then Minister of State for Rural Development in the J&K government, disclosing that as many as 278 people have been killed, 815 people injured and forty-one structures damaged in cross-border gunfire and shelling over one and a half decades since the onset of militancy (Ibid.). The borderlanders in Kashmir passionately narrate their woes in relation to confronting intermittent gunfire and shelling. Ameena, from Rajouri, stated

"My mother was washing clothes in the open yard just outside our house. I was sitting next to her. She collapsed and then I saw blood all over... My mother had been hit by a bullet from across the border... she died on the spot... This is kind of life we all lead as borderlanders, uncertain and insecure."
(Personal Interview August 18, 2012)

Sometimes people are not able to harvest ripe crops due to the gunfire. As per one report, in the Ranbir Singh Pura sector of the Jammu region, 800 to 900 acres of agricultural land came under fire on May 4, 2002, when India and Pakistan were engaged in coercive diplomacy on the border in the aftermath of the attack on the Indian Parliament (Daily Excelsior: May 9, 2002). This skirmish resulted in the burning of ripe crops in the fields.

There were many instances of frequent clashes on the border, especially after the onset of militancy, before the nuclear-armed neighbours agreed to a ceasefire in 2003. Exchange of fire continued intermittently. At the time of writing, in 2014, the year had witnessed more frequent exchanges of fire than in previous years since 2003, and as per one report issued in August 2014, the month had witnessed the heaviest cross-border gunfire since the 1971 war (Times of India: August 26, 2014). Though the casualties from this fighting were limited, cross-border gunfire nevertheless added to anxiety and uncertainty in the lives of the people.

Recurring Displacement

Borderlanders are displaced whenever a border is disturbed due to wars, the rumour of war, heavy gunfire, shelling or even the mobilisation of security forces. Although borderlanders are not participants in such hostilities, they still bear the cost in multiple ways. Border displacement is not always accidental but sometimes deliberately thrust upon borderlanders when they are targeted directly by cross-LOC gunfire and shelling. As Skjelsbaek and Smith argue, "They [civilians] are no longer... part of the 'collateral damage' consigned to the margins as perhaps regrettable and probably unintended, but unfortunately, inevitable casualties of military exigencies... in many wars, the civilians are the targets" (Skjelsbaek/Smith 2001: 3-4). In the case of Kashmir, displacement has become part and parcel of the life of the borderlanders, as they nomadically keep ferrying between their native homeland and camps during periods of violence. Shekhawat, in her study on border displacement in Kashmir, claimed that Kashmiri borderlanders have been displaced seven times since the late 1940s (1947-48, 1965, 1971, 1987, 1999, 2001 and 2002) (Shekhawat 2006: 98). It will be the eighth time the borderlanders will have been displaced, if the year 2014 is taken into account, as cross-border gunfire in August forced hundreds of families to flee to safer locations, away from the border.

The period of displacement, which ranges from a few days to months – and sometimes for years – is largely temporary but recurrent. Borderlanders have to abandon their homes and take shelter in interior parts, when border areas become extremely tense. In the case of Kashmir, the history of border conflict and the history of displacement coincide. In 1947-48, there was an influx of about 50.000 families from the areas of Muzaffarabad, Mirpur, Bagh, Rawalakote, Bhimber, Kotli and Jhanger in the Pakistani side of

Kashmir to J&K. At present, thousands of displaced people from these areas are residing in various parts of J&K, mainly Bhor, Digiana and Gole Gujral in the Jammu district. Initially, they lived in camps with the hope of returning to their native places, but they appear to have reconciled with the fragile terms of their new life and are more or less permanently settled in J&K.[7]

The 1965 and 1971 wars led to the further displacement, and the Kargil war of 1999 added to this forced migration. One study found that about 157.000 people were displaced from various border areas during this particular conflict (Mandal 2009: 34). The war scare of December 2001, after the attack on the Indian Parliament, led to massive movement; a news report suggests that about 100.000 people were exiled from the Jammu region alone (The Kashmir Times: January 13, 2002). The cross-border gunfire in August 2014 again led to massive movement away from the border – something which had been ongoing for many decades. One report claimed that about 15.000 villagers fled in August to temporary shelters established by the government. Although many of them eventually returned home, about 2000 decided to stay in the camps (The Guardian: August 28, 2014). The border residents consider this nomadic life as their 'fate.' Gunfire has led to massive movement away from the border, which in fact has been a recurrent phenomenon since the creation of the border. Moola Ram, from Jammu, in an earlier interview, observed that "Displacement has become a part and parcel of our lives" (Personal Interview: May 11, 2007).

It is a minimalist argument that displacement has saved the lives of borderlanders, because such an argument does not take into account the aftermath of the displacement, the condition of the displaced once they leave their native homes and the destruction that they have to confront when they return to their homelands.

---

7   The Pakistani side of Kashmir witnessed similar movements of people. The displaced in Pakistani part of Kashmir are struggling to settle, like their counterparts on the Indian side. Robinson (2013) argues that this unprecedented forced movement of people in Kashmir is a factor in motivating many young refugees based in Pakistan to become jihadists.

Life of the Displaced in the Camps

Through a survey that I conducted in camps set up on the fringes of Jammu city to accommodate borderlanders from the Akhnoor sector, displaced due to the 2001-2002 standoff between India and Pakistan, I noticed that the situation was deplorable. The displaced are herded together without basic amenities such as proper shelter, water or toilet facilities, and they live in totally impoverished conditions. Often they are at the mercy of public authorities for relief, which is meagre and irregular. Rama Rani told me:

"Don't you think animals lead a better life than us? We have been herded even more pathetically... These pigeonhole-sized tents are even worse than a prison... No privacy, no toilets, no drinking water and no food to eat... we are cut off from the rest of the world... our children's education has been disrupted... there is no social life... actually, there is no life. We keep running from our homes on the borders to these camps and vice versa... We borderlanders are doomed to suffer." (Personal Interview: October 20, 2006)

In 2006, during another survey but this time with people who had to flee their homes during the 1999 Kargil War, I noticed a lack of even minimal infrastructure for decent living, even though these people had been living there since years. Garoo Ram said: "Life in these camps is hell... there is no alternative for the borderlanders" (Personal Interview: October 22, 2006).

Despite the appalling problems in the camps, many borderlanders prefer to remain in them rather than return to their homes, since they fear the return of violence. Sanjeev Kumar, a border resident, expressed this predicament well: "At least we are alive in the camps and do not have to fear losing our life to a bullet" (Personal Interview: October 26, 2006). Ram Pal, living in Naiwala camp, lamented

"We return only to prepare ourselves for another displacement... It is a choice between death and the devil. Life on the border is hell... here in the camps it is no better... but at least we are alive here... in our native place no one knows when a person will get killed by gunfire or even by a mine blast." (Personal Interview: October 28, 2006)

My survey of 2006 revealed that about 48.000 people, who were displaced due to the Kargil War of 1999, had returned to their respective border villages, although about 12.000 had continued to live in one of the three camps set up – Devipur, Naiwala and Rampur (Shekhawat/Mahapatra 2006). The survey revealed that many of those who had returned to their homes did not go back voluntarily. They were forced by the authorities through various tactics, such as closing camp schools and health dispensaries and stopping the supply of drinking water, electricity and the distribution of relief. Since then, the majority of the displaced have returned, and there were no major clusters of the displaced until August 2014, when a fresh wave of displacement was reported.

Fortified Defence

India and Pakistan have fortified the border with a multilayered security structure comprising mining, fencing and the presence of defence personnel, all compounding the ordeal of the borderlanders. Besides its physical presence, the modern border, argues Heyman, also works as a virtual wall. In its narrowest sense, this virtual wall involves "applying advanced surveillance and computer technologies to border law enforcement," and in a broader sense it points to the "massing of police forces, including military and intelligence agencies, in the border region" (Heyman 2008: 305). The presence of both a physical and a virtual wall in Kashmir is probably more acute than in other border regions of the world in terms of the presence of heavily armed security personnel, electrified fencing, security towers, electronic monitoring stations and the wholesale planting of mines.

Fencing

Fencing and floodlighting are considered crucial by the state for maintaining vigilance along the border. Indian security forces have erected barbed wire fencing to check infiltration from across the border.[8] The fence generally has been erected about 150 yards within the Indian side and consists of

---

8   The fortification, however, has not been able to completely check the infiltration of militants. The available information reveals that the infiltration that had consistently decreased since 2005 reversed in 2009 and increased substantially compared to 2008. For details see Annual Report of Ministry of Home Affairs (2011: 6).

a double row of fences and concertina wire, the height ranging from eight to twelve feet. It is electrified and connected at sensitive points to a network of motion sensors and alarms, in order to check violation. The stretch of land falling between the two rows of fencing is also mined. The erection of fencing started all along the J&K border in the 1990s, but it slowed down in 2001-2002 as hostilities increased, resulting in exchanges of fire at the border and thereby disrupting fencing work. Once the November 2003 ceasefire agreement came into force, fence building was resumed, and fencing in the Kashmir Valley and Jammu regions was completed in 2004 (The Times of India: December 16, 2004).

The fence, constructed at a distance of two to five kilometres away from the edge of the contested border, covers large swathes of cultivable land between the actually agreed border and the fencing itself. This has curtailed the mobility of local people and affected access to their land. In many cases, the land remains uncultivable, as the owners have to cover a distance of about two to three kilometres to reach the gates made in between the fences to access their land, and this has to be done during fixed hours. They have to take circuitous routes and abide by a fixed schedule of hours to access their farms which are actually located only a few metres away from their houses and are owned by them. Also, the barbed wire fencing proves dangerous and life-threatening at places where it is electrified, as livestock and stray animals often fall prey to it.

Landmines

During the Indo-Pakistani hostilities in 1965 and 1971, mines were planted all along the border, on cultivated land and pastures, around infrastructure and even houses, to obstruct movement from across the border. In the late 1980s, with the rise of the militant movement in J&K, heavy mining in border areas was undertaken, to halt cross-border infiltration and to stop the support and patronage of militants from across the border. At times of heightened tension, for instance during Operation Parakram[9] in the last week of December 2002, armed forces increase this activity even further. As per one estimate, over 25.000 acres of land has been mined with anti-

---

9   Operation Parakram was the Indian codename for the 2001-2002 military mobilisation along the border in Kashmir. India mobilised its forces in reaction to an attack on its Parliament on December 13, 2001, which was carried out by Pakistan-based terror groups.

personal mines (APMs) and anti-tank mines (ATMs) at a density of about 1000 mines per sqare kilometre. In the Kathua and Jammu districts, the army took over 31.927 hectares of land, of which 23.078 hectares became a "literal minefield" (The Kashmir Times: February 8, 2004). Unlike the mining of 1965 and 1971, the mining of 2002 was widespread. While in the earlier cases only a radius of one kilometre was mined, in the latter case more than three kilometres were mined.

The end of hostilities normally leads to the removal of landmines from inhabited areas, but many devices remain undetected due to land slides, rain and movement of rodents. Hence, deaths and injuries as a result of stepping on mines are commonplace. During a survey in the Kargil border villages in 2007, I noticed active landmines, which were planted as early as in 1965 and 1971, on both sides of a narrow walkway, about six feet wide, towards a village situated on a hill top. Though the visible tin surface of a mine slightly resembles a discarded tin can, the people cautioned me that these devices were powerful enough to take a person's life or permanently incapacitate him. The border people remain cautious in this respect, but occasional straying from the path proves fatal. There are many instances of people being crippled by these mines while collecting firewood or cutting grass: "I was doing my normal activity of grass cutting in the morning. When I lifted my right foot to take the next step, there was a thundering sound, almost making me deaf. Seconds later, I realised I had stepped on a landmine. I lost a leg," said Shabana, from the Jurian area of Jammu (Personal Interview: August 15, 2012). Domestic and wild animals also fall prey to these mines: "I have lost three cows and two buffaloes to these landmines," informed Bablu Singh (Personal Interview: August 12, 2012). The exact number of victims of landmines is not available, but an estimate of heavy physical losses can be gauged from the fact that in Chagia, a small village in Ranbir Singh Pura sector of Jammu, landmines set up during the 1971 war injured as many as twenty-three residents up to 2001 (The Kashmir Times: January 13, 2012). As per another report, more than 2000 victims of landmines had been recorded in the Rajouri-Poonch belt between 1947 and 1989.

Mine blasts due to forest fires have caused heavy damage to flora and fauna in the region. A forest fire in May 2014 in the Poonch region, for instance, spreading over two to three kilometres of border land, led to many explosions from mines planted in the area to check the infiltration (Daily Excelsior: May 22, 2014). Three landmines exploded in the same region in

July 2014, killing one army porter and injuring three others, besides killing two mules carrying goods for security personnel (Daily Excelsior: July 9, 2014). Deepika Singh Rajawat, Chairman of Voice for Rights, an organisation working for the rights of mine victims, argues that New Delhi has downplayed the concerns of victims and ignored compensation claims. According to Rajawat, about 550 landmine victims from the Poonch region are currently waiting for relief and compensation (Daily Excelsior: December 25, 2014). My survey, in the villages of the Akhnoor in 2006 and Kargil in 2007, revealed that mines still remain undetected and, hence, are a continuous threat to the people. They not only cause physical injury, but their potential in terms of generating fear is phenomenal. Though no human casualty was reported during the days of the surveys, I witnessed cases of cattle being injured or killed, due to undetected mines. In October 2004, Indian authorities claimed that demining operations were almost complete. On condition of anonymity, an army official, however, admitted that it was not feasible to demine the area entirely, since mines change their positions due to soil movements caused by rain or rodents.

Mines impact the livelihoods of the border people through loss of cultivable land – one of their major sources of income. As per an estimate made by a local daily newspaper, nearly 350.000 hectares of agriculture land lay uncultivated due to tension-induced dislocation from the border area (Daily Excelsior: June 3, 2002). Moreover, the non-cultivation of land for a long period makes fertile lands barren, thus increasing the burden of loss.

Defence Personnel
The presence of security forces contributes to further rigidity along Kashmir's border. The multi-tiered defence mechanism buzzes as a result of the presence of defence personnel, whose strength varies in accordance with the prevailing situation. This strength may vary, but the presence of armed personnel is permanent in and around the border villages, thereby restricting the mobility of the people. In his study of the US-Mexican border, Dunn provides insights into how militarisation contributes to violating the human rights of people living on the margins (Dunn 2001). The overwhelming presence of security personnel in border villages gives the impression that these places are military cantonments, cordoned off purely for the use of army personnel, thus affecting the freedom of movement and livelihoods of local people. Furthermore, armed establishments in public places have affected the social and cultural lives of the people. My surveys

in the Poonch region revealed that many public places such as schools and medical centres, which should have served the common people, have actually housed security personnel. At the time of my survey in 2007, a Boys' Higher Secondary School in Surankote had been under the control of army since 1990s. Similarly, in Lassanna, one public health centre was sheltering defence personnel, causing inconvenience to local people looking for treatment of diseases (Mahapatra 2007).

There is another less explored dimension of the presence of military personnel in border areas. Military presence has developed a siege mentality among the border people, as they feel their rights and freedom are not theirs but are instead subject to the wishes of the military forces.[10] The continued sight of security forces in uniform has created a deep-seated fear in the minds of the people that violence can grip the area at any time, they can be targeted at any time and their land can be taken at any time. This has led to depression and the development of a sense of resignation, thus hampering creative spirit of the borderlanders.

As Loknath, from Surankote, lamented,

"We are living for the sake of living. I went to Ludhiana [a city not very far from Kashmir] and I did not find gun-toting forces roaming everywhere. Here, it is so different. You see armed forces everywhere – in our schools, in our medical centres and in our fields. Our children cannot play and study properly, and we elders are

---

10 There is a debate about the role of Indian armed forces and Acts such as Armed Forces Special Powers Act (enacted by the Indian Parliament in 1990, under which the armed forces were granted overwhelming power), in the Indian side of Kashmir. India claims that the Act is meant to protect the "sovereignty and territorial integrity of India" and to prevent "terrorist acts" (for the text of the Act, see http://www.satp.org/satporgtp/countries/india/states/jandk/documents/actsandordinances/J&K_Specialpoweract.htm; accessed January 10, 2015). There are, however, arguments that armed forces have used this power arbitrarily, which has resulted in fake encounters, disappearances and other kinds of human rights violations in the region, particularly in the valley. For this side of the debate see Duschinski (2009 and 2010).

helpless. We are in our land, but actually not in our land. We are at the mercy of the armed forces." (Personal Interview: August 14, 2012)

Leading a peaceful life amidst this turbulence has been an abiding problem for border people, as they continue to suffer innumerable losses, in both the short term as well as in the long term, in all aspects of life. Lack of mobility, caused by frequent gunfire and mining, results in a restricted lifestyle wherein people cannot freely perform day-to-day activities. Even the use of basic facilities becomes problematic, as they cannot keep lights on at night, sleep outside during the summer season, a common practice in Indian villages situated on the mainland, or even use toilets freely, which are located outside their houses. The socio-cultural life of border people is restricted. They cannot celebrate festivals and other social functions joyously, invite relatives to their homes or even gossip while sitting out in the open. The relatives of borderlanders from the mainland shy away from visiting them, lest any misfortune of border life befall them. The border residents often find it difficult to find suitable marital prospects for their sons, since people from the mainland do not wish to marry their daughters to a person living in such a tense area of hostility. Education, health services and other essential facilities such as communication and transport are also severely affected.

Conclusion

The Kashmir borderland, one of most violent borderlands on Earth, was forced on the people living in the region. It was created abruptly as a result of war between two states. The unsettled border remains violent even today, sixty-seven years since its inception. Local people, known as 'borderlanders', have experienced the consequences of this violence. In a 21st-century globalised world, where many borders have emerged as lines of contact, commerce and cooperation, the violent and uncertain nature of the forced border in Kashmir has developed as a contrasting phenomenon in juxtaposition to the current border discourse.

The emerging border discourse, focusing on the fluidity and flexibility of borders, has remained contested in Kashmir. The rigid and tense environment in Kashmir's borderland has specific implications for local people, as they suffer problems rarely experienced by the mainlanders. This suffering remains part of only a local discourse, as the state-centred security discourse still remains dominant in this part of the world. This has contributed to the undermining of human security and stymied multiple enabling voices of the borderlanders at the margins. The alienated border continues to be a harsh reality for the people, and until India and Pakistan prioritise human security over border security, the normalisation of lives of people living along borders is unlikely.

Borderlanders' voices need to be mainstreamed and factored into policymaking, which will serve a dual purpose. First, it will highlight the plight of borderlanders in one of the most violent zones of the world and secondly, it will prove amply instructive for other borderland situations. The overfocused state security discourse needs to be questioned centrally, in order to correct the asymmetrical discourse on border and security. The question needs to be asked: security of whom, and by whom? And is the state the sole provider of security, and the sole rescuer of people from violence, even when the violence is committed by the state itself?

REFERENCES

Asiwaju, A. I. (1984): Artificial Boundaries, Lagos: Lagos University Press.
Boucher, D. (1998): Political Theories of International Relations: From Thucydides to the Present, Oxford: Oxford University Press.
Bufon, Milan (1993): "Cultural and Social Dimensions of Borderlands: The Case of the Italo-Slovene Trans-border." In: GeoJournal 30/3, pp. 235-240.
Buzan, Barry (1992): People, States and Fear: An Agenda for International Security Studies in the Post-Cold War Era, New York: Harvester Wheatsheaf.
Daily Excelsior (2002): June 3, 2002 and May 9, 2002.
Daily Excelsior (2003): May 10, 2003 and May 22, 2003.
Daily Excelsior (2004): April 10, 2004.
Daily Excelsior (May 22, 2013): "Fire breaks out in forest, land mines explode along LoC in Poonch." (http://www.dailyexcelsior.com/fire-breaks-out-in-forest-land-mines-explode-along-loc-in-poonch/; accessed September 14, 2014).

Daily Excelsior (July 9, 2013): "Porter killed, 3 injured as militants detonate IEDs." (http://www.dailyexcelsior.com/porter-killed-3-injured-as-militants-detonate-ieds/; accessed September 14, 2014).

Daily Excelsior (December 25, 2013): "Poonch mine blast victims for release of pending compensation." (http://www.dailyexcelsior.com/poonch-mine-blast-victims-for-release-of-pending-compensation/; accessed September 14, 2014).

Dasgupta, C. (2002): War and Diplomacy in Kashmir 1947-48, New Delhi: Sage Publications.

Dixit, J. N. (2002): India- Pakistan in War and Peace, London and New York: Routledge.

Donnan, H./Wilson, T. (eds.) (2010): Borderlands: Ethnographic approaches to security, power, and identity, Lanham: University Press of America.

Dunn, Timothy J. (2001): "Border Militarization via Drug and Immigration Enforcement: Human Rights Implications." In: Social Justice, 28/2, pp. 7-30.

Duschinski, Haley (2009): "Destiny Effects: Militarization, State Power, and Punitive Containment in Kashmir Valley." In: Anthropological Quarterly 82/3, pp. 691-718.

Duschinski, Haley (2010): "Reproducing Regimes of Impunity: Fake Encounters and the Informalization of Violence in Kashmir Valley." In: Cultural Studies 24/1, pp. 110-132.

Ganguly, Sumit (2002): Conflict Unending: India-Pakistan Tensions since 1947, New Delhi: Oxford University Press.

Gupta, Sisir (1966): Kashmir: A Study in India-Pakistan Relations, Bombay: Asia Publishing House.

Heyman, Josiah McC. (2008): "Constructing a Virtual Wall: Race and Citizenship in U.S.-Mexico Border Policing." In: Journal of the Southwest 50/3, pp. 305-334.

Johnson, B. H./Graybill, A. R. (eds.) (2010): Bridging National Borders in North America: Transnational and Comparative Histories, Durham: Duke University Press.

Khan, M. Akbar (1975): Raiders in Kashmir, Islamabad: National Book Foundation.

Kilot, Nurit /Newman, David (eds.) (2000): Geopolitics at the End of the Twentieth Century: The Changing World Political Map, London: Frank Cass.

Kutsche, Paul (1983): "Borders and Frontiers", in E. Stoddard/R: L. Nostrand/J. P. West (eds.), Borderlands Sourcebook: A Guide to the Literature on Northern Mexico and the American Southwest, Norman: University of Oklahoma Press, pp. 16-19.

Lamb, Alastair (1966): Crisis in Kashmir: 1947 to 1966, London: Routledge and Kegan Paul.

Mahapatra, Debidatta A. (2007): "Poonch for Peace: An Eyewitness Account," The Kashmir Times, May 6, 2007.

Mahapatra, Debidatta A. (2013): Making Kashmir Borderless, New Delhi: Manohar and RCSS.

Mandal, Monika (2009): "Internal Displacement in India: Status, Condition and Prospects of Return." In: Refugee Watch 33, pp. 33-47 (http://www.mcrg.ac.in/rw%20files/RW33/3.IDP_Monika.pdf; accessed September 14, 2014).

Martinez, Oscar J. (1994): Border People: Life and Society in the US–Mexico Borderlands, Tucson: University of Arizona Press.

Ministry of Home Affairs (2011): Annual Report, 2010-2011, New Delhi: Policy Planning and Research Division, Government of India.

Ministry of Home Affairs (2012): Annual Report, 2011-2012, New Delhi: Policy Planning and Research Division, Government of India.

Newman, Edward (2001): "Human Security and Constructivism." In: International Studies Perspectives 2/3, pp. 239–251.

Newman, Edward/Selm, Joanne van (eds.) (2003): Refugee and Forced Displacement: International Security, Human Vulnerability and the State, Tokyo: United Nations University Press.

Robinson, Cabeiri deBergh (2013): Body of Victim, Body of Warrior: Refugee Families and the Making of Kashmiri Jihadists, California: University of California Press.

Schendel, Willem Van (2005): The Bengal Borderland: Beyond State and Nation in South Asia, London: Anthem Press.

Schofield, Victoria (2004): Kashmir in the Crossfire: India, Pakistan and the Unending War, New Delhi: Viva Books Pvt. Ltd.

Shekhawat, Seema (2006): Conflict and Displacement in Jammu and Kashmir: The Gender Dimension, Jammu: Saksham Books.

Shekhawat, Seema/Mahapatra, Debidatta A. (2006): Kargil Displaced of Akhnoor in Jammu and Kashmir: Enduring Ordeal and Bleak Future, Geneva: Internal Displacement Monitoring Centre.

Skjelsbaek, Inger/Smith, Dan (2001): Gender, Peace and Conflict, New Delhi: Sage Publications.
Stoddard, E./Nostrand, R. L./West, J. P. (eds.) (1983): Borderlands Sourcebook: A Guide to the Literature on Northern Mexico and the American Southwest, Norman: University of Oklahoma Press.
The Guardian (August 28, 2014): "15.000 Kashmiris take shelter as cross-border tensions escalate." (http://www.theguardian.com/world/2014/aug/28/kashmir-fighting-15000-villagers-shelter-india-pakistan; accessed September 14, 2014).
The Kashmir Times (2002): January 13, 2002.
The Kashmir Times (2004): February 8, 2004.
The Times of India (December 16, 2004): "LoC Fencing Completed: Mukherjee." (http://timesofindia.indiatimes.com/india/LoC-fencing-completed-Mukherjee/articleshow/960859.cms?referral=PM; accessed July 15, 2008).
The Times of India (August 26, 2014): "Heaviest cross-border firing since 1971 war, India lodges protest with Pakistan." (http://timesofindia.indiatimes.com/india/Heaviest-cross-border-firing-since-1971-war-India-lodges-protest-with-Pakistan/articleshow/40936924.cms; accessed September 14, 2014).
Waltz, Kenneth (2000): "Structural Realism after the Cold War." In: International Security 25/1, pp. 5-41.
Wilson, T. M./Donnan, Hastings (1998): "Nation, State and Identity at International Borders." In T. M. Wilson/Hastings Donnan (eds.), Border Identities: Nation and State at International Frontiers, Cambridge: Cambridge University Press.
Wirsing, Robert G. (1994): India, Pakistan and the Kashmir Dispute: On Regional Conflict and Its Resolution, New York: St. Martin Press.

Interviews

The select areas on the border in which interviews were conducted are listed below followed by the months:
Jammu, Akhnoor, Rajouri and Surankote: October 2006, May 2007 and August 2012.
Kargil: July 2006, May 2007 and January 2012.

Exclusionary Infrastructures: Crisis and the Rise of Sectarian Hospitals in Northern Pakistan

EMMA VARLEY

INTRODUCTION

By building on the emerging anthropology of clinics in crisis, this chapter will explore how hospitals are observed and imagined to operate as sites which mirror and perpetuate the social segregations and structural inequalities associated with Shia-Sunni hostilities in Gilgit Town, the capital of northern Pakistan's semi-autonomous Gilgit-Baltistan region. In so doing, I explore the complex ways that Shia and Sunni health infrastructures and the services they provide are mimetic and generative of broader forms of discord and conflict. The chapter first discusses the rise of sectarian hospitals in Gilgit Town, whereby medical services have come to operate as unique sites of Shia and Sunni sectarian capital formation – processes which draw their impetus from insecurity, violence and warfare. Then, through an ethnographic case study examination of the 'Sunni' Kashrote Government City Hospital, my analysis foregrounds how, to an increasing and often exclusive degree, public sector hospitals have been socially, bureaucratically and politically configured as sectarian medical infrastructures, and it also addresses the contestations and concerns associated with this process. The chapter concludes with a discussion on the significance of sectarian medical infrastructures as dynamically heterotopic sites of experience, identity affirmation and boundary-making. Through critical exploration of the ways that Shia and Sunni hospitals serve as spaces of sectarian inclusion and safety, or inequity and exclusion, my research illuminates the diverse ways that health services in Gilgit Town have come to occupy a central role in Gilgitis' political and sectarian imaginations.

My interests in the interrelationship between sectarianism, conflict and health services began as a result of the complex fallouts for Gilgit Town's hospitals from Shia-Sunni hostilities after the January 8, 2005 assassination of Gilgit-Baltistan's Shia religious leader, Syed Zia-ud-din Rizvi, by Sunni militants. Gilgiti Shias, who comprise the majority of Gilgit Town's residents, responded forcefully through the organised use of violence and, by capitalising on their growing dominance in a wide array of socio-political contexts, reduced and excluded Sunnis' access to and control over political and economic resources, including those related to health. Such conflicts are not recent. Gilgit Town has been the scene of protracted sectarian enmities and hostilities for many of the past thirty years, during which time an estimated 3000 people, mostly Shias and Sunnis, have been killed (Interview: March 16, 2012).[1]

---

1 A careful review of the reported numbers of injured and dead in Gilgit's Sunni and Shia communities suggests the conflicts as being symmetrical, even while it can also be argued that Sunnis and Shias experience asymmetrical inequalities and risks in the spaces and contexts dominated by their respective sectarian 'others' (see 'Presentation by Inspector General of Police'; http://urban.unhabitat.org.pk/Portals/0/Portal_Contents/Balochistan/Turbat/Police%20Deptt%20GB.pdf; accessed April 19, 2012). For instance, between 2009 and 2010, the Police registered nineteen Shia and sixteen Sunni deaths as being the result of 'sectarian crimes', fourteen Shias and twenty-five Sunnis were injured, while twenty-five Shias and forty-three Sunnis were accused of murder (Ibid: 37-39). It merits note that the political forces affecting how Shia-Sunni conflicts are recorded and represented, often in an uneven or biased capacity, may also contribute to the under- or over-reporting of those killed in Gilgit's sectarian tensions. For instance, while unofficial estimates place the numbers killed in the thousands, Hunzai (2013) notes that, "according to a recent analysis in Gilgit-Baltistan, 117 sectarian-related murder cases were registered between 1988 and 2010, which does not include an estimated 170 attempted murders. In 2011 alone, another forty-four cases of sectarian killings were registered" (Hunzai 2013: 6). These estimates do not include the "killings of nearly one hundred people in 2012, mostly Shia, travelling between Islamabad and Gilgit, and the

The dissonances associated with Gilgit's Shia-Sunni 'tensions', as the conflicts are called locally, are not predicated merely on questions of doctrinal difference.[2] They also reflect the acute social distortions and political polarisations which arise from the expanding efforts of Sunnis, Shias and also Ismailis to control Gilgit-Baltistan's scarce political and economic capital (see Hunzai 2013). In turn, Pakistan's uneven governance of the region, which Martin Sökefeld aptly qualifies as "post-colonial colonialism" (2005), produces power vacuums at local and regional levels, whereby politicisation processes and power contestations are conceived along, and draw their freight and impetus most forcefully from, explicitly sectarian rather than shared forms of ethnic or regional affiliation[3].

Gilgit Town, the setting for my ethnographic fieldwork since the late 1990s[4], was estimated in 2011 to be populated by 260.000[5] Shia, Sunni and

---

retaliatory killings of Sunnis in town that followed" (ibid). Moreover, Shia deaths were observed to be over-reported, or reported at the exclusion of any recognition of Sunni deaths, thus producing significant complications for researchers attempting to enumerate accurately the loss, debility and death produced by inter-sectarian violence.

2   See Sökefeld (1998b, 1999) and Grieser/Sökefeld (2015) for a concise elaboration of the post-Partition history of sectarian enmities and conflict in Gilgit-Baltistan, and Gilgit Town in particular.

3   While it is beyond the ambit of this paper to attend to the contribution of ethnic, clan (*qom*; also described as denoting 'tribe' and 'caste') and kinship (*khandan*) affiliation and identity to Gilgit's Shia-Sunni hostilities, it is of note that in regional political rhetoric and discourse, ethnic and sectarian identity have come to be largely (but not exclusively) conflated, while the role played by caste and family associations is almost always neglected. (Gilgit Town's Shia, Sunni and Ismaili populations self-identify not only as 'Gilgiti' in terms of their ethnicity, but frequently also prioritise other forms of ethnic affiliation, such as being Hunza, Nagar, Ghizer, Diamer, Astore or Ghanche or Skardu in Baltistan, should their families' origins be non-native to Gilgit). Accordingly, this paper follows from this precedent as well as my interlocutors' narratives, to accord analytical primacy to sectarian identity ahead of other but no less relevant forms of belonging and association.

4   This paper is based on fieldwork conducted in 2004-2005 and between 2010 and 2013. The research on which this chapter is based involved narrative exploration of the experiences of the DHQ's Shia and Ismaili medical personnel, such as

Ismaili residents, with each sectarian community being roughly equal in size[6]. While Gilgiti Shias belong to the Twelver and Ismailis to the Sevener sects of Shia doctrine and practice[7], the majority of Sunnis are affiliated with the Deoband Hanafi *fiqh* (school of jurisprudence). Each sect is differentiated from the other not only according to the degree of their adherence to sect-specific religiously, but also from socially and politically moderate or conservative positions. Although Gilgit's contemporary tensions have their origins in the early 1970s (see Aase 1999; Sökefeld 1998b, 1999), most of my interlocutors, irrespective of sectarian affiliation, remembered 1988 as the year when Shia-Sunni hostilities in Gilgit Town became exponentially worse. In May of that year, purportedly in response to a series of events, including a "rumor alleging a Sunni massacre in Gilgit by Shias, which some say was deliberately spread to provide an excuse for Sunni militants to conduct the attacks" (Hunzai 2013: 5), an armed *lashkar* (militia) of Sunnis from Kohistan District in Khyber-Pakhtunkhwa travelled north along the Karakoram Highway, joined by Sunnis from Diamer and southern Gilgit Districts. With their northward progress largely unchecked by resi-

---

hospital administrators, physicians and Lady Health Visitors, and equivalent cadres of Sunni and Ismaili personnel at the Kashrote Hospital.

5   Population estimates vary considerably for Gilgit Town. For instance, the 1998 Population Census Survey indicated that its population was 56.701, and this was expected to grow to 72.350 by 2008 and 92.365 by 2018 (Karrar, Iqbal and Mubarak 2011: 18). However, "the preliminary findings of a house listing exercise in Gilgit District, conducted in 2011 by the Government of Pakistan," which included neighbouring villages that had been previously excluded from the 1998 survey, found that the population stood at 261.440 residents (Annandale/Hagler Bailly Pakistan [Pvt] Ltd., 2014: 116). Based on an estimated population growth rate (PGR) of 6 per cent, the 2011 survey proposed that Gilgit Town's population would grow to 331.000 people by 2025 (Ibid: 117), further compounding the already unmanageable pressures placed on the city's civil infrastructure and services, inclusive of public sector hospitals.

6   In important contrast to Shias' minority status in the rest of Pakistan, they comprise the majority of Gilgit-Baltistan's residents, followed by Sunnis and then Ismailis (see Ali 2010: 739).

7   Despite sharing a common theological base, Shia and Ismaili cultural practices and modes of worship differ, and Gilgiti Ismailis mark such differences by self-identifying simply as 'Ismaili'.

dents, the Police or the Army, upon arriving in Gilgit Town the *lashkar* attacked several Shia communities and the village of Jalalabad in particular, destroying property and inflicting hundreds of casualties[8] (Aase 1999: 58-60, Ali 2008: 16, Sökefeld 1998: 173). The number of deaths and the scale of destruction were unprecedented and marked a key juncture in Shia-Sunni relations which, until that point, had been characterised by commensality and intermarriage (see Aase 1999, Ali 2008, Sökefeld 1999).

Episodic conflicts followed throughout the 1990s and were often related to ritual observances by Shias in Gilgit's mixed-sect public spaces, as well as the close proximity of the annual Ashura processions to Sunni *masjids* (see Grieser/Sökefeld 2015). Gilgit's sectarian communities were also evermore at odds thanks to the ideologically framed and resource-based competitions inherent in sectarian-aligned projects relating to regional development. Such projects have included the avowedly secular, but in practice and organisational culture sectarian, work of the Aga Khan Development Network (Settle 2010: 14-15, 23; Settle 2011), which has been active predominantly in Ismaili communities across the region since the 1970s. AKDN's activities have been paralleled by the rise of an expanding array of Shia and Sunni civil society, non-governmental and voluntary organisations. Over recent decades, the sum result of Gilgit-Baltistan's sectarian-linked political and social development, inclusive of the "sectarianisation" (Grieser/Sökefeld 2015) of civil infrastructures and, as this chapter explores, health systems and services, has been that inter-sectarian differences and socio-economic inequalities have intensified, and the ensuing Shia-Sunni conflicts have increased in both frequency and duration.

In order to establish the context for Gilgit Town's sectarian medical infrastructures, this chapter first details the conflicts which generated the need for segregated infrastructures[9] and facilities. Through an ethnographic case study of the 'Sunni' Kashrote Government City Hospital, I pull into view the role of hospitals as sites of cultural and religious politics and transformation. In so doing, I seek to address how sectarian health governance raises a number of ethnographic and practical concerns, for instance

---

8   See footnote 1 for a discussion of the politics which affect the enumeration of sectarian losses in Gilgit.

9   For this chapter, my use of the term 'medical infrastructure' follows from Larkin, who qualifies "infrastructures [as] built networks that facilitate the flow of goods, people, or ideas and allow for their exchange over space" (2013: 328).

under what conditions do health services operate as vehicles of sectarian conflict? Furthermore, how do sectarianism's unwieldy politics affect or undermine service provision, and to what degree and in which specific ways can the health sector become a co-participant in the production and exacerbation of sectarian difference? By evaluating the interrelationship between Shia-Sunni conflict and Gilgit's sectarian medical infrastructures, this chapter demonstrates the consequences of sectarianism not only for hospital sites and medical practices, but also for forms of sociality within and across lines of sectarian affiliation. My research is best qualified as hospital ethnography, an approach which occupies an increasingly important place in the anthropology of conflict and crisis. Recent anthropological research confirms the multiple complex roles played by medical infrastructures, institutions and health personnel in mitigating, sustaining or even exacerbating conditions of insufficiency, instability and danger (see Anderson 2004, Brown 2011, Fassin 2008, Hamdy 2008, Jaffre 2012, Pinto 2004, Sousa and Hagopian 2011, Smith 2015, Street 2012, Sullivan 2012, Wick 2008, Zaman 2004). Against this backdrop, my analysis of the hospitals is guided by ethnographies which prioritise how hospital spaces, and the socialities which proliferate within them, are constitutive of and mirror the diverse "identities, imaginations and practices" (Davidson/Milligan 2004: 571) associated with and emerging from conflict.

In order to evaluate the dynamic socio-political and spatial complexities enduring in and arising from Gilgit's sectarian hospitals, my analysis builds on Foucault's notion of heterotopia, which can be defined as "intrinsically ambiguous spaces… [that] are both constituted by their relationship to other spaces and defined in opposition to them; they involve a complex ordering of opening and closing that 'both isolates them and makes them penetrable' (Foucault, 1986, p. 26)" (Street/Coleman 2012: 8). Medical anthropologists who adopt the concept to analyse "the contested and multiple nature of hospital space" argue that as heterotopic sites, hospitals are constituted by multi-layered orderings of power and sociality (Street/Coleman 2012: 4, 5). My analysis is also predicated on the insights garnered both from my fieldwork and my experiences as the wife and mother of Gilgiti Sunnis, which permitted me to see first-hand the different but numerically equivalent ways that Shias and Sunnis experience violence and death during sectarian tensions. It merits note that my work stands counter to, or is at the very least unique from, the majority of regional research (see Aase 1999; Ali 2008, 2009, 2010, 2012, 2013; Stöber 2007, Rieck 1995) and media, which foreground Shia vulnerabilities and loss at the expense of any fuller understanding of the scope and impacts of conflict on Sunnis or Ismailis. Ultimately, through an ethnography of hospitals as heterotopic sectarian institutions through which hostilities are interpreted and experienced, we gain insights into the ways in which healthcare facilities serve as spatial and temporal benchmarks in the larger history of Gilgit's tensions and contribute to demarcating and reinforcing the boundaries of sectarian difference and political subjectivity.

GILGIT'S TENSION TIMES

Among the key precipitating factors in the emergence of Gilgit's sectarian medical infrastructure in Gilgit Town were the January 2005 killings of Sunni patients and physicians at the District Headquarter Hospital, and the subsequent risks faced by all Gilgiti patients whenever they sought medical care across spatial or social lines of sectarian affiliation. The events of January 2005 were the culmination of nearly a year of evolving, intensifying dissent from within Gilgit's Shia community. In the summer of 2004, Gilgit Town was paralysed by a series of protests led by Aga Syed Zia-ud-din Rizvi, the religious leader to Gilgit-Baltistan's Shias, concerning the Sunni tone of the federal educational syllabi (*nisab*). The Nisab Crisis, which began in the spring of 2004, led to acts of vandalism, arson, violence, killings and military curfews. Five months later, on January 8, 2005, Zia-ud-din was killed by non-local Sunni assassins. For the subsequent ten months, the city was wracked by sustained hostilities, protracted curfews, attacks and counter-attacks between Shias and Sunnis. The violence, known locally as the 'tension times', further entrenched and exacerbated the segregations which even prior to Zia-ud-din's death had come to characterise Shia-Sunni relations. Prominent among the after effects of January 2005 was the inability of Shias and Sunnis to travel easily or safely through, or access resources located in, the urban spaces dominated by their sectarian others (see Grieser/Sökefeld 2015, Sökefeld 1999: 420). For instance, in ways which continue to fuel Sunnis' anxieties about hospital settings, on January 8, 2005, the 250-bed government District Headquarter Hospital (DHQ), based in a Shia enclave and the facility to which Zia-ud-din was taken for emergency treatment, was the scene for targeted attacks. Nearly twenty Sunnis were killed on the hospital premises and in the immediately surrounding neighbourhoods. While Shia gunmen threatened to kill Zia-ud-din's Sunni treating physicians, should he die from his injuries, the patient wards throughout the hospital were searched for Sunni male patients and attendants (Varley 2010: 65). Because of the density of Shia homes surrounding the hospital, many Sunni patients and staff were unable to escape the hospital for several days. And even though the Sunni Department of Health Director was shot and killed on January 8th as he attempted to reach the DHQ, in the months that followed Sunni medical officers and paramedical staff were not provided with secure transport to and from the hospital, and thus they often refused to attend their duties on days of tension (ibid).

The diverse risks associated with the DHQ site led to stark differentials in health service access and outcomes for patients from across all sectarian communities, but among Sunnis in particular (ibid: 65-67). For example, hospital attendance among Sunni maternity patients decreased by 90 per cent following the start of the tensions, compounding the region's already high maternal mortality ratio of 500 to 800 deaths per 100.000 live births (Rahman 1999: 12; see Varley 2010: 62). From 2005 to the present, Sunni healthcare providers and patients have been particularly concerned for their security at the DHQ. The unmitigated risks associated with the hospital therefore led to Sunni patients' lasting marginalisation, whether intentional or otherwise, from Shia enclave-based hospitals and, as some interlocutors narrated, their neglectful or abusive medical treatment by the DHQ's non-Sunni providers (see Varley 2010: 67-68). Nor was it only in-town Sunnis who faced challenges accessing the hospital. Because the DHQ is Gilgit-Baltistan's sole tertiary-care referral hospital, serving a patient base of over 1.5 million residents, Sunni patients from across Gilgit-Baltistan were and continue to be affected profoundly by the hospital's insecure spaces. Importantly, the estrangement of Sunnis from Shia-provided or neighbourhood-based health services was argued to signify the reversal of the discriminatory practices[10] historically enacted against Shias, a minority in Pakistan but a majority in Gilgit-Baltistan, by Gilgiti Sunnis in coordination with the Sunni-dominated state (Ali 2008, 2010, 2012).

With Sunnis unable to access easily or safely the DHQ during the tensions of 2005, my doctoral research also documented the early days of the

---

10 For example, see Hunzai (2013) for a discussion of the Sunni community's perspectives concerning their contemporary political and economic marginalisation "by the Shia-majority government in Gilgit-Baltistan" (7-8).

30-bed 'Sunni' Kashrote Government City Hospital, established as a safe but insufficient alternative to the DHQ. Between 2010 and 2013, I returned to Gilgit-Baltistan to explore how sectarian enmities and recurrent violence continued to shape, amplify and politically differentiate Sunni and Shia forms of identity and belonging, and underpinned the post-2005 establishment of additional hospitals. As this chapter will illustrate, Gilgit's contemporary health services exemplify socially, spatially and symbolically the institutionalisation of sectarian difference in striking ways. Moreover, the sectarian-linked disaggregation of regional health systems is not an isolated phenomenon but occurs alongside similar segregations in Gilgit's educational, economic, police and judicial systems, as well as in its jails and media (Unpublished Police Report; Grieser/Sökefeld 2015[11]). Gilgit's hospitals, like all recent sectarian-linked institutional and infrastructural developments, manifest novel modes of governance that owe their existence to broader historical practices of regional sectarian-aligned development and politicisation, as well as the inter-sectarian and resource-driven competitions, discords and enmities to which they give rise. Rather than try to account fully for the diverse sectarian modalities associated with medical services and health outcomes in Gilgit Town, this chapter instead provides an ethnographic snapshot of the impacts of conflict on hospital access and service provision, and reflects on the role played by sectarianism in emergent health infrastructures, economies and the redistribution of public sector resources at the margins of the state (Das/Poole 2004).

SECTARIAN MEDICAL INFRASTRUCTURES

When I returned to Gilgit in 2010, the DHQ had become associated with Sunni vulnerabilities and deaths. This was more than simply because the DHQ had been the epicentre of January 2005's violence and the targeting and killing of Sunnis in the years to follow (see Express Tribune: March 28,

---

11 Sökefeld/Grieser (2015) provide a detailed discussion of the "sectarianisation" of social space and resources, including the temporary implementation of sectarian transport routes in those areas spatially associated with and politically controlled by Shia and Sunni communities during the renewal of Shia-Sunni tensions, violence and targeted killings in spring 2012 (see Express Tribune: March 28, 2012; Pamir Times: March 31, 2012, April 1, 2012).

2012, Pamir Times: July 20, 2010, March 28, 2012). In explaining why they avoided the hospital, many Sunni interlocutors spoke not only of their on-site insecurities, but also the hospital's conflict-instigated reconfiguration and reimagining as a primarily 'Shia' facility. The DHQ's reconceptualisation in Shia social and political terms arose not merely from the hospital's location in a Shia neighbourhood[12], or from the predominantly Shia and Ismaili composition of its administrators, staff and medical personnel, with many Sunni providers having left to join the Kashrote Hospital after the events of 2005. Because of the DHQ's centrality to Shia accounts of Zia-ud-din's mortal wounding and his ultimately failed emergency treatment, the hospital serves as a space of Shia community loss and the instigative 'flashpoint' for the subsequent tensions of 2005. In turn, the Shia ritual, political and protest practices taking place on and around the site ensure that, for Sunnis, the DHQ operates to symbolise and actualise Shia political agency.

For example, during my fieldwork between 2010 and 2013, Shia religious posters, political graffiti and religio-political flags (some for the Imamia Students Organisation [ISO], whose members were purportedly responsible for the majority of Sunni deaths in January 2005) were found on and around the DHQ site. The congested residential streets surrounding the hospital have also been the scene for Shia political protests and religious commemorations, such as the intense Muharram mourning cycles. Such mourning events are accompanied by collective acts of ritual self-flagellation and mortification, by which Shia histories of injustice and marginalisation during the days of early Islam are evoked in ways which potently corroborate Gilgiti Shias' contemporary experiences of vulnerability and loss. In ways that further illustrate the quotidian interlacing of sectarian and state spaces, a Shia religious flag, emblazoned with the name of Hazrat Ali, the revered first Imam and spiritual progenitor of Shia Islam, was erected 30 feet atop the fortified concrete Army bunker which stands at the DHQ's main entrance. Not coincidentally, this is the location where Sunnis

---

12 Although my interlocutors uniformly referred to the DHQ's location as being in lower Bermas, a Shia-dominated village, the hospital may be more accurately described as being situated at the intersection of Bermas and a number of adjoining neighbourhoods, including Hospital Colony and Majini Mohalla (Personal Correspondence: March 14, 2015). *Mohalla* can be roughly translated to mean 'neighbourhood'.

were injured and killed immediately after Zia-ud-din's 2005 assassination. Sunni physicians and patients remarked that the Army's apparent inability to remove the flag or, at the very least, to prevent Shia rallies from being held at the hospital site, evidenced Sunnis' ongoing logistical vulnerabilities at the DHQ. Sunnis, in turn, understood such practices and events as indicating not only Shia religiosity, but also their socio-spatial and political capture of the DHQ and the "symbolic accretion" (Dwyer 2004: 422) of Shia identity to the site itself.

In response to the post-2005 security challenges associated with the DHQ, and in order to meet the Sunni community's health needs, between 2005 and 2010, two 'Sunni' public sector civil hospitals were built: one in the Sunni-dominated Kashrote Mohalla, a neighbourhood in central Gilgit Town, and the other in Baseen, a predominantly Sunni village located at Gilgit's western edge. While my ethnographic case study of the Sunni 'Kashrote' Hospital is the focus of the latter half of this chapter, the 'Sunni' Baseen Hospital also merits mention. The 30-bed 'Sunni' Civil Hospital in Baseen, for example, was initiated in 2006 using the development funds allocated to Baseen's elected Member of the Legislative Assembly (MLA) and was inaugurated in December 2009. Its origins were instigated, one Medical Officer said, as much by the Baseen community's health impoverishments as by the tensions which hazarded locals' access to the DHQ (Interview: July 9, 2010). However, Baseen's health inequities were poorly remedied by the hospital's services. When I first visited the site in 2010, its general Out-Patient facilities were still under-construction – its services barely functional and manned by one physician assisted by a handful of male volunteers. By 2013, its In-Patient facilities were completed but remained poorly resourced, and the hospital employed few permanent staff. Notwithstanding such deficiencies, a Medical Officer at the Baseen Hospital explained the facility's importance thusly: One patient, who needed surgery, refused to go to the DHQ from his home in Baseen, saying, "I can accept dying a natural death here, but I refuse to accept dying an unnatural death and being killed by a bullet there" (July 9, 2010).

Importantly, it is not only Sunnis whose hospital access has been restricted by Gilgit's tensions. Irrespective of sectarian affiliation, during civil curfews all patients experience profound challenges accessing the DHQ. In turn, this has led to the rise of 'Shia' health facilities. Shia Gilgitis, whose hospital access was hazarded or disrupted by the risks posed by travel to the DHQ through Sunni *mohallas* and villages, have agitated for the diversion of civil, regional and federal funds, in order to construct alternative access routes as well as 'Shia' health facilities, such as the post-2005 development of hospitals in Danyor, a Shia-dominated village located across the Gilgit River from Gilgit Town[13]. In April 2007, Danyor's elected Member of the Legislative Assembly allocated a portion of his development funds to initiate the construction of a 30-bed 'Shia' Civil Hospital. Although its completion was originally slated for the spring of 2008, in 2015 the hospital remains unfinished and non-operational. However, in July 2006, the Sehhat Foundation, a Shia non-governmental organisation based in Karachi, inaugurated a small Maternal and Child Health (MCH) Centre in Danyor. In 2009, construction began for the 25-bed Sehhat Foundation Hospital, which by summer 2011 was completed, well-resourced and operational. Despite its highly regarded clinical services, because of the hospital's location in a village in which Sunnis have been attacked and killed, it acts as a site of symbolic and actual health exclusion, and is considered by Sunnis to be socially inaccessible and unsafe. Conversely, Shia interlocutors justified the establishment of the Danyor Civil Hospital and the completion of the Sehhat Hospital not only through reference to the region's problematic maternal morbidity and mortality ratios, which persist despite the near total medicalisation of reproductive and childbirth health, but also to the Sunni "terrorists" (Interview: June 12, 2012) and *mohallas* which stand between Danyor's residents and the DHQ.

Between 2004 and 2013, I also researched the role played by Gilgit Town's 'Ismaili' health services. Whether during times of peace or crisis, Gilgit's Ismaili community has been considered by Shias and Sunnis to be largely peripheral to the region's violent sectarian contestations. Ismaili interlocutors explained their 'in between' positioning as being the result of their theological solidarity with Shias and social commensality with Sunnis, as well as the ethnic, caste and kinship ancestries which historically overlap and bind each community to the other. The notions of neutrality attributed to Ismailis carried over positively to Ismaili providers, with Ismaili women comprising the majority of paramedical staff in all local public and private hospitals, and Ismaili-affiliated institutions such as the Aga Khan Health Service, Pakistan's (AKHS,P) 40-bed Gilgit Medical Center. But because of its location in the Shia Chenar Bagh Mohalla, Sunnis had experienced

---

13 Danyor is located less than ten kilometres from the site of the 1988 Sunni-orchestrated massacre of approximately 200 Shias in Jalalabad.

challenges accessing and using the hospital's fee-based services, and consequently they made less use of the hospital than Shias and Ismailis. Ismailis, in turn, were comparatively less affected by the conflict's worst outcomes and restrictions than either Shias or Sunnis, with medical personnel and patients able to access and remain at hospital sites regularly, even during times of conflict. However, Ismaili interlocutors spoke of their fear of being caught up in spontaneous violent protests or crossfire during active hostilities. And when military curfews were enacted to contain and prevent violence during tensions, restrictions were imposed on all in-city movements, leading Ismailis to report experiencing health access deprivations on the same scale as Shias and Sunnis.

KASHROTE GOVERNMENT CITY HOSPITAL

Two weeks after Syed Aga Zia-ud-din's assassination in January 2005, Gilgiti Sunnis sought to generate alternative health facilities for those patients and providers now unable to safely access or work at the DHQ site. Sunni politicians and physicians, displaced from their work at the DHQ, proposed the ad hoc establishment of the no- and low-cost Kashrote Hospital, popularly known as the 'Sunni' Hospital. Using community donations, and with services provided on an initially voluntary basis, a Forestry Officer's residence in the Sunni-dominated Kashrote Mohalla was rented and converted into a rough surgery, labour room and 10-bed In-Patient ward. According to Hafeez-ur-Rehman, a Kashrote resident and then-elected Member of the Northern Areas Legislative Assembly (NALA), in its earliest days the facility 'borrowed' the public sector status of a nearby government dispensary so as to facilitate the temporary reallocation and delivery of much-needed medical supplies and equipment from the DHQ:

"The shift happened due to [the] situation.... There was a dispensary in Kashrote Girls' High School. People suggested [to] me to shift the dispensary to outside [of] the school. Then, we went and took over the Forest Office [building] which was nearby." (June 27, 2010)

By summer 2005, Hafeez-ur-Rehman personally funded the construction of an additional 12-bed ward for the women and paediatric patients admitted to the hospital. By this time, the facility was identified as the Kashrote

Government Civil Hospital. However, because there were no facilities for X-rays, ultrasound and most laboratory tests, many patients were forced to continue relying on the DHQ or costly private clinics. Approximately 1500 patients came from across Gilgit-Baltistan to seek treatment each month (Varley 2010: 67), overwhelming the small hospital site and its staff. Despite profound equipment and supply deficits, the facility's services were provided primarily by unpaid Sunni and Ismaili volunteers and healthcare providers. Many of the hospital's Sunni staff had been DHQ employees who had narrowly escaped being killed on January 8th and were thereafter unwilling or unable to return to their posts at the DHQ. (Complicating matters further, for many months after joining the Kashrote Hospital, the staff who had joined from the DHQ received only partial disbursements of their government salaries.) In 2006, the site for a new facility was formally approved by the regional Annual Development Plan (ADP), and by 2007 permission had been granted to start constructing the foundations of a permanent 30-bed hospital on a small plot of land adjacent to the Gilgit River at Kashrote Mohalla's northern edge. In addition to the funds allocated to the hospital by the Regional Administration, support was provided by Hafeez-ur-Rehman's Development Fund and the monies donated by prominent community members. In June 2012, construction began on an additional wing and upgrade to the hospital, which by summer 2014 had been further enlarged to fifty beds and was near completion. In becoming the Kashrote Government City Hospital, the facility's positioning and enfolding into the regional public sector health system and its associative infrastructures was effected.

Notwithstanding the undeniable political advantages and spatial securities afforded by sectarian hospitals, not all Gilgitis were in favour of the establishment of the Kashrote and later the Baseen and Danyor Hospitals. Especially in 2005, many Sunni interlocutors also expressed their concerns that while the Kashrote Hospital provided them with an inarguably safer space in which to seek medical care, it also confirmed their community's failure to assert and protect their 'right' as citizens of Pakistan to access government health services at the DHQ. Many Sunni staff also argued that after January 8th, the hospital was their only safe and viable opportunity for employment in a region they felt was increasingly dominated by Shia and also by Ismaili 'control' over hospital administrations and hiring committees. In these ways and more, the 'Sunni' Hospital operated as a resistive structure which pragmatically countered and also reified Sunni alienation from 'Shia' public sector sites, as well as their experiences of political dispossession, not only in matters of health, but also in regional governance (see Hunzai 2013: 7-8). However, by 2012, and the return of inter-sectarian hostilities[14], Shias, Sunnis and Ismailis seemed equally resigned to the need for the hospital's existence, even if it was also apparent that the reallocation of scarce government health resources to Gilgit's emerging sectarian medical infrastructures, combined with the sectarian demographics inherent in Gilgit-Baltistan's health systems, had resulted in striking difficulties.

For example, the state and degree of functionality of the DHQ and the Kashrote Hospital (as well as Gilgit's other sectarian hospitals) were seen as evidence of the uneven division of regional resources along lines of affiliation. Issues of resource allocation were then made manifest by the types of care available to each community, with the DHQ's services used predominantly by Shias and Ismailis, and the Kashrote Hospital almost wholly attended by Sunnis. For example, the Kashrote Hospital's establishment and initial status as a 'dispensary' led to the impoverishment of the DHQ's stores of medication, supplies and equipment. Moreover, because Gilgit's cadre of public sector specialist physicians were predominantly Sunnis, following 2005, the DHQ lost most of its specialists to the Kashrote Hospital. Notwithstanding the DHQ's larger resource and equipment base, the exodus of Sunni specialists led to critical deficits in service coverage for its patients. In comparison, the health and security benefits ostensibly afforded by the Kashrote Hospital and its larger cadre of specialists have been historically offset by high patient loads and a lack of essential medicines, supplies and working equipment.

Echoing the views of many Sunni community members, interlocutors from across the sectarian divide spoke angrily of the Kashrote Hospital's condition:

---

14 My 2010 return to Gilgit-Baltistan, for additional ethnographic fieldwork, coincided with the renewal of protracted hostilities and bloodshed. Then, in ways which further compounded the politics and practices of inter-sectarian dissention, in the spring and summer of 2012, upwards of thirty Shias, Sunnis and Ismailis were killed in targeted attacks in Gilgit Town, while an estimated fifty Shias and five Sunnis were massacred on three separate occasions on the Karakoram Highway and the Naran-Kaghan Route interconnecting Gilgit to Islamabad, Pakistan's capital.

"Sunnis are basically cut off from basic resources, because they can't go to the DHQ, and even though they've built an alternate hospital, it's in a terrible condition. If you go, there is no oxygen, no medication [and] no surgical preparedness." (July 27, 2012)

Such deficiencies produced particularly acute challenges for maternity patients, for whom there has been erratic specialist coverage for complex cases and those requiring surgical intervention in particular. As is true for nearly all public sector facilities across Gilgit-Baltistan, in deference to Islamic and traditional concerns for gender segregation, gynaecological and obstetrical services are provided by female paramedical staff, nurses and physicians. However, the historic shortage of female physicians working in the region has resulted in public hospitals being forced to rotate and overburden a small cadre of short-term and permanent Sunni, Ismaili and Shia obstetrician-gynaecologists (OB-GYNs). It has also meant that between 2005 and 2013, the DHQ, Kashrote and Baseen Hospitals' Labour Room services were provided predominantly by Lady Health Visitors (LHVs), midwives with advanced clinical training who are typically tasked to work in those facilities across Gilgit-Baltistan where specialised providers were not usually available[15]. At the Kashrote Hospital, for instance, maternity services were provided nearly exclusively by LHVs, who were intermittently supported and supervised by a series of Ismaili and Sunni public and contracted private sector physicians[16]. However, when physicians left the hospital because of its challenging working conditions, or for safer or more lucrative opportunities, the hospital's Labour Room operated for stretches without any specialist coverage. (In 2006, the hospital's first obstetrician-gynaecologist, a Sunni who had joined the facility in January 2005, refused to continue providing services at the facility, citing her concerns for the multiple dangers posed to patients by the hospital's services [Interview: Ju-

---

15 Though used to handling complex and often dangerous obstetrical cases because of insufficient physician coverage, LHVs in Gilgit are an inadequate substitute for advanced clinical and surgical care.

16 By summer 2013, a permanent specialist physician was seconded to join the Kashrote Hospital from her full-time duties at the District Headquarter Hospital, which left each clinically overburdened hospital with only one specialist woman obstetrician-gynaecologist.

ly 2, 2010].) In 2011, an Ismaili nurse at the DHQ spoke of the Health Department's apparent lack of commitment to the hospital and its patients:

"They are not doing justice with them [at]... the Kashrote Hospital, because the Sunni community are not coming [to the DHQ] because they're scared due to these clashes. There should be a gynaecologist there, too, because they are also human beings.... They're not taking care of them. The government is not paying attention to them and to that hospital." (July 2, 2011)

Uneven healthcare provider coverage, the risks of which were compounded by the hospital's insufficiencies, meant that a significant number of complicated obstetrical cases were routinely referred to the DHQ. Indeed, it was precisely because of the Kashrote Hospital's poor services and the high costs of Gilgit's private sector hospitals[17] that many Sunnis continued to seek care regularly at the DHQ, albeit in lesser numbers than they had before January 2005. The DHQ's greater degree of medical resources therefore ensured a continued degree of inter-sectarian contact, however fraught and high-risk it may have been for Sunnis. Yet, as the DHQ and Kashrote Hospital records, my interlocutors' narratives and my own observations attest, during tensions, Sunni patients and attendants hastily evacuate the hospital, often without notifying providers, in order to escape to the socially 'safer' but medically inefficacious Kashrote Hospital.

Sunni patients often reserved their harshest criticisms for the Kashrote Hospital's healthcare providers, whose work, they felt, was characterised by a lack of investment in or a commitment to their patients. Such claims were not far removed from the critiques offered by physicians' former colleagues at the DHQ, one of whom argued, "We are doing duties [while] they are resting. I mean, [the Kashrote Hospital's providers] are in their homes, they are not working!" (Interview: July 2, 2011). Such commentaries highlighted what interlocutors from across the sectarian divide perceived was Sunnis' moral disregard for one another, showing that the quali-

---

17 Other than the Kashrote Hospital, for Sunnis the only other physically accessible, but for many economically inaccessible, hospitals have been the Family Health Hospital, run by the Rahnuma-Family Planning Association of Pakistan (FPAP), and the Pakistan Army's Combined Military Hospital (CMH), both of which are located in Jutial Mohalla, an inter-sectarian neighbourhood which abuts Gilgit Town's Army Cantonment.

ty of care or its absence were capable of indexing what many argued was the tension-instigated weakening of in-community social, political and also therapeutic bonds. These findings also indicated that the Sunni preference for same-sect care was often more reflective of the logistical securities afforded by the hospital site than the medical benefits derived from same-sect treatment. In response to such critiques, the Kashrote Hospital's Sunni providers contested characterisations of their work by their patients, as well as other sectarian actors, as being erratic, unfocused or risky. They spoke vehemently of their inability to provide safe medical care amidst the hospital's stark insufficiencies, and they pointed to the challenges they faced even reaching the hospital from their homes in other *mohallas* during crises, confirming that providers, like patients, were not exempt from conflict-related restrictions in relation to their social mobility and hospital access. In turn, physician fatigue and burnout compounded the increasingly regular absences of key specialist personnel from their duties. This was especially true for those healthcare providers who were tasked with multiple, complex responsibilities and clinical supervision for hundreds of patients a day, such as when physicians provided coverage for both In-Patient and Out-Patient Department services.

My Sunni interlocutors were aware of the potent challenges posed by unevenly practiced and sometimes dangerously under-resourced services. With nearly 1000 patients seeking treatment at the facility every day (Interview: June 11, 2012), the hospital had the obvious potential to further compound Sunnis' already imperilled community health indicators. I observed how the adverse health outcomes arising from the hospital's services were poorly captured by, intentionally misreported or excluded entirely from the clinical records maintained in each ward. Such risks have also not gone unnoticed by Gilgit's broader publics, local politicians and the media. For example, recent coverage of the hospital has focused on protests by community members following acts of purported malpractice and patient death (see Dawn: February 6, 2012; Express Tribune: May 31, 2013; IHROGB: February 1, 2014; Pamir Times: January 20, 2014; Right Now: January 20, 2014), and it has also identified the hospital as a site for the production of bio-hazards and disease, rather than their alleviation (see IHROGB: March 23, 2013; Pamir Times: November 13, 2010).

On one level, the Kashrote Hospital's structural and medical dysfunctions were conceived as representing the fractured state of Sunni community integrity and self-governance, thereby permitting Sunnis dynamic, if also discomforting, forms of political reflection and cultural self-critique. Importantly, many such narratives contrasted the Sunni community's politico-moral impoverishments against their understanding of Shias' in-community allegiance and political integrity[18]:

"Sunnis, they don't know what to do... they're disorganised. I've never seen anything like it. Disorganised.... Many of our own [people] think only about their own families, about our own lives; if we can do something, we will do something. But in one united way, like the other [sects] in Gilgit, we can't do it." (March 16, 2012)

Sunni political incapacity was also thought to be evidenced by the hospital's infrastructural and security deficiencies. For instance, in early 2010, the Medical Superintendent acknowledged the site was smaller than the regulated allotment required for a hospital of its size. Built as it was on sandy soil, only metres from the Gilgit River, the hospital's precarity was exacerbated by the summer 2010 monsoon floods. In late July, the rising Gilgit River first washed away the rock-built retaining wall that had been constructed to protect the site from erosion, and then it inundated the hospital and damaged its foundations. Then, during violent sectarian tensions in April 2012, the hospital was caught in crossfire between Sunni police officers and the residents of a Shia *mohalla* on the opposite side of the river, which led to additional protections being built atop the hospital's roof. By 2013, many portions of the hospital, then only a few years old, were in a poor condition because of the sub-standard quality of construction materials and workmanship; cracks zigzagged across the inside of the facility's rooms, leaks resulted in blooms of mould on interior walls and ceilings and electrical outlets frequently short-circuited.

When such problems first became evident in early 2010, the politician Hafeez-ur-Rehman, who had initiated the hospital in 2005, held little hope that they would be remedied on account of the multiple dysfunctions of Gilgit's political process:

"You know, so much corruption is in us these days; it very strongly embedded in our people. [The Health] Secretary visited and I have shown [him] all [the] departments.

---

18 Interestingly, Sunnis' critiques appear to parallel other researchers' findings concerning the ways in which Gilgit-Baltistan's Shias and Ismailis, like Sunnis, are critical of their community's unity and organisation.

There [will be] an inquiry about the hospital, and the inquiring people will take money and nothing will happen." (June 27, 2010)

Because the facility relied on the same broader civil infrastructures that support all of Gilgit's public sector services, it also regularly went without water or electricity, and it had no formal waste management structure in place to deal with the sometimes highly contaminative refuse. Instead, biohazardous materials were dumped in a pit on the hospital's perimeter, with the result that much of the waste was ultimately washed into the Gilgit River, which is a source of irrigation and drinking water for a number of residents (see Pamir Times: November 23, 2010).

Concerns for the Sunni community's haphazard planning, maintenance and securitisation of the site were often secondary to more strident complaints from community members and politicians regarding the hospital's resource deficiencies, which were definitively correlated with the quality and effectiveness of treatment and implicated in clinical health outcomes. Indeed, with Shias especially having gained significantly more governmental representation and control over politico-economic capital and public sector resources in the 2009 elections, the paucity of medical supplies at the Kashrote Hospital, especially in its early years of operation, was argued to signal the under-prioritisation of Sunnis' security and health needs by Gilgit-Baltistan's now predominantly Shia and Ismaili government officials. With Gilgiti Sunnis being historically, if not always accurately, understood to be more closely affiliated with, or 'loyal' to the Sunni-majority State of Pakistan (see Ali 2009, 2010, 2012), one interlocutor described the state's failure to intervene and remedy either the inequities experienced by Sunni patients at the DHQ or the Kashrote Hospital's deficits as a betrayal of Sunnis' political "sincerity" (*mokhlees*) (Interview: July 27, 2012) and pro-state orientation. Through such sectarian optics, the Kashrote Hospital's supply deficits were described by Sunni interlocutors as manifesting the enactment of harm against them, not only by 'Shias', but also by the Gilgit-Baltistan administration and the 'Sunni' state. As was also true for many Shias and Ismailis, for a growing number of Sunnis the state's failures, absences and corruptions added political credence to and hardened their calls for the region's independence (*azaadi*) from Pakistan.

Sunni frustrations with and critiques of Gilgit's sectarian medical infrastructures and economies were echoed to an important degree by those shared by many Shia interlocutors. For instance, several claimed that the

DHQ's post-2005 lack of specialist service coverage constituted evidence of the ways in which the State of Pakistan was in its own way 'guilty' of differential investments in Gilgit's Shia community. With a share of its medication, equipment and also personnel siphoned off to support the Kashrote Hospital, the DHQ was also a site bereft of necessary administration and resources (see Dawn: October 15, 2008, July 15, 2011; Brooshal Times: December 2, 2013; Pamir Times: October 3, 2010, October 3, 2012, June 29, 2014). Such shortages were in many striking ways similar to those at the Kashrote Hospital, and they were also described as signalling the state's neglect of Pakistan's ethnic and religious minorities – and Gilgit-Baltistan's Shias in particular. Gilgiti Shias' experiences of health marginalisation and adverse health outcomes at the DHQ (see IHROGB: May 24, 2013), in turn, were invoked as mirroring the burden of bodily threat and political disempowerment endured by Shias country-wide. More problematically, the DHQ's expanding insufficiencies were attributed to the predominantly Shia health officials and administrators who, some argued, mismanaged the facility. Alternatively, they were described as representing the regional government's disinvestment in the hospital and its patients. In turn, some Shia interlocutors pointed to the challenges they faced in critiquing the Health Department[19] which, after 2009, was predominantly populated by Shia bureaucrats and elected and appointed health officials, the reservation to speak against other members of the Shia community having become bound up with the heightened importance of in-community 'loyalty' during crisis.

Despite the proven consequences of the tensions in relation to Sunnis' use of public health services, even as late as 2013, few Shia government officials or healthcare providers were willing to speak directly about the ways in which Sunni patient migrations away from the DHQ, and the establishment of the Kashrote and Baseen Hospitals, were the by-products of unresolved inter-sectarian tensions and civil insecurities. For example, an Ismaili nurse recounted how her Shia colleagues at the DHQ had protested against the Kashrote Hospital's establishment using funds, resources and

---

19 Between 2009 and 2015, the Health and Population Welfare Department was helmed by a Sunni, the Minister for Health, Hajji Gulbar Khan; an elected member and the leader for the Jamiat Ulema-e-Islam (JUI-F) from the Tangir Valley in Diamer District.

staff diverted from the DHQ. They also criticised Sunnis' subsequent patronage of the hospital:

"[They] are saying, 'Why are they making a hospital over there? Why are they not coming to the [DHQ]? Are we murdering them? We are not murdering them!' But... look, how can we tell them that if they have any problem, that under that condition, [Shias] will [not] do these things again. Why won't they come over here? Because their lives are also important. I know the whole situation. I know each and everything. In 2005, I was here." (July 2, 2011)

Not all interlocutors were unwilling to recognise the undeniable risks bound up with inter-sectarian relations and hospital sites during tensions, and many were deeply saddened by the transition from shared to segregated lives. The narrative accounts shared by one Sunni physician, who had maintained her primary duties at the DHQ while also providing auxiliary surgical coverage to the Kashrote Hospital in 2005 and 2006, were inflected both by trauma caused by the crisis as well as her loss of the social and, as Gilgitis' prior shared use of hospitals had demonstrated, therapeutic commensalities which had joined each sect to the other.

"Before the tension, we all treated each other equally and we used to go to each community's houses [for] eating and dining.... We used to help each other. At that time we put aside all differences. Now the situation has totally changed." (July 2, 2010)

While the tensions eroded some commensalities in a number of key respects, they nevertheless afforded other commensalities to be established or built back up in meaningful and novel ways.

One retired Ismaili nurse, who had served at the Kashrote Hospital when it was first established in 2005, remembered how it had facilitated site-specific affirmation of Ismailis' and Sunnis' commensalities, which were at once professional and also informed by the broader forms of peace and stability historic to Ismaili-Sunni relations[20] across Gilgit-Baltistan:

---

20 The comparatively more amicable relations between Sunnis and Ismailis, a subsect of Shia Islam, serve as compelling proof that Gilgit's tensions are not always solely religious in nature but also reflect the social, economic and political contestations specific to Shia-Sunni relations.

"We were friendly, and it had a good atmosphere. It was very good back then, but we were *majboorh* [helpless]. There was no equipment. Patients came from everywhere, and Sunni patients couldn't go to the DHQ." (Nurse: July 8, 2010)

Importantly, in the spring of 2005, a number of physicians proposed to establish an inter-sectarian community medical outreach service which, because the hospitals were difficult or impossible to access during conflict or curfews, would help resolve patients' unmet treatment needs. More than this, such an outreach provision was envisioned as a means of rehabilitating and renewing the commensalities undermined by the tensions, thereby offsetting the cultures of exclusion emerging from the DHQ and the 'Sunni' Kashrote Hospital. For instance, one Sunni senior Medical Officer recounted her efforts in 2005 to start medical camps, named after the most prominent victims of January 8th: Syed Zia-ud-din Rizvi and Dr Sher Wali Khan, the Sunni Director of the Health Department:

"After the curfew, I asked my colleagues here to start medical camps in Bermas named 'Sher Wali' Camps, and another camp should be started in Kashrote called 'Zia-ud-din.' Yes, I thought this would be a wonderful step towards peace, you know? But they said it was a critical time, not a good time, for such a thing. Who knows, maybe when things get better... What agencies and departments can fix this situation? I don't know." (September 7, 2005)

The comradery afforded by serving together during periods of acute crisis and insufficiency facilitated, albeit in different ways, Ismailis' relations with Sunnis at the Kashrote Hospital and Shias at the DHQ. The commensalities which resulted, though, were not merely medico-professional in nature; they also reaffirmed the political and economic importance of some sectarian connections rather than others. In turn, the distances forged between Shias and Sunnis by conflict resulted in complex forms of alienation, meaning that over the last two decades each sect has become increasingly emotionally disconnected, 'strange' (*ajaib*) and unfamiliar to the other, as one Sunni physician lamented during an administrative meeting at the DHQ:

"Now, since the last 15 years, or 20 years, there is a sect-wise exclusion.... There [are] Ismaili community schools, Sunni community schools and there [are] Shia community schools... [Children have] got no communication with each... other.

Their parents have got no communication with each... other, and they've got no sympathy for each other." (July 17, 2012)

In her analysis of the aftermath of the 2005 tensions, Nosheen Ali (2008) qualifies how such processes of estrangement and 'othering' reflect and are generated by sectarian imaginaries, through which "Shia and Sunni Muslim communities in Gilgit imagine, feel about and relate to each other, and the subtle ways in which sectarian anxieties are experienced and reproduced in everyday life" (Ali 2010: 739)[21]. As my interlocutors' narratives confirm, such imaginaries were not unique to times of tension, and to an important degree they were sustained by the politico-sectarian qualities, affiliations and forms of display unique to each hospital. Indeed, in much the same way that the DHQ site served as a site for Shia commemoration, ritual display and signalling, the Kashrote and the Baseen hospitals also took on distinctively Sunni 'traits'. Over time, Sunni accoutrements, such as the flags of the predominantly Sunni Jamiat Ulema-e-Islam (JUI-F) party, or 'wallchalking' (graffiti) promoting Sunni politicians' campaigns or anti-Shia slogans and militancy organisations (such as the banned Sipah-e-Sahaba [SSP]), have appeared in and around each facility. And where Shia voluntary and charitable organisations circulated at the DHQ, the presence of Sunni-affiliated organisations, such as the Al-Khidmat Trust, helped reify the Kashrote Hospital's sectarian affiliation. The interconnections between sect and site have become so fixed that when the local media is unable or unwilling to note victims' sects during tensions, simply knowing to which hospital a patient or body is transferred establishes their sectarian identity.

---

21 Where Ali (2010) speaks of the sectarian imaginaries, in his analysis of Gilgitis' relations with and thoughts on Pathans, who formerly comprised a significant proportion of Gilgit Town's traders, Sökefeld (1998a) attends to the imageries, prejudices and stereotypes animating inter-ethnic relations. These, he remarks, serve to prevent closer social contact and are ultimately self-enforcing, in that "stereotypes and interaction are interdependent [and] connected by relations of mutual structuration" (297).

Discussion and Conclusion

In many of the same ways that armed ethnic or sectarian conflicts expose identity-related fault lines and socio-spatial precarity in divided cities such as Belfast and Beirut, Gilgit Town's Shia-Sunni hostilities demonstrate how identity risks and violence are distributed among and over-represented by some of Pakistan's most economically, politically and logistically marginalised citizens. In turn, the social segregations and health deprivations observed and imagined to be produced through and sustained by differential service provision, and reinforced by recurrent acts of violence on hospital sites, mark sectarianism's pervasive and often inescapable effects. And while the emergence of sect-specific medical infrastructures, and the inequitable patterns of illness and death they produce, call our attention to the enduring impacts of conflict on the organisation and distribution of healthcare resources, the violent atmospherics and lasting insecurities associated with Gilgit's tensions illustrate the need for ethnographers to question the analytical distinction typically applied to distinguish between conflict and post-conflict states (see Varma 2014). Such realities destabilise popular understandings of hospitals as neutral facilities, capable of reducing Shia-Sunni enmity through medical care which is guided by the therapeutic rather than sectarian impulse, and they have meant that not only during crisis but also in the uneasy periods which follow, the states of the Kashrote Government City and District Headquarter Hospitals mirror the condition of Gilgit's sectarian body politics.

With health facilities acting as sites for the enactment of conflictive sectarianism, providers' and patients' experiences crystallise the cultural, moral, political and sectarian imaginaries by which local hostilities are interpreted and the state assessed. For instance, the DHQ's numerous insecurities, when considered in conjunction with the hazards posed by Gilgit's under-staffed and poorly resourced sectarian facilities, serve as analytical and narrative platforms for Gilgitis' understandings of state dysfunction and governance gaps. Indeed, the failure of the regional and national governments to ensure equitable service provision, improve civil security and, more importantly, reduce hospital-based hazards reinforced my interlocutors' broader dissatisfaction with the state's neglect of Gilgit-Baltistan and its people; discontent which is shared by and to an ironic degree unifies Gilgit's otherwise at-siege sectarian communities. Hospitals also operate as forums for novel forms of sectarian biosocial and political organisation, as well as conflict-enabled professional commensalities such as those between Ismailis and Sunnis or Shias. In turn, the unique deprivations experienced by each hospital and its staff and patients are reflected in Gilgitis' political imaginaries as evidence of the imposition of exclusions, neglect and harm, however differently configured and operationalised, against each community by their sectarian others or the state – or both. Further interwoven into my interlocutors' critiques were their concerns for the ways in which hospitals upheld, rather than reduced, the sectarian intransigencies dividing Sunnis from Shias, as well as their abiding concerns for the quality and effectiveness of the services offered at each site.

Furthermore, sectarian hospitals demonstrate the failure of the state to enforce either civil security or the basic principles of non-discriminatory medical service provision. The existence of Gilgit's public sector sectarian hospitals highlights the peculiar and often irreconcilable tension between citizens' need for security and the principles of secular health governance, whereby Pakistan's government hospitals are explicitly configured as 'neutral' institutions which are affected by, but not productive of, forms of exclusionary governance and politicisation. So, while Gilgit's hospitals are constitutionally mandated to provide "medical relief for all such citizens irrespective of sex, caste, creed or race" (Zafar 2007: 16), it is a mandate which has become pragmatically impossible to achieve. Instead, the town's sectarian hospitals serve as sites for identity formation and the emergence of new forms of sectarian sociality, as well as the sometimes traumatic spaces in which the values specific to conflict and which drive sectarian rather than inter-sectarian commensality and politicisation are generated. In turn, the incapability of Gilgit's health systems to meaningfully accommodate sectarian differences, or to stand as a bulwark against Shia-Sunni hostilities, represents the government's inability or unwillingness to adequately secure hospital sites and thereby permit inter-sectarian care or, at the greater level, quell or develop lasting responses to the hostilities. Gilgit's sectarian hospitals should not be understood only in terms of their safeties, as sites commensurate with areas of sectarian-exclusive spatial and social control, because, as inescapably and inherently sectarianised spaces, they are also incommensurate with the political and moral aspirations of many Gilgitis for an end to the hostilities, and for secular public sector services once more to be freely available and accessible to all citizens.

The permeability of hospitals to sectarianism, and my interlocutors' narrative assessments of hospitals as products of sectarian history and socio-spatial extensions of communities themselves, guides us to another level of interpretation. Recent medical ethnographies of hospitals, especially in Global South settings that are characterised by poverty or instability (see Street/Coleman 2012, Street 2012, Sullivan 2012), demonstrate a growing appreciation for Foucault's concept of heterotopia, which permits critical analysis of the complex, multi-layered, socio-spatial and temporal qualities of hospital spaces. Where traditional ethnographies of hospitals tend to overemphasise them as places "set off and isolated from everyday social space" and governed by their own "complex systems of social control and order" (Street/Coleman 2012: 5), Street and Coleman argue this is an analytical fiction (Ibid: 5). In countering the myopia of prior analysis, they draw on Foucault to define hospitals as heterotopic "spaces of multiple orderings" (Ibid: 5) in which "social control and… alternative and transgressive social orders emerge and are contested" (Ibid: 4). Their work displaces treatments of hospitals as being "a place apart" (Ibid: 5), in favour of an analysis thereof as "simultaneously bounded and permeable" and where "the core values and beliefs of a culture come into view" (Van Der Geest/Finkler 2004: 1996). Indeed, by evaluating the socio-sectarian texture of medical services at the Kashrote Hospital, my work responds to Street and Coleman's call for medical anthropologists to mobilise heterotopia, in order to attend better to the "'multiformality' [and] complexity, variability, and unpredictability inherent to" (2012: 6) clinical facilities and health systems. Heterotopia therefore facilitates my analysis of Gilgit's hospitals, not only in their integrity and uniqueness, but also as microcosms of the social domains and cultural contexts in which they are embedded.

Ultimately, Gilgit's sectarian hospitals are more than simply ethnographic "truth spots" (Gieryn 2006 in Street/Coleman 2012: 5) or vantage points. Their very presence, when combined with the conflict-instigated recalibration of their services and the sites on which they are located, signifies the evermore intractable condensation, intensification and "hardening" (Dwyer 2004: 422) of Shia-Sunni enmity. As segregated infrastructures, they also serve as sites for the formation of broadly political, professional as well as intimately therapeutic social collectives. Gilgit's sectarian hospitals are also the spaces in which we may more closely "examine the shifting boundaries between material and immaterial structures" (Lokrem/Lugo 2012) in everyday and exceptional contexts, and assess the forms of power, identity and belonging they produce. And rather than seeing sectarian hospitals as a temporary phenomenon, Gilgit's ongoing tensions confirm they are likely to endure for the long term. Because Gilgit Town's sectarian medical infrastructures owe their existence to conflict, hospitals manifest sectarian-linked forms of power and represent the comparatively greater investment of Gilgitis in the perpetuation of conflict than in processes of peace and reconciliation. With medical resources harnessed as vehicles for the rise and concretisation of sectarian privilege or exclusion, 'Shia' and 'Sunni' hospitals therefore serve as symbolic, material and eminently political evidence of the divisive consequences of violent sectarianism. And by functioning as safe sites for some sectarian actors rather than all, they also signify the emergence of novel modes of medico-political segregation and securitisation which are likely to endure as long as sectarian tensions remain.

REFERENCES

Aase, Tor H. (1999): "The Theological Construction of Conflict: Gilgit, Northern Pakistan." In: Leif Manger (ed.), Muslim Diversity: Local Islam in Global Contexts, London: Curzon Press, pp. 58-79.

Ali, Nosheen (2008): "Outrageous State, Sectarianized Citizens: Deconstructing the 'Textbook Controversy' in the Northern Areas, Pakistan." In: South Asia Multidisciplinary Academic Journal, Special Issue - Nb. 2, 'Outraged Communities': Comparative Perspectives on the Politicization of Emotions in South Asia. (http://samaj.revues.org/document 1172.html, accessed January 1, 2009).

Ali, Nosheen (2009): States of Struggle: Politics, Religion, and Ecology in the Making of the Northern Areas, Pakistan, Cornell University: Department of Sociology, Unpublished Doctoral Thesis.

Ali, Nosheen (2010): "Sectarian Imaginaries: The Micropolitics of Sectarianism and State-making in Northern Pakistan." In: Current Sociology 58/5, pp. 738–754.

Ali, Nosheen (2012): "Poetry, Power, Protest: Reimagining Muslim Nationhood in Northern Pakistan." In: Comparative Studies of South Asia, Africa and the Middle East 32/1, pp. 13-24.

Ali, Nosheen (2013): "Grounding Militarism: Structures of Feeling and Force in Gilgit-Baltistan." In: Kalpana Visweswaran (ed.), Everyday Occupations: Experiencing Militarism in South Asia and the Middle East, Philadelphia: University of Pennsylvania Press, pp. 85-114.

Anderson, Helle Max (2004): "'Villagers': Differential treatment in a Ghanaian hospital." In: Social Science & Medicine 59, pp. 2003-2012.
Annandale, David D./Hagler Bailly Pakistan (Pvt) Ltd. (2014): Strategic Environmental Assessment of the Master Plan for Gilgit City, Islamabad: IUCN Pakistan.
Brooshal Times (December 2, 2013): "All DHQ hospitals in tatters." (http://urdu.brooshaaltimes.com/popup.php?lang=en&r_date=12-02-2013&story=12-02-2013page-1-4 and http://brooshaaltimes.com/dhq-hospitals-tatters; accessed December 11, 2013).
Brown, Hannah (2011): "Hospital domestics: Care work in a Kenyan Hospital." In: Space and Culture 15/1, pp. 18-30.
Das, Veena/Poole, Deborah (2004): "State and Its Margins: Comparative Ethnographies." In: Veena Das/Deborah Poole (eds.), Anthropology in the Margins of the State, Santa Fe, NM: School of American Research Press, pp. 3-33.
Davidson, Joyce/Milligan, Christine (2004): "Embodying emotion sensing space: Introducing emotional geographies." In: Social & Cultural Geography 5/4, pp. 523-532.
Dawn (October 15, 2008): "DHQ Hospital at Gilgit.", (http://www.dawn.com/news/867902/dhq-hospital-at-gilgit; accessed January 2, 2015).
Dawn (August 3, 2010): "Bashir Ahmed elected opposition leader in GBLA" (http://www.dawn.com/news/550908/bashir-ahmed-elected-opposition-leader-in-gbla; accessed August 11, 2010).
Dawn (February 6, 2012): "Gilgit plunges into darkness." (http://dawn.com.news/693538/gilgit-plunges-into-darkness; accessed February 7, 2012).
Dwyer, Owen J. (2004): "Symbolic accretion and commemoration." In: Social & Cultural Geography 5/3, pp. 419-435.
Express Tribune (March 28, 2012): "Daring escapade: Police escort under fire, prisoner escapes with accomplices." (http://tribune.com.pk/story/356100/daring-escapade-police-escort-under-fire-prisoner-escapes-with-accomplices/; accessed March 2, 2014).
Express Tribune (May 31, 2013): Endless deaths: Inquiry ordered into infant, maternal mortality at G-B hospitals." (http://tribune.com.pk/story/556588/endless-deaths-inquiry-ordered-into-infant-maternal-mortality-at-g-b-hospitals/; accessed June 2, 2013).
Fassin, Didier (2008): "The elementary forms of care: An empirical approach to ethics in a South African hospital." In: Social Science & Medicine 67, pp. 262-270.

Grieser, Anna/Sökefeld, Martin (2015): "Intersections of sectarian dynamics and spatial mobility in Gilgit-Baltistan." In: Stefan Conermann and Elena Smolarz (eds.), Mobilizing Religion: Networks and Mobility, Berlin: EB-Verlag, pp. 83-110.

Hamdy, Sherine F. (2008): "When the state and your kidneys fail: Political etiologies in an Egyptian dialysis ward." In: American Ethnologist 35/4, pp. 553-569.

Hunzai, Izhar (2013): "Conflict Dynamics in Gilgit-Baltistan", United States Institute of Peace December 9, 2013 (http://www.usip.org/sites/default/files/SR321.pdf).

International Human Rights Observer Gilgit-Baltistan (March 23, 2013): "The heaps of garbage inside the City Hospital Gilgit speaks in volumes about the inability of Health Department Gilgit Baltistan." (https://www.facebook.com/pages/International-Human-Rights-Observer-Gilgit-Baltistan; accessed March 25, 2013).

International Human Rights Observer Gilgit-Baltistan (May 24, 2013): "The death of a mother and child from Nagar in DHQ Hospital Gilgit due to the negligence and child indifference from a Lady Doctor is human and atrocity." (https://www.facebook.com/permalink.php?id=302681576524970&story_fbid=335749796551481; accessed May 25, 2013).

International Human Rights Observer Gilgit-Baltistan (February 1, 2014): "A new born child breathed his last due to the negligence of GYN at City Hospital Gilgit." (https://www.facebook.com/pages/International-Human-Rights-Observer-Gilgit-Baltistan; accessed February 1, 2013).

Jaffre, Yannick. (2012): "Towards an anthropology of public health priorities: Maternal mortality in four obstetric emergency services in West Africa." Social Anthropology/Anthropologie Sociale, 20 (1): 3-18.

Karrar, Mariam/Iqbal, Affan/Mubarak, Sarosh (2011): Report on Gilgit City: October 2011, Urban Research & Design Cell: Karachi, 243 pages.

Larkin, Brian (2013): "The Politics and Poetics of Infrastructure." In: Annual Review of Anthropology 42, pp. 327-343.

Lokrem, Jessica/Lugo, Adonia (November 26 2012): "Infrastructure: Editorial Introduction." Curated Collections, Cultural Anthropology Online: http://www.culanth.org/curated_collections/11-infrastructure; accessed January 2, 2015.

Pamir Times (July 20, 2010): "Patient shot dead in Gilgit hospital, alleged Burqa clad culprit flees." http://pamirtimes.net/2010/07/20/patient-shot-dead-in-gilgit-hospital-alleged-burqa-clad-culprit-flees/; accessed April 3, 2014.

Pamir Times (October 3, 2010). "Secretary Health GB visits DHQ Hospital in Gilgit." (http://pamirtimes.net/2010/10/03/doctors-to-be-appointed-on-contarct-in-gilgit-baltistan; accessed October 20, 2010).

Pamir Times (November 23, 2010). "Field based study: Solid waste assessment of Gilgit town." (http://pamirtimes.net/2010/11/23/field-based-study-solid-waste-assessment-of-gilgit-town/; accessed January 29, 2015).

Pamir Times (October 3, 2012). "Pictorial: Inside and around the DHQ Hospital Gilgit." (http://pamirtimes.net/2012/10/03/pictorial-in-and-around-the-dhq-hospital-gilgit/; accessed October 10, 2012).

Pamir Times (March 28, 2012). "Gilgit: Masked men free murder convict, two police officials injured." (http://pamirtimes.net/2012/03/28/gilgit-masked-men-free-murder-convict-two-police-officials-injured/; accessed February 27, 2014).

Pamir Times (January 20, 2014). "Residents of Kashrote staged a protest demonstration against the MS of City Hospital. They demanded inquiry into the death of two people at the hospital." (https://www.flickr.com/photos/ptgallery/12053405284/; accessed January 30, 2014).

Pamir Times (June 29, 2014). "[Pictory] A day without electricity at DHQ Hospital Gilgit." (http://pamirtimes.net/2014/06/29/pictory-day-without-electricity-dhq-hospital-gilgit/; accessed July 7, 2014).

Pinto, Sarah (2004): "Development without institutions: Ersatz medicine and the politics of everyday life in rural North India." In: Cultural Anthropology 19/3, pp. 337-364.

Presentation by Inspector General of Police (2011): http://urban.unhabitat.org.pk/Portals/0/Portal_Contents/Balochistan/Turbat/Police%20Deptt%20GB.pdf; accessed April 19, 2012.

Rahman, A. (1999): Northern Health Project (NHP): Northern Areas baseline survey, Karachi: Abdur Rahman Associates.

Rieck, Andreas (1995): "Sectarianism as a Political Problem in Pakistan: The Case of Northern Areas." In: Orient 36/3, pp. 429-448.

Right Now (January 20, 2014): "Protest against MS City Hospital Kashrote." (http://www.rightnow.io/breaking-news/gilgit-ms-city-hospital_bn_1390235340957.html; accessed February 2, 2014).

Settle, Antonia (2010): "Paper presented at the First International Development Conference of Syria, organised by the Syria Trust for Development, Damascus 23-24 January 2010." (www.syriatrust.sy/sites/default/files/u19/antonia%20settle.pdf; accessed January 17, 2012).

Settle, Antonia (2011): "The new development paradigm through the lens of the Aga Khan Rural Support Programme: legitimacy, accountability and the political sphere." In: Community Development Journal 47/3, pp. 386-404.

Smith, Catherine (2015): "Doctors that Harm, Doctors that Heal: Reimagining Medicine in Post-Conflict Aceh, Indonesia." In: Ethnos: Journal of Anthropology 80/2, pp. 272-291.

Sousa, Cindy/Hagopian, Amy (2011): "Conflict, health care and professional perseverance: A qualitative study in the West Bank." In: Global Public Health 6/5, pp. 520-533.

Sökefeld, Martin (1998a): "Stereotypes and Boundaries: Paṭhān in Gilgit, Northern Pakistan." In: V.V. Kushev/N.L. Luzhetskaia/L. Rzehak (eds.), Central Asia, Eastern Hindukush, St Petersburg: Oriental Studies, pp. 280-299.

Sökefeld, Martin (1998b): "'The people who really belong to Gilgit' – Theoretical and ethnographic perspectives on identity and conflict." In: Irmtraud Stellrecht/Hans-Geor Bohle (eds.), Transformations of Economic and Social Relationships in Northern Pakistan, Cologne: Köppe-Verlag.

Sökefeld, Martin (1999): "Debating Self, Identity, and Culture in Anthropology." In: Current Anthropology 40/4, pp. 417-447.

Sökefeld, Martin (2005): "From Colonialism to Postcolonial Colonialism: Changing Modes of Domination in the Northern Areas of Pakistan." In: Journal of Asian Studies 64/4, pp. 939-973.

Stöber, Georg (2007): "Religious Identities Provoked: The Gilgit 'Textbook Controversy' and its Conflictual Context." In: Internationale Schulbuchforschung 29, pp. 389–411.

Street, Alice (2012): "Affective Infrastructure: Hospital Landscapes of Hope and Failure." In: Space and Culture 15, pp. 44–58.

Street, Alice/Coleman, Simon (2012): "Introduction: Real and imagined spaces." In: Space and Culture 15, pp. 4-19.

Sullivan, Noelle (2012) "Enacting spaces of inequality: Placing global/state governance within a Tanzanian hospital." In: Space and Culture 15, pp. 57-67.

Van Der Geest, Sjaak/Finkler, Kaja (2004): "Hospital ethnography: introduction." In: Social Science & Medicine 59, pp. 1995-2001.

Varley, Emma (2010): "Targeted doctors, missing patients: Obstetric health services and sectarian conflict in Northern Pakistan." In: Social Science & Medicine 70, pp. 61-70 (http://link.springer.com/article/10.1007/s11013-015-9456-5).

Varma, Saiba (2014): "Interrogating the 'Post-conflict' in Indian-occupied Kashmir." In: Fieldsights - Hot Spots, Cultural Anthropology Online March 24, 2014 (http://www.culanth.org/fieldsights/506-interrogating-the-post-conflict-in-indian-occupied-kashmir; accessed February 7, 2015).

Wick, Livia (2008): "Building the infrastructure, modeling the nation: The case of birth in Palestine." In: Culture, Medicine & Psychiatry 32, pp. 328-357.

Zafar, Syed Furqan (2007): Understanding Pakistan, Reforms in Health Care: An Equitable and Comprehensive System, SPO Conversation Series, Strengthening Participatory Organization: Islamabad.

Zaman, Shahaduz (2004): "Poverty, violence, frustration and inventiveness: hospital ward life in Bangladesh." In: Social Science & Medicine 59, pp. 2025-2036.

Notes on the Contributors

Khushbakht Hojiev is a PhD Fellow at the Center for Development Research (ZEF) at the Rheinische-Friedrich-Wilhelms University of Bonn, Germany. He has M.A. degrees in Political Science, from the OSCE Academy, and Peace and Conflict Studies, from Otto-von-Guericke University of Magdeburg, as well as a diploma in International Relations. Khushbakht has previously worked as an OSCE officer in conflict zones, such as the OSCE Mission to Moldova, specialising in conflict prevention/resolution, and has held research and consultancy positions at UN organisations in Tajikistan. His past research concentrated on regional integration processes and political transition in post-Soviet countries and normative implications of humanitarian intervention and the norm of sovereignty in post-Cold War international relations. His current research projects include the prosessual approach in conflict analysis, mobilisation in ethnicised conflicts and the politics of nation-building in Central Asia, particularly in Kyrgyzstan and Tajikistan.

Aksana Ismailbekova is a post-doctoral researcher at the Zentrum Moderner Orient in Berlin and a member of the competence network Crossroads Asia project 2011–2014. For her postdoctoral project, Aksana conducted research in Osh during 2011-2014. During her project on Uzbek communities, her research revealed the importance of marriage among Uzbeks as a coping strategy in the face of community unrest and violence/conflict. Aksana conducted her research in rural Kyrgyz communities for her doctoral project, completed in 2011 at the Max Planck Institute for Social Anthropology (MPI). In her first research project, she examined the overlapping interlinkages between Kyrgyz kinship and networks of political patronage, and she has published papers on kinship, marriage, patronage networks, coping strategies, migration, conflict and women. These articles have appeared in peer-reviewed journals such as Central Asian Survey, Focaal, Nationalities Papers, etc. Recently, Aksana's book manuscript, "Blood Ties and the Native Son: Poetics of Patronage in Kyrgyzstan," was accepted by the Indiana University Press, and it contributes to the ethnography of kinship politics in the region. Finally, Aksana, together with Jeanne Féaux de la Croix, will soon publish a Special Issue on Futures and Belongings in Kyrgyzstan in the Anthropology of East Europe Review (AEER).

Jan Koehler is researcher at SFB 700 Freie Universität Berlin. He received his first degree from the Freie Universität Berlin in Social Anthropology and did his PhD in Political Science on an institution-centred conflict research methodology and application. The current geographical focus of Jan's activities is Afghanistan, Central Asia and the Caucasus region, with special emphasis on longitudinal impact assessments, conflict and governance context analysis and capacity development on empirical research methods in those regions. He is lead researcher for two ongoing impact assessments in Afghanistan, one dealing with the impact of the intervention on local security, acceptance and state-society relations, and the other one on the stabilisation effects of specific development programmes. Recent articles include Koehler, Jan/Gosztonyi, Kristof 2014: The international intervention and its impact on security governance in North-East Afghanistan, in: International Peacekeeping 21: 2, 231-250; and Böhnke, Jan/Koehler, Jan/Zürcher, Christoph 2014: Assessing the Impact of Development Cooperation in North East Afghanistan 2005-2009: A repeated mixed-method survey, in: Bull, Beate/Kennedy-Chouane, Megan/Winkler Andersen, Ole (Eds.): Evaluations in Situations of Conflict and Fragility, Routledge, 105-129.

Debidatta Aurobinda Mahapatra, after receiving a PhD in International Studies from Jawaharlal Nehru University, New Delhi, in 2005, taught and researched at Central University of Punjab, University of Mumbai and University of Jammu, India, from 2005 to 2012. He received the Scholar of Peace Award (New Delhi) in 2007 and the Kodikara Award (Colombo) in 2010. He was Visiting Fellow at the Institute for Conflict Research, Belfast, UK, in November 2008, Charles Wallace Fellow at Queen's University Belfast in March-April 2010 and ICSSR-RAS Fellow at the Institute of

Oriental Studies, Moscow, in September 2010. He worked as a consultant for the Internal Displacement Monitoring Center, Geneva, in 2006 and 2010. He has published on issues related to conflict and peace-building. His recent publications include Conflict and Peace in Eurasia (editor, Routledge, 2013) and Making Kashmir Borderless (RCSS, Colombo, 2013). Dr. Mahapatra is currently pursuing a second PhD at the Department of Conflict Resolution, Human Security and Global Governance, University of Massachusetts, Boston. He is a Fellow at the Center for Peace, Development and Democracy and alternatively teaches two courses – Introduction to Conflicts in South Asia and the Kashmir Conflict: Dynamics, Costs and Peace Prospects – at the Osher Lifelong Learning Institute at the same university.

Katja Mielke works as a senior researcher at the Bonn-based think-tank Bonn International Center for Conversion (BICC). She earned a PhD in Development Research from the University of Bonn and has been conducting long-term fieldwork in Afghanistan since 2006. Her academic interests lie in the field of political sociology at the intersection of conflict and development research and include questions on norm transfer, social mobilisation and conflict, inequality and social im/mobility, local governance (politics, power, legitimacy and representation) in rural and urban contexts, social order and non-institutionalised forms of power and movements. Her regional expertise covers Russia, Central Asia, Afghanistan and Pakistan. The research for the contribution to this volume was undertaken as part of her post-doc project "Sub-urban movements: Social inequality and dynamics of micro-mobilization in Kabul, Karachi and Lahore" as a member of the Crossroads Asia research network at the Center for Development Research (ZEF) of Bonn University. Recent articles include Mielke, Katja 2014: Social Order as a Boundary Concept: Unveiling Dichotomies, Conceptualizing Politics, in: Asien – The German Journal on Contemporary Asia, 35-52; Wilde, Andreas; Mielke, Katja 2014: Order, Stability, and Change in Afghanistan. From Top-Down to Bottom-Up State-Making, in: Goodhand, Jonathan; Sedra, Mark (eds.): The Afghan Conundrum. Intervention, State-building and Resistance. London, New York: Routledge, 353-370.

Nick Miszak is a doctoral candidate at the Department of Anthropology and Sociology of Development, Graduate Institute of International and Development Studies, Geneva. He is writing his dissertation on the military and peace-building intervention in Afghanistan, focusing particularly on the interactions of local, state and international actors in land-based conflicts in Nangarhar and Kabul provinces. Nick has worked as a researcher in Afghanistan since 2007 for The Liaison Office and as a consultant. He has extensive policy-oriented research experience on the political economy of land, formal and informal justice, internal displacement and peace and reintegration. Nick completed his Master studies at the University of Fribourg in Switzerland (2006) and holds a bilingual (German/French) MA in Social Science.

Martin Sökefeld is chair of the Department of Social and Cultural Anthropology, Ludwig-Maximilians University, Munich. His main field of interest is the anthropology of politics, particularly in the politics of migration and diaspora, ethnicity and the politics of identity and recognition, as well as the politics of disasters. His main area of fieldwork is Gilgit-Baltistan, where he started research in 1991, but he has also done fieldwork in Azad Kashmir and among Azad Kashmiris in the UK, in the Kashmir valley, in Turkey and among Turkish Alevis in Germany. Recent publications include Diaspora und soziale Mobilisierung: Kaschmiris in England und Aleviten in Deutschland im Vergleich: In: Nieswand, Boris; Heike Drotbohm, eds. (2014): Kultur, Gesellschaft, Migration. Die reflexive Wende in der Migrationsforschung. Wiesbaden, Springer VS: 225-253; Jammu and Kashmir: Dispute and diversity,in: Berger, Peter; Frank Heidemann, eds. (2013): The modern anthropology of India: Ethnography, themes and theory, London, Routledge: 89-105. He also edited a special issue of Contemporary South Asia on Jammu and Kashmir: Boundaries and Movements (Vol. 23, no. 3, 2015).

Emma Varley is a medical anthropologist whose research explores the impacts of conflict and political instability on global maternal health interventions and women's use of medical services for pregnancy and childbirth in northern Pakistan. Over the course of eight years of fieldwork in the Gilgit-Baltistan region, she has researched the cultural, ethical and experiential texture of medicine and the political etiologies underlying women's health outcomes during times of crisis and emergency. Her ongoing research and

publications critically analyse the health ramifications caused by sectarian discrimination, exclusionary health service provision and other forms of structural violence in community and hospital settings, and she also addresses how issues of gender, politics and religion are expressed through the medium of maternal health practices, beliefs and behaviours and narratives. Emma has her BA and MA degrees from the University of British Columbia, her PhD from the University of Toronto, and she completed a post-doctoral fellowship at Dalhousie University. She is an Assistant Professor in the Department of Anthropology at Brandon University in Canada.